grow
herbs

grow
herbs

JEKKA McVICAR

**LONDON, NEW YORK, MUNICH,
MELBOURNE, DELHI**

PROJECT EDITOR   Sarah Ruddick
PROJECT ART EDITOR   Vicky Read
MANAGING EDITOR   Esther Ripley
MANAGING ART EDITOR   Alison Donovan
PRODUCTION EDITOR   Maria Elia
PRODUCTION CONTROLLER   Erika Pepe
ASSOCIATE PUBLISHER   Liz Wheeler
PUBLISHER   Jonathan Metcalf
ART DIRECTOR   Peter Luff

First published as *New Book of Herbs* in Great Britain in 2002
by Dorling Kindersley Limited,
80 Strand, London WC2R 0RL
A Penguin company

First paperback edition 2013

2 4 6 8 10 9 7 5 3 1

001-192363-April/2013

A CIP catalogue record for this book is available from The British Library

ISBN 978 1 4093 2493 5

Printed and bound in China by Leo Paper Products

Discover more at
www.dk.com

Author's note Herbs contain natural medicinal properties and should be treated
with respect. This book is not intended as a medical reference book, but as a
source of information. Do not take any herbal remedies if you are undergoing any
other course of medical treatment without seeking professional advice. Before
trying herbal remedies, the reader is recommended to sample a small quantity
first to establish whether there is any adverse or allergic reaction. The reader is
advised not to attempt self-treatment for serious or long-term problems without
consulting a qualified medicinal herbalist. Neither the author nor the publisher
can be held responsible for any adverse reactions to the recipes,
recommendations, and instructions contained herein, and the use of any
herb or derivative is entirely at the reader's own risk.

In loving memory of William

Contents

A catalogue of Jekka's favourite herbs for the kitchen, home, and garden. This beautifully illustrated A–Z offers essential information on propagation, maintenance, and harvesting for each specific herb and suggests culinary, medicinal, and household uses.

INTRODUCTION

What is a herb?

The answer to the apparently simple question "What is a herb?" is not as straightforward as you might think. The Royal Horticultural Society's definition of a herb, according to its Dictionary of Gardening, is "a plant of which the stem dies to the ground at the end of the season". This definition seems to me to be rather too narrow, considering that some plants I regard as herbs, like bay (*Laurus nobilis*), are evergreen, and so I prefer the explanation given in the Oxford English Dictionary, where the term "herb" is applied to "plants of which the leaves or stem and leaves are used for medicine, or for their scent or flavour".

The properties of herbs

Herbs have a history that is steeped in myth and magic, and there is much bogus information regarding their potency and properties. But if we put aside the superstitions attached to herbs and concentrate on the many medicinal and culinary benefits they have brought us over the past 1,500 years, we cannot but conclude that they are the most extraordinarily diverse and useful plants. Herbs come in all shapes, sizes, textures and perfumes, and they can be incorporated into any size of garden or container. You may think of a particular herb like sweet basil (*Ocimum basilicum*) as a delicious cooking herb, only to discover its value in the garden as a companion plant for deterring pests from tomato plants or its ability to act as a fly repellent when planted in pots for the home. The same applies to a herb like chamomile (*Chamaemelum nobile*), which is wonderful in beauty products for lightening hair but is also a healing herb to relieve insomnia when drunk as a tisane.

The future for herbs

Research into the properties of herbs and how people around the world use these plants is now high on most people's agenda, and I am aware of a herb revival at a time when we are more knowledgeable about the damaging effects of our lifestyles on our bodies and the environment. I think that there is a new respect for herbs, and that they have a vital part to play in a healthier approach to modern living.

This informal, aromatic herb garden combines culinary and medicinal herbs with herbaceous perennials.

◄◄ **Foxglove** (*Digitalis purpurea*) is a traditional medicinal herb that has been used since the 18th century to treat various heart conditions.

◄ **Narrow-leaved sage** (*Salvia lavandulifolia*) leaves have a strong aromatic flavour in casseroles and stews. They are also good for making a herbal infusion to help the memory.

◄◄ **Lemon balm** (*Melissa officinalis*) has lemon-scented leaves that can be added to salads or made into an infusion to relieve tiredness and tension.

◄ **Purple basil** (*Ocimum basilicum* var. *purpurascens* 'Dark Opal') has highly aromatic leaves that are good eaten raw in salads or added to pasta sauces.

◄◄ **Borage** (*Borago officinalis*) attracts bees and other pollinating insects to the garden, and the seeds are high in polyunsaturated fats.

◄ **Sweet Annie** (*Artemisia annua*) is a natural herbicide and an important medicinal herb used in the treatment of malaria.

Growing herbs organically

"The organic approach to gardening and farming recognizes that the whole environment in which plants grow is much more than the sum of its individual parts, and that all living things are inter-related and inter-dependent."
– *Garden Organic*

Organic methods and principles respect the environment and work in harmony with nature. Organic gardeners build up the sustainability of the soil by feeding it with home and garden waste. This encourages the microbes in the soil to turn this waste into plant food. The plants flourish and attract beneficial insects for pollination. Seeds are produced, fall to the ground, and in turn grow into new plants. As life is a cycle, so is the garden.

Benefits of organic herbs

Herbs are one of the most beneficial groups of plants to have in the organic garden. Grown without pesticides and chemical fertilizers, organic herbs attract many beneficial insects, bees, birds, and butterflies to the garden and vegetable plot, achieving a high level of pollination and increased yields. So by growing your herbs organically you not only create a beautiful garden that is teeming with wildlife, but also increase the productivity and the health of the plants you grow. You can enjoy picking and using delicious fresh herbs in cooking without the worry of introducing pesticides into your diet.

Personally, I prefer to eat organic herbs because I think that they taste better. Herbs grown in the sun, rain, and soil – instead of being grown on a large scale under artificial lights – contain more nutrients as all these environmental elements help boost the natural oil content in the plants. When used in cooking, the organic herbs often go further because they have a more intense flavour and a lower water content. For common ailments, too, organic preparations are less likely than conventional medicines to cause adverse reactions, and many are gentle enough to treat small children and pets. You can also make your own herbal cleaning products for the home that are free from synthetic pollutants.

The best way forward

"Organic systems work in harmony with nature, not against it, keeping harmful chemicals out of our land, water, and air, creating a healthy environment."
– *The Soil Association*

The organic approach to farming was practised widely until after World War II when mechanization, a growing population, and the demand for more intensive production and cheaper food increased. However, with the BSE (bovine spongiform encephalopathy) scare in the UK in the 1980s and the wider concern about genetically modified (GM) food, we are becoming more aware of the consequences of intensive farming. Organic systems, for me, represent the best way forward. Growing herbs organically will help to keep our environment as well as our gardens, safe, enjoyable, and healthy places to be.

Balancing the ecosystem

BENEFICIAL PLANTS When choosing herbs for your garden, consider what the plant can contribute to the garden. For example chamomile (*Chamaemelum nobile*), as well as making a soothing cup of herb tea, will repel flying insects when planted next to onions, and will improve their crop yield. A chamomile infusion can also be sprayed on seedlings to prevent "damping off", or leaves can be placed on the compost heap to help speed up the process (see page 37).

COMPANION PLANTING When planted next to other species, certain herbs will deter pests or have a healing effect. Plant basil next to tomatoes and this will inhibit whitefly, because the pest prefers basil to tomatoes. Or plant yarrow (*Achillea millefolium*) near an ailing shrub or tree and the herb will help the plant rebuild its natural disease resistance.

ATTRACTING BIRDS Birds eat pests and insects, so to encourage birds into the garden, plant seed-bearing herbs to give them a supply of food for the winter. For example, evening primrose (*Oenothera biennis*) attracts all members of the tit family and elecampane (*Inula helenium*), the finch family.

BEES AND BUTTERFLIES Both are good pollinators, so plant herbs to attract them. Planting borage (*Borago officinalis*) with runner beans helps to increase the yield. Angelica Vicar's Mead (*Angelica sylvestris* 'Vicar's Mead') is a beneficial late-season nectar plant, so consider growing it in the garden.

Biodiversity in the garden

Every species, no matter how small, has an important role to play in the garden. They are all part of the jigsaw that is the ecosystem and just one missing piece can cause disease, the loss of a crop, or even extinction. The preservation of biodiversity – the existence of a wide variety of plant and animal species in their natural environments – can be critical to the health of our surroundings, and ultimately to that of our planet.

The bee population, in particular, is in severe decline in the northern hemisphere. Bees depend upon a flower-rich habitat for food, the loss of which, as a result of the intensification of agricultural systems over the past century, has caused a drop in population levels. This, in turn, means that there are fewer bees to pollinate flowers and maintain the populations of the fruit and vegetables we take for granted. By acting quickly to ensure a balanced environment in the garden, we can help to stop this decline.

What can we do?

We can all contribute to biodiversity – most gardens already play their part, offering a small haven with a combination of habitats, soils, and native and exotic plants, all of which create a unique environment. Even windowboxes make a difference, offering nectar and pollen to bees and butterflies. By adopting some good general gardening practices, the biodiversity in your garden can be further enhanced. Whatever you choose to do, remember that the ecosystem is a fine balance, reliant on complex interactions, and that the tiniest insect, lichen, or fungus can make a huge difference to the natural equilibrium.

◄◄ **Flowering herbs**, like marjoram, are important for their ability to draw bees, providing food for the insect as well as pollinating the plant.

◄ **As well as looking beautiful**, oregano's flowers will benefit the many butterflies native to the UK.

Ways to enhance the biodiversity in your garden

Choose a range of plants, annuals, vegetables, shrubs, and trees that provide a food source over a long period. Include nectar- and pollen-rich plants to provide food for bees, butterflies, and other flower-visiting insects. Night-flowering or -scented species will benefit moths, and fruiting trees and shrubs offer a range of fruit and berries for mammals and birds. Where possible, include climbing plants to provide a nesting habitat for birds. Try to add a few native plants to your selection – these will survive in the local climate and offer a valuable food source.

■ **Delay cutting your hedges back** until the early spring; this will provide a good winter habitat and shelter for birds. Leave a few logs out, as dead wood is a great habitat for invertebrates, fungi, birds, mammals, reptiles, and amphibians.

■ **Leave some structural grasses** and perennials, rather than cutting them back in the autumn. These will provide a winter food source for birds and mammals, and will enhance the overwintering potential and survival rates of beneficial species.

■ **Follow organic gardening** practices, especially concerning herbicides and pesticides; all insects are an important part of the natural food chain in your garden. The chain also includes beneficial natural predators, such as ladybirds, lacewings, and hoverflies, which would be killed by pesticides.

■ **Water in a garden is important**. Not only is it essential for birds, but in the spring it will provide a place for amphibians to spawn; they will return the favour by controlling slugs and snails. You need not create a large water feature – a bowl sunk into the ground would suffice.

■ **Reduce the size of your lawn**, or consider leaving part uncut. Long grass is beneficial to many species, and reducing mowing cuts emissions and saves fossil fuels.

Garden birds need a year-round food source – help them with a simple feeder like this one. The more wildlife you can attract to your garden, the better.

■ **Turn all or part of your lawn** into a wildflower meadow. This will require careful management but can be hugely rewarding.

■ **Install bird feeders**, as well as bird, hedgehog, and bat boxes, solitary bee nests, and ladybird and lacewing homes. Birds should be provided with food and water throughout the year, not just in winter. Many birds will benefit from the wide range of insects, worms, and other invertebrates in your garden.

■ **Think carefully** about materials that you use in your garden. Consider where, for example, your potting compost, plants, and wooden furniture come from. Are they from sustainable sources, or are their habitats under threat?

■ **Recycle the plant material** in your garden; leaf litter, in particular, makes superb compost. Always check your compost heap for wildlife before disturbing, as compost waste and heaps can provide a valuable wildlife habitat for slow worms and many other invertebrates. Use your own compost instead of peat-based products.

Managing herbs the natural way

The art of good organic management is constant vigilance. I regularly tour my farm on the look-out for signs of pests or disease. If I notice anything amiss, I can act quickly before the problem spreads, either by introducing a predator to control an infestation of pests, or by cutting back the plant if it is diseased.

Another organic, but time-consuming method is to remove or squash any pests as you see them. When I first started the farm the ecosystem was out of balance (as will your garden be in its first year without chemicals) and I had to perform slug patrols at night. If you have previously used slug pellets, pay special attention to that area where you laid pellets because they are designed to draw slugs to them. If collecting up slugs is not working, introduce the parasitic nematode *Phasmarhabditis hermaphrodita*; however, this only works well at temperatures above 5°C (40°F) on moist soil.

To control insects like greenfly, try growing a companion plant like buddleia mint to attract hoverfly, whose larvae will then eat the greenfly. Alternatively,

Spring

Summer

Remove moss and weeds from wintered container plants in spring. This will prevent the weeds from taking over the pot and stop them taking all the nutrients from the substrate. Also it allows the wind and rain to get to the plant, which makes a stronger specimen.

Feed pot-grown herbs in spring, to encourage the plant to put on new growth. After clearing off all the winter debris and roughing up the surface of the substrate, add a small amount of organic fertilizer to the surface, then lightly cover this with a layer of new substrate.

Start controlling pests from spring onwards – pick off any that you see, and look under the canopy of the shrubs to see if there are any slugs. Check containers for vine weevil damage and repot, removing all contaminated soil. Check the glasshouse or conservatory for whitefly or red spider mite, introducing predators if required to control the problem.

Cut back flowers of your herb plants in summer to prolong the harvesting season. This is an especially good idea for soft-leaved herbs like lovage, chives, mint, and lemon balm. After cutting back give the herbs a liquid feed with comfrey (see page 39), which will encourage rapid new growth to produce a second crop of leaves.

collect ladybirds and introduce them into the infested area. A diseased plant will drop its leaves on to the soil so cut out infested or damaged parts of the plant to inhibit the spread of disease. Act quickly, especially in the case of rust, which infects herb plants like mint, tarragon, and chives. Once the rust spores are in the soil it is difficult to get rid of them organically (see page 149).

In autumn and spring, check the weather forecast for frost. Use horticultural fleece to cover and protect established tender plants and newly emerging seedlings. Before feeding the soil in autumn or spring with well-rotted manure, pick up a handful of soil and smell it. If there is only a faint aroma, the soil is deficient and needs a generous manure feed. Above all else try to enjoy the work and do not try to fight against nature – go with it.

Buddleia mint flowers attract the beneficial hoverfly, which then acts as a predator to black- or whitefly.

Autumn

Cut back established plants in early autumn to regain shape. Evergreen herbs like thyme, lavender, and cotton lavender benefit from being cut back, not only to stop them from becoming woody and shapeless but also to protect them from adverse weather conditions. It also encourages light new growth for winter protection.

Lift tender plants in autumn to protect them from frost. Small herbs like scented pelargoniums (shown here) are well worth lifting. Cut them back quite hard, pot up using a loam-based substrate, water in, then place the container in a frost-free environment. The plants will then need minimal watering until the following spring.

Feed established plants in the garden in autumn. Use either well-rotted manure or well-rotted compost and dig in around the established plants, avoiding areas of soft growth. By doing this in autumn, the feed will slowly nourish the soil and, at the same time, give the roots added protection.

Winter

Protect exposed plants in the garden in winter. Tender plants that have become too large for moving may need extra protection from inclement weather. Horticultural fleece is ideal. It is light so will not damage the plant, and it is permeable so the plant can breathe. On warm days, remove the fleece to allow better air circulation, especially if it has become wet.

THE GARDEN

Your garden environment

The key to a successful organic herb garden is to work with nature, and remember that every garden has a unique set of growing conditions that distinguish it from any other, which goes some way to explaining why a neighbour may be able to grow certain plants that you have tried to grow with little success. Perhaps your garden is sheltered by the house and the soil does not get much rain. Or it could be exposed to a prevailing wind that makes the soil drier than the garden next door. Before you plan a new herb garden or re-design an existing one, it is a good idea to familiarize yourself with your plot.

Assessing the site

When considering the site of your planned herb garden, note down any environmental factors that may influence the herbs you select. The native trees, shrubs, and weeds that are already growing well in the garden or its immediate surroundings will offer clues to your soil type. The presence of horsetail and comfrey are signs of a damp, heavy soil, while shrubs like rhododendrons and azaleas indicate acid soil, and beech trees thrive in

A well-planned herb garden will encourage the plants you choose to thrive, and will be a pleasure to work in.

chalky soil. Herb gardens, particularly those that feature Mediterranean culinary herbs such as sage, need plenty of sunshine to thrive. Note the position of the sun in relation to the growing beds in the garden. Where does the sun rise, and how does it move across the garden during the course of the day? Which areas of the garden are in permanent shade, and is there anything you can do to improve the situation? Perhaps a shadow is being cast by a large tree which needs pruning.

Planning a new herb garden

If your proposed herb garden site has been neglected for years, or you are starting a new garden from scratch in a field site – as I did – try to find old maps of the area to give you some background information on what has gone before so that you will have some knowledge about what you can grow there. When I looked at an old Ordnance Survey map of the area, I found that the site was formerly called "clay fields", so I knew from the outset that I would have to work with heavy clay soil and have to find herbs that could adapt to these conditions, or else work hard to improve the soil. Make lists of herbs that suit your soil, and another list of herbs that suit your position, ie sun or shade. Once you have these lists, see which herbs overlap between the two – these will be the easiest to grow in your particular site. So by finding out as much as you can about your site and conditions before you start, you will have all you need to plan a thriving herb garden.

◄◄ Comfrey plants
(*Symphytum officinale*) growing
wild along the edge of the field,
signalling heavy soil.

◄ Hops (*Humulus lupulus*) are
happy climbing up a sheltered
wall. Walls protect the soil
directly beneath from rain, which
is of benefit when growing hops
in heavy soil because they favour
drier conditions.

◄◄ Tree spinach
(*Chenopodium giganteum*)
and borage (*Borago officinalis*)
were found growing on my
waste compost heap, having
happily self-seeded in these
nutrient-rich conditions.

◄ Horseradish (*Armoracia
rusticana*) grows on the roadside
close to the farm. This is a sign
of heavy soil.

◄◄ Elderberry (*Sambucus
nigra*), like horseradish, also
grows along the lane where
there is heavy alkaline soil.
Elderberry will grow happily
in these conditions.

◄ Horsetail (*Equisetum
arvense*) is an indicator of
damp soil, as these are the
only conditions it enjoys.
Beware – horsetail roots
can reach a depth of 2m (6ft).

Soil analysis

The easiest way to analyse your soil is to pick up a handful and ask yourself the following questions: does it fall through your fingers, or does it form a solid lump? Does it have a sweet, warm, earthy smell? Or is the soil poor with no odour or even a slightly sour smell? A healthy soil is teeming with life and should have worm channels, which indicate that the soil is aerated and not compacted. Good plant growth is dependent not only on the nutrient content of the soil, but also on its structure. Sandy soil is often low in nutrients because the rain washes them away. Clay soil can be rich in plant food but heavy and waterlogged, so plant roots find it difficult to establish a foothold. Use bulky organic matter to improve soil structure, to help sandy soil retain water, to aerate clay soil, and generally to produce healthier herb crops.

Soil condition

The soil is the engine of your garden, so it is important to know its condition before you start planting. Check by putting a spade into the soil to see if it has become compacted – if it has, it will need to be dug over prior to planting. Ideally, this should be done in the autumn before planting in the following spring, and layered with well-rotted compost to encourage microbes (see page 10).

Checking the pH

The pH of the soil refers to its acidity or alkalinity. It is a vital factor in the plant's ability to obtain all types of plant foods and essential chemicals via its root system. For example, an alkaline soil can produce stunted plants with yellowing leaves because minerals like iron cannot be absorbed. At a neutral pH of 7, most of the essential chemicals and plant foods become available, so producing healthy plants.

Soil testing

To test your soil, buy a soil-testing kit from a garden centre. The majority of amateur soil-testing kits are very simple and rely on colour rather than the numerical pH scale. Acid soil turns the indicator orange, neutral turns it green, and alkaline dark green.

A soil-testing kit is a quick and easy way to check the acidity or alkalinity of your garden's soil.

Improving soil structure

■ All soil improvers can be added as a mulch or dug into the top 15cm (6in), which is the main feeding area for the plant roots.

■ Stand on a wooden plank while you dig. Do not stand or walk on the soil as compacted soil has little air, which makes it difficult for the roots to penetrate.

■ Dig only when necessary – over-digging can destroy soil structure.

■ Keep the soil covered with mulch to maintain structure.

■ Overfertilized plants will produce lush top growth but no flowers, and therefore no fruit.

Basic soil types

Soil can vary from acid (pH 3.5) to alkaline (pH 8.5). Most herbs will tolerate a range of pH 6.5–7.5, which is fairly neutral. Here, I am holding a clay soil in my right hand – the soil particles stick together – and a good-quality loam soil in my left hand. The four basic soil types and their properties are outlined below. They are all suitable for growing herbs, but some may require extra help to ensure successful growing.

SAND (pH 4.5) This soil feels gritty. It is free-draining, so plants' nutrients are washed away. One advantage is that it warms up quickly in spring so sowing and planting can start early. To help retain moisture, feed in winter with leafmould and well-rotted manure.

LOAM (pH 5.5–8.5) This is often considered the optimum soil for herb growing. There are various types of loam. A sandy loam is the best for growing Mediterranean herbs, but herbs like soapwort, comfrey, angelica, valerian, Joe Pye weed, meadowsweet, and purple and yellow loosestrife grow best in moist to marshy loam.

CLAY (pH 6.5) This soil has tiny particles that stick together when wet, making the soil heavy and difficult for roots to penetrate. In summer, when dry, it sets hard. Even though it can be rich in nutrients, improve its structure by working in well-rotted leafmould. This will enable young plants to establish themselves.

CHALK (pH 8.5) This soil is light and has lumps of flint or chalk. It drains well and is often shallow in depth. It has a high pH, making it alkaline. Nutrients can be increased with compost, but it is harder to reduce alkalinity. Many herbs tolerate chalk, but for root depth and moisture it may be easier to grow them in raised beds.

Preparing new beds for planting

The time you spend preparing your new beds before planting will be repaid over the years to come, giving you a bumper harvest. Having fed and dug over the beds the previous autumn (see page 20), watch out for the weeds that will appear as soon as the soil warms in spring – make sure you remove them before planting.

Weeds, especially perennial ones like bindweed, can be persistent and deep-rooted and should be eradicated. Dig heavy soil in early winter after rain, when the top soil is easier to work but before it becomes waterlogged. Frosts will also help to erode and break up clods of soil. Leave light soil undug until early spring so that nutrients do not leach out of the soil in wet winter weather. Once cleared, cover the soil (see below) to inhibit weed seed, which lies dormant until exposed to light. This way you will avoid having to weed the site before planting. When newly planted up with young herbs, do not irrigate the area with a spray hose or sprinkler – jets of water can spread weed seed. Use leaky pipes or seep irrigation instead, which will also reduce water consumption.

Plastic sheeting to cover new beds

1 **Cover newly prepared soil** with mulch or plastic sheeting once clear of weeds. By excluding the light from the soil, you are effectively preventing weed growth. Here, I am using black polythene sheeting (400 gauge) which is excellent for keeping the ground clear before planting. Lay the sheet over the newly prepared soil for a month to exclude light, lock in moisture, and warm up the soil before planting. A permeable membrane like coir matting (see opposite), which allows the soil to breathe and water to permeate, is best as a long-term cover for herb beds.

2 **Anchor plastic sheeting** by burying the edges in soil or under stones or planks to stop the polythene from lifting in strong winds. Planks are good because they give you access to the site and spread your body weight without compacting the soil structure – which is, after all, what you are trying to improve. Cardboard is another suitable soil cover – place torn-up strips between rows of annual herbs like coriander and dill to inhibit weeds. It is biodegradable, so when it is no longer useful in the herb bed, break the cardboard up and add it to the compost heap (see page 37).

Preparing existing beds

The best time for maintaining an existing bed is in the spring, when the soil has started to warm up and seedlings are starting to grow. Start by keeping your herb garden as weed-free as possible, which will not only make it easier to see any new seed-raised crops, but will also make it easier to harvest later in the season.

Clear the ground of weeds, add any soil improvers or fertilizers (see pages 36–39), then apply a mulch to inhibit further weed growth. Suppress weeds with a permeable plastic membrane or bark chippings, leafmould, gravel, coir, or cocoa shells. I personally do not like cocoa shells because they have a strong smell, are environmentally unsound, having been transported across the world, and

there is little information on whether the cocoa bush is sprayed with pesticides. I have similar ecological concerns about excessive use of coir, the coarse fibre from coconut shells, and find that it does not break down well. When applying mulch around established plants, always leave some soil bare close to the plant crown and roots to allow air to circulate and so prevent rot.

Mulch and coir matting on mature beds

1 **Spreading leafmould mulch** will help to improve the soil condition as well as stifling weeds; the mulch in an established garden should be both nutritious and moist. My favourite mulches are leafmould and bark (see page 36) because herb plants prefer these relatively low-nutrient versions. As well as being of benefit to the soil, a layer of mulch will smarten up the appearance of the flower bed.

2 **Fit permeable mulch covers** around plants to suppress weeds. Permeable mulches made from fibrous matting materials are also available from garden centres. Fibrous coir matting (shown above) is useful for suppressing weeds around established low-growing herbs, where it is often awkward to weed. The coir mat will also help to protect the plant's root system in winter from cold and damp. Avoid old carpet or sacking because they look unattractive and may encourage pests like mice or other rodents, which feed on herbs.

Designing a herb garden

Herbs are very versatile plants, and the pleasure in designing a herb garden is that there is a species of herb to suit every soil type and location. Whether you are planning to give over the whole of your garden to herbs, or you just want to plant up herbs in individual pots, take time deciding how you want to use your chosen species. Are you growing herbs purely for their colour and fragrance? Or do you want to be able to harvest herbs all year round to flavour cooking, or be able to pick herb leaves for use in summer salads? Maybe you just want to grow a selection of medicinally beneficial herbs to make tisanes? Perhaps a combination of all of these? Whatever you choose to grow in your herb garden, make sure that your design leaves you space to harvest them, and try to choose some herbs that will give your garden structure in the winter months.

Planning the design

Before you start planting, consider your soil type and which way your garden faces (see page 18 for more information). Plan the best position for each plant in the garden design by researching the growth habit of each one. Information on specific herbs can be found in my Top 100 herbs (see pages 74–215). Consider height; for example, angelica reaches 2.5m (8ft) so is best placed at the back of the herb bed, while some herbs, such as mint, spread very quickly, so you may wish to grow them in containers rather than in the herb bed to keep their growth in check. Another factor is the growing cycle; for example, herbs like salad rocket are short-lived and are only productive for a few months, while others such as box are evergreen and will remain in leaf throughout the year. Also consider which herbs grow well together and make good companion plants. Think of your garden ecosystem, and which herbs attract birds, bees, and butterflies. By their very nature, all herbs are born survivors and self-seed freely. To keep the herb garden looking its best, you will need to maintain it, clipping evergreen foliage to shape and cutting off flowerheads before they run to seed.

If you already have an existing herb garden that you have inherited from a previous owner, do not be afraid to replace old plants, such as lavender and rosemary that have become woody and are now no longer productive. Equally, if you do not particularly like certain herbs, remove them to create more space for herbs you are keen to grow. Making an existing herb garden your own is an opportunity to grow the plants that you will make the best use of, so do think carefully about the plants you would like to retain or replace.

Sources of inspiration

To help you plan a successful herb garden design, try to visit established herb gardens for inspiration. The Herb Society in the UK (see Resources) has information on herb gardens that are open to the public. You may be inspired by a Mediterranean-style rockery for herbs like thyme, oregano, sage, and prostrate rosemary, for example. A raised herb bed provides a good solution if your soil type is unsuitable for the herbs you wish to grow; an aromatic border can be planted with low-growing herbs like sage, or a herbaceous border with a mix of other shrubs and trees. Flower shows also offer a wealth of ideas for planting schemes, and often have ideas on how to use herb plants to provide structure, or as path edges and hedges. Armed with this information, you will be equipped to make an enthusiastic start.

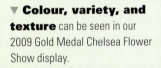

▶ **Paths through gardens** give access and make it easier to pick and tend to the plants.

▼ **Colour, variety, and texture** can be seen in our 2009 Gold Medal Chelsea Flower Show display.

Traditional herb garden design

Herbs have been cultivated for thousands of years as medicine and as a food, and were also planted near temples for use in religious rituals. Today, herbs are grown in beds and as part of formal herb gardens, the design of which reflects their history, as well as in mixed herbaceous borders and incorporated into vegetable gardens. They are grown not only for use in the kitchen but also for their ability to increase biodiversity (see pages 12–13), which attracts pollinating insects, in turn helping to increase the yield of fruit and vegetables grown in a kitchen garden.

Herbs in history

By 1066 AD, the custodians of medicinal herbs were European monasteries. After their dissolution, herbs became the province of the manor house garden and by Elizabethan times herb gardens had become very formal. In 1621, the first Botanic Garden in the UK opened at Oxford University, and in 1673 the Chelsea Physic Garden followed. By the 18th century, herbs had become an informal part of the flower border and vegetable plot.

ROMAN Geometrically precise, Roman herb gardens had raised beds filled with coriander, dill, parsley, rosemary, and fennel. These elaborate formal gardens disappeared during the Dark Ages.

MEDIEVAL Monastic gardens were rectangular and divided into four specific areas with paths running between each bed for easy access. The "physic" area was placed next to the infirmary, and each bed grew a medicinal plant. The vegetable garden area also had a system of rectangular beds. The third area contained fruit trees, and the fourth – the kitchen garden – had walled or raised beds.

TUDOR Most large houses grew a variety of sweet-smelling herbs to cut for nosegays. The herbs were combined with the flower garden for household use along with vegetables and fruit trees. This developed into the formal knot garden of the Elizabethan era.

STUART Formal European garden designs had a major influence during this period. The chief features of this style were broad avenues, flanked by rectangular parterres made up of formal low hedges. Herbs were often set apart in their own section.

20TH- AND 21ST-CENTURY DESIGN Early on, garden designers like Gertrude Jekyll treated herbs like other herbaceous perennials and incorporated them into the flower border, as shown in the photograph below. By the end of the 20th century, herbs were once again recognized for their own culinary and medicinal merit and the dedicated herb garden plan has now undergone a huge revival.

A mixed herbaceous, herb, and shrub border that was first created by Gertrude Jekyll.

Herb garden styles

The three main styles of herb garden still exercise their influence on design today. The dedicated physic garden had its origin in medieval monastic gardens; the formal knot garden can be seen at flower shows every year, and the culinary herb garden has become ever more popular.

PHYSIC The design of this herb garden is influenced by the monastic gardens. The beds are rectangular and divided by grassy paths, giving access to each area of the garden. Herb beds were carefully ordered and divided up so that each bed was planted with herbs from one family, or with herb plants that healed specific areas of the body such as the head, heart, or the circulatory system.

FORMAL KNOT In the early 16th century, knot gardens became fashionable. The feature of this style of planting is that regular geometric and symmetrical patterns are picked out in evergreen herbs like cotton lavender (*Santolina chamaecyparissus*), thyme (*Thymus vulgaris*), hyssop (*Hyssopus officinalis*), or hedge germander (*Teucrium* x *lucidrys*). An "open knot" garden was filled with flowers: a "closed knot" was a more complex pattern with no flowers but with a sand or brick dust infill to enhance the pattern. Box (*Buxus sempervirens*) was only introduced as a hedging plant in the 17th century.

CULINARY Over 200 years ago, herbs were a staple food of everyday life. The term "herb" had many different meanings: vegetables were known as "pot herbs", because they added bulk to the cooking pot; "salad" (salet) herbs and "sweet" herbs were used for flavouring, and "simples" were medicinal herbs. The culinary herb garden evolved from being primarily a combined vegetable and herb garden, to a garden that now contains mainly evergreen and annual herbs. The design of a culinary herb garden ensures that the plants are easily accessible for picking, so stepping stones or paths running between narrow beds are an important feature.

▲ **Box hedges** (*Buxus sempervirens*) punctuated by columns of clipped yew (*Taxus*) give structure to the garden all year round.

▲ **A modern-day apothecary's garden**, with a thyme (*Thymus*) centrepiece; the wide paths give shape and ease of access.

Formal versus informal design

Every gardener has a different idea of the style of herb garden they would like to create. Formal designs generally follow traditional lines and feature clipped evergreen hedges infilled with perennials and annuals. They give clear paths and a strong sense of direction, while informal gardens are often more relaxed with meandering paths that encourage you to stop and take in the colours and fragrances. As with formal designs, paths running through the informal garden are important for picking and maintaining the plants, which grow in large groups and self-seed rather than being restricted to a specific area or bed.

FORMAL SQUARE DESIGN

Based on the principles of an "open knot" garden, this offers a successful low-maintenance design for a small town garden or a "room" in a larger garden. The path ensures easy access to all four beds.

In the first year, the garden will establish itself. In the second year, trim the hedge to keep the plants at a uniform height. Pinch out growing tips of the bay trees to maintain shape. Lightly cut back sage, thyme, and oregano after flowering, and ensure that they do not smother the bay trees. After winter, check that herbs in the beds have room to spread; remove plants to create space if necessary. Fill any empty spaces. In late summer, cut back herbs after flowering to prevent self-seeding and stop the stems from becoming woody. By the third year, the box hedge will have started to knit together, and the bay trees will have grown up.

INFORMAL RECTANGULAR DESIGN

This fragrant, relaxed-style garden is planted with mint and lemon verbena, bordered by a silvery hedge of cotton lavender and has a slow, winding path running through, planted with a selection of thymes.

In the first year, trim sages, thymes, and oreganos after flowering to maintain their loose shapes, as well as the cotton lavender hedge. Protect tender plants like lemon verbena in winter. In the second year, check that the sorrel, wood sage, and oreganos have not spread too much. Lift and divide if they have (see page 53). Cut back lemon verbena and southernwood and remove growing tips from bay, myrtle, and luma. By the third year, the garden will have filled out and the hedge established. If you wish your garden to keep its shape, cut it back in spring. The thyme plants on the path may also need replacing.

Choosing a shape

Before you decide upon a shape, consider the space available and whether you want to plant up your whole garden with herbs, or would you like them to occupy a "garden room" within a larger garden, or just a flower bed or corner? Round or oval-shaped gardens are a lovely solution; the curved edge also allows access from all sides. A triangular herb bed is a good solution for the corner of a larger garden. A rosemary hedge along two or three sides protects Mediterranean herbs like oregano and thyme from exposure to cold winds and driving rain, and they will thrive. Clip the hedge to give a more formal appearance.

OVAL GARDEN

Oval and round gardens are good for making the most of a small space. This design has an S-shaped path edged with golden box, which runs like a golden ribbon through the design. The path creates the illusion of space, and makes picking the culinary and medicinal herbs a pleasure.

As the plants mature, a tapestry effect will be produced as the different herbs blend together. To achieve this effect, keep invasive plants like buckler leaf sorrel in check, and trim tall plants so that they do not dominate this small garden. Cut back lavender, sage, and thymes after flowering to maintain their shape, and cut off feverfew flowers to prevent self-seeding. Protect wild rosemary if the weather is cold, and mulch between plants in autumn. By the third year the box hedge should be established and the thyme plants cascading over the edge of the oval.

TRIANGULAR CORNER GARDEN

Here, the border of rosemary plants has only recently been planted and needs time to grow into a hedge. Creeping thymes have been planted in the centre of this simple design to create an aromatic carpet. In summer, when the thymes and rosemary are in flower, they will attract butterflies to this aromatic garden. The garden has been mulched with gravel to inhibit weeds and enable thyme to gain a foothold.

In the first year, only trim the top growth of the young rosemary hedge. In summer, trim the thymes after flowering to encourage new protective growth for the winter. In spring, check to see if any gravel has been washed away, and spread more if necessary. By the third year, the hedge can be properly trimmed and shaped to the required height. Make sure that there is a gap for access to the thyme plants.

Herbs and planting design

Describing how she first sets out a planting design, the influential plantswoman Beth Chatto says she treats the garden like any other room in the home – large plants are the "furniture", creeping plants the "carpet", and decorative plants the "ornaments". This simple yet effective approach is, in my experience, the key to successful planting and design in the herb garden. When clipped and trained into shape as hedges, plants such as box (*Buxus sempervirens*) provide the furniture for the garden and create the necessary height and structure for the design, while paths of creeping thyme or lawn chamomile make a wonderfully fragrant carpet. For ornament and decoration, groups of annual and perennial herbs will bring the garden alive with their changing colours and textures, coming into flower and dying back as the year progresses.

Herb ideas

The following herbs can be combined to create the herb garden you want, according to your planting plan (see opposite). Choose herbs you will make use of, as well as those that will work best in your garden.

HEIGHT AND STRUCTURE *Angelica archangelica* (angelica); *Angelica sylvestris* 'Vicar's Mead' (angelica Vicar's Mead); *Buxus sempervirens* (box); *Calomeria amaranthoides* (incense plant); *Chenopodium giganteum* (tree spinach); *Cynara cardunculus* (cardoon); *Eupatorium purpureum* (Joe Pye weed); *Humulus lupulus* (common hops); *Juniperus communis* (juniper); *Laurus nobilis* (bay); *Myrtus communis* (myrtle); *Olea europaea* (olive); *Sambucus niger* (elder); *Ugni molinae* (Chilean guava).

LEAF TEXTURE *Anethum graveolens* (dill); *Artemisia abrotanum* (southernwood); *Foeniculum vulgare* (fennel); *Meum athamanticum* (meu); *Perilla frutescens* var. *purpurascens* (purple shiso).

GROUND COVER *Centella asiatica* (gotu kola); *Chamaemelum nobile* 'Treneague' (lawn chamomile); *Satureja douglasii* (yerba buena); *Sempervivum tectorum* (houseleek); *Thymus* species (thyme).

DECORATIVE HERBS *Achillea millefolium* (yarrow); *Agastache foeniculum* (Anise hyssop); *Alchemilla mollis* (lady's mantle); *Allium schoenoprasum* (chives); *Cichorium intybus* (chicory); *Echinacea* species (echinacea); *Hyssopus officinalis* (blue hyssop); *Lythrum salicaria* (purple loosestrife); *Malva sylvestris* (common mallow); *Monarda fistulosa* (wild bergamot); *Oenothera biennis* (evening primrose); *Primula vulgaris* (primrose).

This magical walled garden combines a wonderful freedom of planting with a sense of structure. Masses of lady's mantle (*Alchemilla mollis*) overrun the gravel between clipped box "lollipops".

Creating a plan

The key to a successful planting is to work with nature. Look carefully at your previous planting and take note of which plants grew well without needing constant attention. The secret is to understand your garden environment (see pages 18–19) and learn to work within your specific site. Once you know where to position herbs in the garden, the creative process of planting design becomes much simpler. When selecting herbs for your planting scheme, consider each plant's characteristics, such as height and structure, leaf texture, and flower colour, and which herbs will provide year-round interest. A thoughtful planting plan with a range of heights and shapes will, in my experience,

look most effective (see pages 28–29), as will a scheme that has been designed to evolve over time as the plants mature.

Look to the work of garden designers for inspiration. If you want to inject your herb planting design with colour, consider Sandra and Nori Pope's planting combinations with their striking colour contrasts. If you favour the wild, naturalistic approach, look to Piet Oudolf's country garden designs, or to Beth Chatto for wonderful gravel-garden plantings. When you have decided on the effect you wish to achieve and have considered the shape and scale of the site, you are ready to put your planting plan into action.

◀ **After** – this photograph was taken in early summer, three months after planting. It shows how careful preparation of the soil in the previous autumn, along with detailed planning, can give a productive culinary herb garden in the first season.

▼ **Before** – this was the space chosen for the herb garden. It had not been used as a garden for a number of years, and the soil was very compacted.

Herbs in existing borders

Herbs can be successfully planted into existing flower borders. Their subtly coloured foliage and flower colours combine well with trees and shrubs. Equally, they look stunning in decorative vegetable gardens planted in formal patterns. In flower borders herbs mix well with wild flowers, especially in gravel gardens where they can self-seed and enjoy well-drained Mediterranean-type growing conditions. If the reason you like a herb is purely because of its colour or leaf shape, rather than its culinary or medicinal value, feel free to grow it for its appearance with other plants that you enjoy. Another reason for growing herbs with flowers in the garden is that they are popular with insects and butterflies. Plants such as angelica Vicar's Mead (*Angelica sylvestris* 'Vicar's Mead') and cardoon (*Cynara cardunculus*) are particularly attractive to beneficial insects.

Herbs with other plants

HERBS AND VEGETABLES In an organic garden, herbs make good companion plants for flowers and vegetables. For example, blue borage (*Borago officinalis*) grown alongside climbing beans will attract bees, which will pollinate the beans, producing large harvests. Chives (*Allium schoenoprasum*) planted next to rose bushes deter blackspot and help fix nitrogen in the soil. Catnip (*Nepeta cataria*) grown in between rows of carrots distracts carrot root fly and flea beetle from brassicas.

The swathe of painted sage (*Salvia viridis* var. *comata*) through this border complements the colours of the other herbs.

HERBS AND ROSES Historically, when monks were planting medicinal herb and vegetable gardens they would plant a rose bush at the edge of the herb bed to symbolize themselves at work. I have seen this use of roses and herbs in a number of historic gardens, notably the famous potager at Barnsley House, in Gloucestershire, UK, where white standard roses are underplanted with lavender to stunning effect.

HERBS AND FLOWER COLOUR In a formal garden, flowerbeds filled with black tulips and sweet woodruff (*Galium odoratum*) and edged with clipped evergreen box hedges look striking. I also enjoy the skilful use of tall silver-grey cardoons (*Cynara cardunculus*) as architectural plants, giving structure and height in grey and pink colour-themed borders. In the flower bed next to my house, I have mixed ceanothus (*Ceanothus thyrsiflorus*), jasmine (*Jasminum officinale*), and tree peony (*Paeonia delavayi*), and underplanted this with lungwort (*Pulmonaria officinalis*) and lady's mantle (*Alchemilla xanthochlora* syn. *vulgaris*). This combination of herbs and flowers works well, giving colour interest through the seasons.

An attractive border of colour and texture can be created with a balance of shrubs and perennials.

Good combinations

WHITE HERBS *Allium ursinum* (wild garlic); *Carum carvi* (caraway); *Chamaemelum nobile* (Roman chamomile); *Meum athamanticum* (meu); *Myrrhis odorata* (sweet cicely); *Valeriana officinalis* (valerian).

SILVER-GREY HERBS *Artemisia absinthium* (wormwood); *Cynara cardunculus* (cardoon); *Marrubium vulgare* (white horehound); *Nepeta* x *faassenii* (catmint); *Olea europaea* (olive).

BLUE HERBS *Borago officinalis* (borage); *Centaurea cyanus* (cornflower); *Cichorium intybus* (chicory); *Hyssopus officinalis* (hyssop); *Lavandula* x *christiana* (lavender Christiana); *Linum perenne* (flax); *Nigella sativa* (black cumin); *Salvia clevelandii* (Jim sage).

MAUVE/PURPLE HERBS *Allium schoenoprasum* (chives); *Lavandula stoechas* 'Willow Vale' (lavender Willow Vale); *Mentha spicata* var. *crispa* (curly mint): *Monarda fistulosa* (wild bergamot); *Origanum vulgare* (wild marjoram); *Symphytum* x *uplandicum* (Russian comfrey); *Thymus pulegioides* (broad-leaved thyme); *Thymus serpyllum* (creeping thyme).

PINK/RED HERBS *Angelica sylvestris* 'Vicar's Mead' (angelica Vicar's Mead); *Cedronella canariensis* (Balm of Gilead); *Centella asiatica* (gotu kola); *Pelargonium* 'Attar of Roses' (rose-scented pelargonium); *Sanguisorba minor* (salad burnet); *Teucrium chamaedrys* (wall germander); *Thymus coccineus* (creeping red thyme); *Tropaeolum majus* 'Empress of India' (nasturtium Empress of India).

Herbs in containers

By growing herbs in containers you can choose the soil and position to suit the plant. Containers of culinary herbs by the back door or on a windowsill are easy to access and are an effective way to grow herbs if space is limited. Most herbs adapt well to growing in containers. Details of the best conditions for growing individual herb species in pots are provided in my Top 100 herbs (see pages 74–215). Tender herbs like lemon grass are best grown in containers; they can be sunk into the flowerbed for the growing season and then lifted in winter and moved under cover for protection against frost, without damaging their roots. The rampant spread of invasive herbs, such as mint and horseradish, can be kept in check when grown in pots too, as their roots are contained and prevented from dominating the herb garden.

Maintaining herbs in containers

Choose a quality substrate so that the plant will thrive in this restricted environment; this will also help to prevent the fertilizer from leaching out. I find that the most reliable all-round substrate is a loam mix. To make your own loam-based potting substrate, mix seven parts loam, three parts composted fine bark, and two parts coarse sand. Alternatively, buy an organic multi-purpose potting substrate from a garden centre.

Seaweed and liquid comfrey are ideal fertilizers for feeding container plants (see page 39) or you can make your own fertilizer mix using: 225g (8oz) seaweed meal;

110g (4oz) bonemeal; 85g (3oz) hoof-and-horn, and 50g (2oz) ground limestone. This fertilizer mix will make enough for 35 litres of potting substrate. Use the feed once a week during the growing season.

It is difficult to judge how often a container plant needs watering as too much or too little can cause stress or long-term damage. Watering is dependent on the size and type of the plant, and the container material. Do not allow container plants to dry out, as once the substrate is dry it is very difficult to get it to take up water again. One of the easiest ways to check is to lift the container, and add water only if it feels light.

◄◄◄ **Creeping pennyroyal** grown on a windowsill is a good herb for repelling ants and for treating insect bites.

◄◄ **Common thyme** likes well-drained soil. If your garden soil is heavy clay, container growing in a loam-based potting substrate may offer a solution.

◄ **Cultivate parsley** in terracotta pots for use in cooking.

Choosing containers

DRAINAGE Make sure that your chosen container has adequate drainage holes. Add broken terracotta ("crocks") or large stones to the bottom of the pot for extra drainage, and to prevent the plant's root ball from sitting in water and rotting.

SIZE Choose the container to suit the plant. A tall plant will need a wide-based container to prevent it from becoming top-heavy and blowing over in strong winds. Also, plants such as bay and olive trees like to have their roots confined and thrive when pot-bound, so do not plant them in too large a container.

MATERIALS Terracotta pots look wonderful but can harbour disease from previous use. Scrub them out well before planting and, if they need sterilizing, dry them in an oven at 120°C (245°F) for 30 minutes. To give brand-new terracotta pots an aged look, cover the outside of the pot with live yoghurt to encourage moss to grow. Glazed pots are not as porous as plain terracotta and retain water better, but they may be prone to cracking in frosty weather.

Plastic offers the lightest and least expensive of container materials. However, sunlight can make plastic brittle. Woven willow containers look lovely but will only last a couple of seasons as they rot in wet weather. Line woven willow containers with moss before planting up with herbs to hold the substrate in place and retain moisture. Make sure that metal containers have adequate drainage holes and position them out of the midday sun, because the hot metal will heat up the soil and may damage the root ball of the plant.

◀ **Nasturtium** Empress of India (*Tropaeolum majus* 'Empress of India') was a show-stopper in this selection of unique containers from our 2008 Gold Medal display at the Chelsea Flower Show. As an annual, it gives flexibility and allows a change of colour emphasis for the following year.

Feeding the soil

Bulky organic waste products can be added to the soil in winter or spring, or both, to improve soil structure (see page 20) and increase its supply of food. Organic material is spread over the soil as a mulch or dug into the top 15–20cm (6–8in). Spring feeding gives a boost at the start of the growing season, while winter feeding offers a slow, steady release of nutrients before the next year's planting. Recycled organic waste forms the basis of all organic soil improvers; if you have a small garden, it may be difficult to generate enough to make your own compost. Make sure that any compost you buy is approved by an organic body such as the Soil Association or Garden Organic.

Compost and mulches

Compost is made from recycled garden waste that has been given time to rot down into a friable substance of medium fertility, which feeds the soil when added in spring or autumn. Mulches, on the other hand, are made from low-fertility waste, such as leafmould or compost bark, both of which inhibit weeds and prevent the soil from drying out in summer.

MANURE This is available from organic or non-intensive farms, and from garden centres. Make sure that the manure is well rotted before use as this stabilizes the nutrients, preventing them from being washed away by rain. To check the quality, smell the farmyard manure. It should have a sweet smell, not a strong and acrid one.

LEAFMOULD This is a useful soil improver and mulch. It has a low nutrient content so suits most herbs. Dug into clay soil, it improves the structure and the airflow and, when added to sandy soil, it helps retain moisture. As a mulch, leafmould is effective for suppressing weeds.

COMPOSTED BARK This mulch is useful for weed control as it is low in nutrients. Make sure that it is well rotted as fresh green bark has a high content of ammonium nitrate and can burn young seedlings and tree trunks.

COMPOSTED WASTE This organic compost is made from a mixture of garden waste, woody stems, and household waste such as fruit and vegetable peelings. Once composted, it has medium fertility, ideal for feeding all plants. It is best applied in spring, either as a mulch or dug into the soil.

Natural compost accelerators

Chamomile, yarrow, and comfrey plants can be added to the compost heap to speed up the decomposition process. The heat they release accelerates decay and kills weed seed. Comfrey leaves rot down quickest and are high in minerals.

Chamomile plants are placed on the compost heap, to act as a compost accelerator and kill weed seed.

Making compost from organic waste

1 **The key to healthy compost** is a good mix of materials. Only using kitchen waste or grass cuttings will create wet slurry. I start off my compost with woody prunings, which are slow to compost and allow air to circulate in the compost bin.

2 **Next add a layer** of organic kitchen waste, 8–10cm (3–4in) deep, then straw or cardboard. Repeat layers. If too dry, add grass or kitchen waste. If too wet, add straw or prunings. The compost is ready when dark brown and crumbly. This will take about 16 weeks in summer.

Making leafmould

1 **In autumn, gather up** fallen leaves from deciduous trees and shrubs in your garden. Do not take leaf material from woodland as this will upset the natural ecosystem. If you have few trees, ask your local council for a supply of leaf material.

2 **Place leaves** in an open bin, or lay sheeting over the mound to stop them from blowing away. Leave them to rot down to a mulch. One-year-old leafmould is a good mulch, two-year-old leafmould is an excellent soil improver when dug into the soil in spring or autumn.

Seasonal use of compost

The soil is the engine of the garden, and to maintain healthy plants it needs to be fed with organic compost: ideally, twice a year. In spring, dig in compost with a spade for an instant feed, if you have lifted herbs from the soil and wish to replace them with new ones. Compost again in autumn when the herbs have flowered and died back.

In autumn, a layer of compost on top of the soil will feed it with nutrients and improve its structure over the winter months, in preparation for the next year's planting. I discourage the use of chemical fertilizers as, unlike organic versions, they can upset the micro-organisms in the soil which, in turn, will upset the natural ecosystem of the garden. If you do not make your own

organic compost (see pages 36–37) or do not have access to organic farmyard manure, there are now organic fertilizers available from garden centres. "Hoof-and-horn", made from the finely ground and sterilized hooves and horns of cattle, is an organic source of slow-release nitrogen, while seaweed meal adds nitrogen, phosphorus, and potassium.

Preparing the ground

Autumn

Spring

1 Weeding is an important first step before you start adding compost to the soil. It is important to remove as many as possible, or the rich compost will feed the weeds and encourage their rapid growth. Use a fork to lift them, and carefully pick them out by hand.

2 Turn over the topsoil by digging over the ground with a spade to help aerate the soil. Always stand on a wooden board when turning over the soil to spread your body weight evenly and avoid compressing the soil and damaging its structure. Turning the soil also makes it easier to dig at a later date, when planting up the garden.

3 Lay on compost by spreading the compost over the soil with a fork in a thick layer. I recommend feeding the soil with compost in autumn to activate the micro-organisms in the soil. The action of the micro-organisms in the compost warms up the soil, while rainwater helps to release nutrients into the soil.

4 Digging in compost, the following spring, will mix in any compost remaining on the soil surface that has not been absorbed or washed away. Established herb plants and newly planted annuals will all benefit from the composted soil. If you have not laid compost on your soil the previous autumn, you can still dig in compost in spring to provide an instant feed for newly-planted herbs.

Organic liquid feed

Comfrey (*Symphytum officinale* or *S.* x *uplandicum*) is perhaps the best natural fertilizer as it is rich in potassium, calcium, iron, and manganese. The comfrey plant provides an abundant crop of leaves, which are available to harvest from spring through to late summer and can be simply and quickly made into a liquid feed.

The liquid feed made from this herb is ideal for foliar-feeding salad herbs, such as wild rocket and chicory, for root-feeding container plants such as box, and as a tonic for restoring mature garden plants such as southernwood or liquorice to health. For root feeding, dilute the liquid feed concentrate to 25ml (1 fl oz) per litre (1¾ pt) of rainwater. For foliar feed, dilute the concentrate to 12ml (½ fl oz) per litre (1¾ pt) of rainwater. Comfrey leaves can also be placed on the compost heap to speed up decomposition (see page 36), or added directly to a trench when planting potatoes. Always wear gloves when dealing with comfrey; some people are allergic to the hairs on the leaves, which can bring them out in a rash.

Making liquid comfrey leaf feed

1 Pick comfrey leaves, wearing gloves, in the early morning when they are at their freshest. Choose a bucket that will not rust and contaminate the liquid, and which has a tight-fitting lid to contain the strong odour of the comfrey leaves as they start to break down. To make approximately 1.2 litres (2pt) of liquid feed concentrate, use a bucket that holds 8 litres (14pt). Pack with the leaves, weigh them down with something heavy like a concrete block and pour over 600ml (1pt) of rainwater. Cover with the lid and place in a warm position but not in direct sunlight. Leave for three to four weeks.

2 After three weeks, remove the bucket lid to check the progress of the comfrey liquid feed. The leaves should have started to rot down, producing a murky brown liquid. If you cannot see any brown liquid, or the leaves are still taking up more than half the bucket space, replace the lid and leave to mature for a further week.

3 Sieve the liquid through a piece of muslin or a pair of old tights into a clean bucket or bowl. Discard any leaf material that collects on the muslin. This concentrated comfrey liquid feed will keep for up to six months if stored in a screw-top bottle, out of direct sunlight. Dilute as described above to make a root or foliar feed.

Herb propagation

For me, propagation is the most exciting job on the farm. I never cease to be amazed that from a cutting you can produce a new plant, and there is nothing more satisfying than to see the seedlings emerging in rows upon rows of trays. From the start, I taught myself how to grow plants without growth-promoting hormones like rooting powder. It is not necessary for herb cuttings, and is particularly harmful for women, upsetting their delicate hormonal balance. The first few weeks are critical and will determine both the health of the plant and its resistance to disease in later life.

When to propagate?

Propagation is not a complicated science. For successful seeds and cuttings, simply watch and imitate the natural cycle. The fruity mellow scent of autumn in the air is the signal to sow autumn seeds, such as angelica and foxgloves. Leave them outside in their containers to expose them to winter weather, especially fluctuating temperatures, which will encourage them to germinate. The change in the air temperature is also the signal to cut back hardy perennials to encourage them to put on

new growth that not only gives protection in winter but also ensures strong new shoots in spring from which successful softwood cuttings can be taken. In spring, look for the first signs of weeds growing. As soon as weeds appear you know the soil is warming up, and that day length is increasing, so it is time to sow annual herbs in open ground and to take softwood cuttings from established plants.

Greenhouse propagation

Balancing the natural ecosystem in an artificial environment, such as a greenhouse or conservatory requires constant surveillance as soft, lush seedlings that have no natural protection are easy pickings for pests. Also, the more seedlings you grow in one site, the more food there will be for pests and they will thrive in the warmth of this sheltered environment. To save having to check under every plant leaf and examine every tray for pests, you can hang yellow sticky traps throughout the glasshouse as an organic method of pest control. Any pest present will stick to the traps making it easier to diagnose the problem, be it an infestation of whitefly, scarid fly, or greenfly. If you find signs of pest damage, you will need to introduce some form of biological control to restore the balance, such as a natural predator that will prey on the pest. For whitefly the best predator is the parasitic wasp, *Encarsia formosa*. Both sticky traps and predators are available from garden centres.

Fennel seedlings need to be sown under protection in the spring, and kept indoors until the threat of frost has passed.

Propagation tips

Growing herbs from seed and cuttings under protection is very different from planting them out in open ground. In an artificial environment, you can control the soil, water, and temperature, and mimic the plant's preferred germinating conditions.

LIGHT Plants need light to grow, but seedlings and cuttings do not like being exposed directly to the hot midday sun as this scorches young leaves. Cover seed trays with lightweight horticultural fleece to shade them.

TEMPERATURE Cuttings need warmth to encourage roots to form and grow. Every seed has an optimum temperature for germination. Although most seeds germinate within a fairly wide temperature range, some have limits so it is worth checking (see pages 74–215).

WATER Cuttings need to replace moisture lost to put on top growth and to encourage roots. Seeds need water to penetrate the outer seed coat to begin the germination process.

AIR On the occasional warm day in winter and in early spring, open your home or greenhouse windows. Good ventilation encourages growth and helps to prevent disease. Oxygen is needed for plant respiration and carbon dioxide for photosynthesis.

▲ **Mint plants** are potted up from small pots to a larger one, ready for the growing season.

◀ **Borage seedlings** (*Borago officinalis*), almost ready for potting, emerge through a layer of perlite (see page 46).

Propagation methods

There are five key techniques used to propagate herbs, and the one you choose depends on the time of year and each plant's growing cycle. For example, sweet cicely (*Myrrhis odorata*) can be propagated by one of three techniques: it can be raised from seed sown in winter; from root cuttings in spring; or by division in autumn or spring. I have indicated the most appropriate method for each herb in my Top 100 herbs section (see pages 74–215).

◀ From seed

Any herb that produces flowers will produce seed. Seed is the only propagation method for annual herbs (see pages 45–49). Biennials – herbs that survive for two years – are also only propagated from seed. In the first year they produce leaf, and in the second flowers, then seed. For perennial herbs, cuttings are the best method of propagation.

▲ From root cuttings

Herbs that spread by creeping roots are propagated from root cuttings (see page 52); the best time to take cuttings is spring or autumn. For tap roots, a slice of root is taken, for creeping roots a thin piece of root with two growing nodes, and for roots that have both, like mandrake, a piece of root is sliced off with a growing node.

▲ From soft- or hardwood cuttings

Cuttings (see page 50) are a successful way to propagate herbs, especially those slow to develop from seed or whose seed is sterile. It works well for herbs that come from warmer climates and do not set seed because the day length is too short, the temperature too cold, or too damp.

▲ By root division

This involves digging up the root ball and breaking it up to produce smaller plants (see page 53). It is suitable for hardy herbaceous herbs that can, in time, die off at their central core. By dividing the plant you keep it vigorous and healthy. Like root cuttings, the best time of year to divide the roots is spring or autumn.

▲ By layering

With this method (see page 51), one of the oldest forms of propagation, you encourage the plant to form roots while attached to the parent plant. Herbs successfully propagated by layering include sage and rosemary, as they have low-growing branches. Layer in spring or autumn when soil is warm.

Choosing seed and seed containers

Take care when buying herb seed, as many producers offer enhanced germination and have used fertilizers and pesticides to achieve this. For example, "pelleted" seeds have an added outer case of nutrients and "primed" seeds have been modified to germinate more quickly. An established herb garden offers the best source of seed because you know its origins. First, check that harvested seeds have no signs of pests or diseases. Keep a record of when they were collected because some only remain viable for a year.

▲ **Pot** Sowing directly into pots is ideal for seeds that are slow to germinate. A pot is also suitable if you only intend to grow one type of herb, as it occupies far less space than a seed tray. They also offer more space for large seeds. The disadvantage of pots is that you can only grow one species from seed at a time.

▲ **Seed tray** These should be sturdy, and 5–7cm (2–3in) deep. The disadvantage of seed trays is that you have to "prick out" (see page 48) each seedling and, when doing so, it is very difficult not to damage the fine roots. Seed trays do not dry out as quickly as modules and they are useful for propagating seedlings whose germination is erratic.

▲ **Ground** Sowing seed into a prepared open site in the garden is ideal for those herb seeds, like dill and coriander, that dislike being disturbed and need to establish a taproot before they produce a crop. The disadvantage of sowing into open ground is that you have to wait until the soil is warm enough before you can begin.

▲ **Plug or modular tray** These are multi-celled trays with 6–200 cells made from plastic, polystyrene or pressed peat. Plastic modules are perhaps the easiest to use as once rooted, the seedling can be slipped out of the container. These trays are useful for plants that dislike having their roots disturbed, but they do dry out quickly.

Choosing seed-growing substrate

To give plants the best start in life, choose a quality seed-growing substrate. Do not take soil from the garden – this is not sterile and seeds will have to compete with weed seed. Last year's proprietary substrate is not an option either, because it may harbour pests or disease. Each year, I make up my own mix from the following ingredients: one part fine bark + one part perlite (or one part vermiculite) + two parts coir. As seeds have their own food supply, I do not add fertilizer, as it can inhibit seed germination and growth.

▲ **Fine bark** Tree bark is available in many different grades. For seed sowing you will need a fine- or propagating-grade bark. If using your own composted bark, ensure that it has rotted down – this usually takes six to eight months. Fresh, green bark is harmful to seedlings; it contains ammonium nitrate, which can burn them or stunt their growth.

▲ **Perlite** This is naturally occurring siliceous rock, heated to produce light, sterile granules. Perlite's structure encourages strong root growth. It is also mixed with other substrates to improve drainage and protect young root systems. It has a neutral pH which means that it will not upset the acid or alkaline balance of the chosen substrate.

▲ **Vermiculite** This is the mineralogical name for hydrated laminar magnesium-aluminium-iron-silicate. It has properties similar to perlite, but retains more water and less air and can be added to substrates to improve drainage or aeration. It can also be used as a seed covering to keep moisture in, but in my opinion, is not as good as perlite for this.

▲ **Coir** This is the outer layer of husk surrounding the shell of the coconut. It improves aeration and water retention in the substrate, and is ideal for encouraging roots to form quickly. It can be difficult to tell if seedlings need watering because the surface of the coir dries out quickly, while further down the substrate is still wet.

Germinating seed

For successful germination, try to mimic the natural conditions the seed will experience in the wild. These will vary according to whether it grows in the cold of the mountains (with extreme temperature fluctuations) or the humid climate of the Tropics. Copying these will improve your chances, especially with seeds that are difficult or erratic germinators. In spring, germination is triggered by a temperature increase, but some seeds require extra triggers, such as extreme cold.

Scarification

Some seeds have hard outer coats that are impervious to water. In the wild, the coat can be broken by the seed falling from the tree, by a sudden change in temperature, or by being ingested by an animal and passing through its digestive tract. In a controlled situation, you can break down the coating by placing the seeds into freshly boiled water. Allow the seeds to soak until the water cools to room temperature. Other methods of scarification include rubbing the seed coating with fine-grade sandpaper (shown here), or using a knife to nick the outer seed coating, taking care not to damage the "eye" (the little depression where the seed is attached to the ovary). Scarified seeds do not store well and should be planted immediately after treatment. Herbs that require scarifying include: *Ginkgo biloba* (ginkgo); *Laurus nobilis* (bay); *Olea europaea* (olive).

Stratification

By subjecting seed to sudden changes in temperature from cold to warm or vice versa, stratification breaks down the seed's protective coating. This mimics winter followed by spring, or summer followed by winter.

NATURAL STRATIFICATION: Where winter temperatures drop below 0°C (32°F) for a period of three weeks, sow the seeds into a container and leave outside to experience all weathers. The temperature change will help break down the protective outer coat.

ARTIFICIAL STRATIFICATION: Where winter temperatures remain warm, you may need to use an artificial stratification technique. Mix the seed with some moist vermiculite, sand, or coir (contact with a cold, damp substrate will make the seed colder). Place the seed mixture into a plastic bag, label it clearly and place it in the refrigerator. Keep it at a constant temperature of 0–5°C (32–41°F) for three to four weeks. Turn the bag from time to time to allow air to circulate.

HERB SEEDS that need stratifying include: *Angelica archangelica* (angelica); *Digitalis purpurea* (foxglove); *Meum athamanticum* (meu); *Myrrhis odorata* (sweet cicely); *Solidago virgaurea* (golden rod); *Viola odorata* (sweet violet).

Sowing seed

Before you start sowing, gather up the equipment you will need, including clean pots, trays, or modules, plant labels and a waterproof pen, the seed substrate mix (see page 44), the seeds for sowing, and a paper clip to reseal the seed packet when you have finished. Make sure your hands are clean and that you work on a clean surface so as not to infect the seed or contaminate the substrate. Seal and store any packets containing leftover seed in a dry, cool environment so that they remain viable.

Fine seed on the surface

Very fine seeds are usually sown on the surface and left uncovered, allowing contact with the maximum light, air, and water. Mix very fine seed with flour or fine sand so that the seed becomes more visible, then place this mixture into the crease of a folded piece of card. Gently tap to sow the seeds thinly on the surface.

▶ **Fine seed** *Calomeria amaranthoides* (incense plant); *Viola odorata* (sweet violet); *Viola tricolor* (heartsease).

Seeds to cover in perlite

Perlite is a useful cover for small seed. To sow, tip a small amount of seed into the palm of your hand. Allow it to settle in the crease of your palm, then carefully control the flow of the seed on to the surface of the substrate. Cover the seed with a thin layer of perlite to approximately the same depth as the seed.

▶ **Small seed** *Agastache foeniculum* (anise hyssop); *Allium fistulosum* (Welsh onion); *Foeniculum vulgare* (fennel); *Hyssopus officinalis* (hyssop); *Lavandula angustifolia* (lavender); *Ocimum basilicum* (basil).

Seeds to cover in substrate

Some medium-sized seeds benefit from being sown in a dark environment. These are often the seeds of plants that self-seed naturally in open ground; their leaves would have fallen in autumn, covering and protecting the seed and blocking out the light. Space seed evenly on the surface, gently press in, and cover with substrate.

▶ **Medium-sized seed** *Eupatorium purpureum* (Joe Pye weed); *Filipendula ulmaria* (meadowsweet); *Phytolacca americana* (pokeroot); *Primula vulgaris* (primrose); *Saponaria officinalis* (soapwort).

Seed-growing techniques

The most important factors for germinating and growing seedlings are water, light, and temperature. Before germination, keep watering to a minimum or the seed will rot, or "damp off", but equally do not allow the substrate to dry out. Germination takes an average of 10–14 days, but varies from species to species. Once the seedlings emerge, water the container in the morning so that it is not sitting in the cold and wet at night, when temperatures fluctuate. Water the substrate, not the seedlings, to avoid fungal disease.

Growing inside with extra warmth

PROPAGATOR This will enable you to control conditions to suit the seed's needs. Make sure that the lid has a vent for regulating humidity.

WINDOWSILL Use only east- or west-facing windows to raise seedlings; turn daily to stop them bending towards the light.

CONSERVATORY OR GREENHOUSE A conservatory is usually hotter. Ensure good ventilation, and protect seedlings in cold weather.

Growing outside with protection

COLD FRAME Use a cold frame structure to propagate seeds that need cold to germinate (see page 45), and to protect tender perennial herbs. Cold frames can be moved from site to site.

CLOCHE These are now available in all shapes and sizes. You can create a mini-cloche from a sawn-off plastic bottle, or buy a glass cloche to protect single plants. Alternatively, you can use an A-shaped cloche in the same way as a cold frame.

Covered with horticultural fleece

Horticultural fleece is available in different weights, depending on how much protection you wish to provide. On a cold spring morning on my farm you will see the young, tender herb plants covered with fleece to protect them during nights when frost is forecast. Always remove fleece during the day to prevent the plant from becoming too soft, and to check for weeds and slugs. Fleece is also an organic way to deter pests. I use it to cover parsley seedlings as a protective barrier against carrot root fly attack, and to protect wild rocket crops from flea beetle.

Pricking out to potting on

After nurturing your seedlings through germination, the next stage is pricking out and potting on. The seedlings are ready when they have formed their second set of leaves and are well rooted. To check if the roots are well formed, lift up the container and see if they are growing out of the bottom, or gently tap and ease the seedlings out of the pot.

After germination, the roots of the seedlings become more intertwined each day while they grow in their pot, and they will suffer stress and damage when transplanted if they have been left for too long before pricking out. Equally, if you leave seedlings in a module for too long, the root ball will become too tight for the seedling to grow and plant growth will be weak. Once they are transplanted, it is very difficult for the new, young roots to emerge from the tight root ball, and this can cause the young plant to die.

Pot seedlings on into a proprietary organic potting substrate or make your own substrate by combining one part coir; one part fine composted bark; one part sterilized loam, and one part vermiculite.

Pricking out seedlings

1 **Seedlings in modules** are ready for potting when you see their roots emerging from the bottom of the module. Seedlings in pots are ready for potting once they have formed their second set of leaves and have started to grow, making them easier to handle.

2 **Fill a container** with substrate, doing this correctly by scooping the chosen substrate into the container so that it is overflowing. Do not pat or tap it down – you are trying to maintain as much air as possible within the substrate.

3 **Remove seedlings** from modules by gently squeezing the base of the module with one hand and pulling the seedling from the module with the other. If you are pricking out seedlings from a seed tray or pot, water the substrate first to make this process easier. Then, using a stick, carefully lever the seedlings out of the substrate. Hold the seedlings by the leaves, not the stems.

I also make my own fertilizer to encourage the newly potted-up seedlings to put on root- and top-growth. To make enough fertilizer for four litres of substrate, mix together: 25g (1oz) seaweed meal; 15g (½oz) bonemeal; 15g (½oz) hoof-and-horn and 5g (¼oz) ground limestone. Alternatively, purchase a good commercial organic fertilizer. Add the fertilizer to your substrate mix at the recommended rate.

You will find that herbs raised in modules will grow twice as fast when potted on as those grown in seed trays or pricked out from pots. The root ball of seedlings grown in modules is hardly disturbed when it is transplanted so the plant does not go into a state of shock in its new surroundings, and the growth of a module-raised plant remains unchecked. This is unlike those seedlings raised in trays or pots, which need to regenerate roots before starting to grow on. When potting on, do not compress the substrate because this will remove the air from the soil and so make it harder for the root system to develop. Instead, simply tap the pot down on the potting bench or another hard surface when full of substrate, then water in.

Once potted up, the young plants will need to be watered regularly. When you are ready to plant them out in open ground, move them first to a protected site to "harden off" for at least one week, prior to planting. Hardening off is a gentle introduction to outdoor growing conditions and prevents herb plants from becoming stressed by the abrupt change when they have been planted out early in the season.

Potting on into a container

5 **Position the module** in the newly filled pot of substrate by tapping the container hard on a firm surface.

6 **Water in well** using a fine rose on a watering can so as not to flatten the young leaves. When ready to plant out, place the young plant in a cold frame or under a cloche to harden off.

4 **Pot up the seedlings** by making a hole in the substrate with one finger, then gently positioning the module into it. Do not push the module down into the substrate because this will compact the newly formed roots and reduce the air flow to the root ball, which will inhibit growth.

Propagation from cuttings

There is something miraculous about creating a new plant from a cutting. The secret of success with cuttings is to use fresh material, preferably collected before midday, then used as soon as possible to prevent it from drying out before it can be moved to a humid environment, under cover. In a matter of weeks, you will have a replica plant.

Herbs such as mint, oregano, and thyme can all be grown from cuttings. The technique for taking softwood (spring to early summer), semi-hardwood (summer to early autumn), and hardwood cuttings (autumn) is the same, with the only difference being the time of year that the cutting is taken from the plant. To grow your cuttings on, make up a cutting substrate mix to fill the modules using one part coir, one part fine bark, and one part perlite. I also use a small amount of organic fertilizer to encourage root growth without stimulating too much top growth. To make up your own fertilizer (enough for a four-litre volume of substrate) mix: 15g (½ oz) seaweed meal; 5g (¼ oz) bonemeal; 3g (⅛ oz) hoof-and-horn and 3g (⅛ oz) ground limestone. Use within six weeks.

Taking softwood cuttings

1 Selecting cuttings
Choose healthy, strong stems with fresh growth. Cut them with clean sharp scissors or secateurs. To keep the cuttings moist, mist the inside of a plastic bag with water, add the cuttings, then seal to prevent them from drying out. It is best to take cuttings early in the morning before the sun has started to dry them out.

2 Preparing cuttings
Remove the lower leaves from the stem with care, so as not to tear the stem – torn stems attract disease. Then, using a clean, sharp knife, cut the stem just below a leaf node. The length of the space between nodes can vary from species to species but try to include the growing tip, plus some leaf plus some stem.

3 Planting cuttings
Gently push the stem end of each cutting into the substrate in a module until only the leaves are visible. Spray-mist the cutting with water to keep it moist.

4 Growing on cuttings
Cover the cuttings. I use a small propagator (shown here). Alternatively, cover the cuttings with a plastic bag, but remember to turn it inside out each day to prevent the bag from becoming too moist. In the morning and again early evening, mist the cuttings with water. They should root within 14–21 days depending on the time of year – cuttings taken late in the year take longer.

Propagation by layering

This traditional method encourages the plant to form roots while still attached to the parent plant, and requires a well-established plant with strong growth hanging down to the ground. For this reason, it is a useful method for shrubby herbaceous herbs, where lower branches often root anyway when they come into contact with the ground.

All you are doing by layering the stem is encouraging the plant's natural tendency to propagate itself. The best time for this is in spring or autumn, when the soil is warm. Water in well afterwards, leaving at least one growing tip above soil level. Throughout the year, check the layered stem and the ground around it. Remove any weeds which may have grown up, and water the stem

layer because it is probably sheltered from the rain by the parent plant. After at least a year, check to see if the stem has rooted, if not, leave it alone for a further year. If it has successfully taken root, cut the stem that joins it to the parent plant. A few weeks later, dig up the rooted layer and replant it into a new well prepared site, where it will grow into a new plant.

How to propagate by stem layering

1 Scrape the stem
For large shrubs like sage (shown here), choose a strong, healthy stem and remove all side shoots and leaves from a 30cm (12in) section. For smaller herbs with much shorter branches, such as thyme, scrape away only 10–15cm (4–6in).

2 Prepare the ground
Dig over the soil well, removing all weeds and stones. For woody herbs like sage, bay, and elder, feed the ground with organic fertilizer to provide the cuttings with extra nutrients so that they will take better. For thyme and Vietnamese coriander, good drainage is the most important factor for successful propagation by layering. To improve soil drainage, add fine grit or sharp sand to the prepared site.

3 Anchor to the ground
Remove a slice along the side of the stem that is going to come into contact with the earth. For herbs with fine stems, peg the stem into the soil with a U-shaped piece of wire – this is more than adequate to hold it in place. For thicker herb stems, anchor the stem with metal pegs and bury in a trench to ensure successful propagation.

4 Cover up the stem layer
Spread a layer of soil over the stem, leaving the growing tip exposed. Herbs like thyme and Vietnamese coriander will put down root within one growing season (if you layer the stem in spring, you will be able to separate it from the parent plant by autumn). However, do not replant the layered stem outdoors in autumn. Instead lift it, pot it up, and place in a cold frame to protect it over the winter months. Plant out the following spring.

Propagation from root cuttings

The technique you use to propagate a herb plant from a root cutting depends on the size and type of root the plant produces. All root cuttings are taken in autumn or early spring when the maximum energy of the plant is in the roots. Collect and use cuttings on the same day to prevent the root from drying out.

Plants with thick taproots, such as comfrey and horseradish, can be propagated by taking a slice of root from the parent plant which is then placed in a pot and covered in substrate – the root slice is too big to grow in a module. Herbs with long, thin creeping roots, such as French tarragon, sweet woodruff, and mint, can be propagated by cutting off a section of the root about 2.5cm (1in) long that has at least two root nodes; this is known as an inter-nodal root cutting (see below). A nodal root cutting is a mixture of the two techniques described above. This technique works well for plants that produce a solid mass of roots, such as mandrake, and involves slicing off a section of root while making sure you take a growing node.

Sliced root cuttings

1 Taking a slice of root
Wash excess soil from the root. With a sharp knife, cut the root up into approximately 2.5cm- (1in-) thick slices.

2 Planting
Using the cutting substrate mix (see page 50), fill your pot two-thirds full with substrate. Make a small hole in the substrate with your finger, drop the cutting into the hole and cover with more substrate to just below the rim of the pot. Water in well and label.

Inter-nodal root cuttings

1 Cutting a node
Having selected your thin roots, wash well to remove excess soil so that the growing nodes are visible. Use a sharp knife to divide the cuttings up so that each length has two growing nodes. If you look carefully at these sweet woodruff cuttings, you will see that at each root node small roots have begun to grow.

2 Planting the cutting
Using the cutting substrate (see page 50), half-fill a module tray. Then lay the root cuttings on the surface of the substrate. Cover the cuttings with more substrate to just below the rim. Do not compact the substrate into the modules as this may damage fine roots. Water well.

Propagation by division

Dividing established herbaceous herbs is a useful way to produce more stock and to keep herb plants healthy. Often herbaceous herb plants, such as lemon balm, become invasive, and as the plant ages the central core can die away. Propagation by division prevents these problems from occurring.

Divide herbaceous herb plants in early autumn when they start to die back, or in early spring before they put on too much top-growth – any later in the season and you could inhibit flowering. When propagating by division, carefully dig up the whole plant plus its root ball, and shake off any excess soil. Divide the root ball in two with your hands, or use two garden forks placed back to back if some extra leverage is required to separate the roots. If you wish to replant one section of the plant back in the same site, dig some well-rotted compost into the soil to give the plant a boost when it is replaced. Replant the other section of the plant in a suitable spot, or, if you don't have the space, offer it to a friend with a garden to grow on.

How to propagate by division

2 Divide roots
Either shake the excess soil off the root prior to dividing or hold the root ball under a running tap to loosen the soil.

3 Replant
The divisions should be replanted into a prepared site as soon as possible to prevent them from drying out. Always water the plants in well. Divisions can also be potted up, either for insurance against bad winter weather, or to create a container plant.

1 Dig up roots
The plants to be divided should be dug up in spring or autumn. Both wild garlic and French tarragon are best divided in the autumn, but for different reasons. The garlic needs time to settle in for winter and to mature sufficiently to provide a crop the following spring. The French tarragon can be put in a cold frame to ensure it survives the damp, cold winter weather. See pages 74–215 for advice on individual plants.

Propagation problems

The main reason seeds and cuttings fail is because of fungal diseases contracted from either too much water, a contaminated supply, or the wrong substrate. Too much water causes seedlings to "damp off" – the term to describe a fungal disease that thrives in cool, wet, poorly ventilated substrates. Even in winter, it is important to maintain good air circulation to prevent this problem. On very cold days, when doors cannot be left open, use an electric fan to circulate the air instead. Hygiene can also cause problems, as fungal

Overcrowded seedlings

It is very easy to sow fine seed too thickly, causing the seedlings to crowd each other out, which in turn inhibits their development into strong, healthy specimens. For sowing techniques, see page 46. If one seedling becomes diseased, the problem can spread very quickly through such close contact with the other seedlings. If you have sown too thickly by mistake, thin the seedlings out as soon as they emerge so that you only have two or three seedlings per 2cm (1in) module.

▶ Watchpoints

Mix fine seed with flour or sharp sand for a thin sowing. Avoid sowing seedlings too close together to prevent the leaves of individual seedlings from touching one another, which may spread infection (see right).

Overwatered cuttings

Growing young plants from cuttings brings out the worst in the enthusiastic gardener. If their "offspring" look poorly, the gardener tries to help the ailing cuttings by watering them. Too much water puts young plants under stress, as they do not have an established root system that can cope. Overwatering also attracts pests, especially sciarid fly, which thrives on wet substrate. The fly lays its eggs in the substrate, and the larvae hatch within a week, feeding on the plant's roots and killing off the cuttings.

▶ Watchpoints

The tray or pot feels heavy with water. When you lift a cutting from the tray, water seeps out. The cuttings start to die. Clouds of black sciarid fly appear when you knock the tray – a sure sign of a very wet substrate.

infections persist in dirty trays and unsterilized substrates between rounds of propagation. It is essential to choose a substrate with the right nutrient content to suit the seedling or cutting, especially when sowing seeds, as a multi-purpose potting substrate often has too high a nutrient content for the young plants. This will cause the seedlings to grow too quickly, producing thin, weak growth that is vulnerable to fungal disease and prone to attack from pests.

Cuttings taken at the wrong time

As a general rule, it is best to take cuttings when the herb is not in flower so that the leaves and stems are in peak condition. When in flower, all of the plant's energy is taken up by flower production. For herbaceous herbs, it is best to take cuttings before flowering; by autumn the herbs will have started to die back. Evergreen herb cuttings are best taken in summer or early autumn. Any earlier and the sap will not have risen, so the cuttings are much slower to root.

▶ **Watchpoints**

Cuttings taken at the wrong time may take a long time to put down roots. Look out for cuttings that are weak and die, or those that root but do not put on new growth.

Disease in cuttings

Cuttings taken from plants that have been attacked by pests are best avoided because the cutting is weak from the outset and will attract disease. Use a clean, sharp knife to take cuttings to avoid diseases like blackleg, which can occur if plant cells in the stem are crushed. Blackleg spreads rapidly, and the only organic solution is to throw away the cuttings and start again. Always wash propagation trays thoroughly after use, especially if previous stock was diseased or attacked by pests.

▶ **Watchpoints**

Look out for the stem of the cutting turning black, or the growing tip of the cutting bending over. If you notice mould growing on the leaves, this could be the first sign of mildew.

Seasonal maintenance

I find it useful to keep a record each year of when we take cuttings, when we sow seeds, and what pests have caused problems during the year. The maintenance routine changes very little; in an organic herb garden there are always jobs to be done as you have only natural methods for keeping pests and weeds under control. The secret of a well-managed herb garden is to keep the ecosystem in balance, stay vigilant, and not be fooled by nature. If spring comes early, for example, be prepared to guard against frost at night – have a roll of horticultural fleece ready to cover up tender plants.

A year in the herb garden

Spring

While you prepare the ground for sowing annual herbs in spring, take time to mulch around mature plants to suppress weed growth and to save time spent weeding. Container plants also require attention at this time – they may need repotting, pruning, or carrying outdoors. As summer approaches, growing tips need pinching out to keep plants bushy, and flowering herbs require regular deadheading to keep them in flower. Tender herbs are ready to plant out when the risk of frost has passed.

Summer

By midsummer, every herb plant in the garden is gearing up for harvest. Now is the time to choose which herbs you are going to let run to seed for propagation, and which ones you wish to keep in cultivation through winter. Summer is also the time to cut back hardy herbs to encourage them to produce extra growth for winter protection and late pickings.

Autumn and winter

As winter approaches, tender plants need protecting from frost. Clear away annual herbs. Dig over and mulch the soil to feed and protect it. In winter, plants under protection are prone to disease so ensure good ventilation. Take time in winter to select healthy seeds and plan next year's herb garden.

The maintenance calendar

See the pages that follow for more detailed information on maintenance throughout the year, whether you have a young or mature herb garden. Below is a quick reference guide to refer to for your maintenance tasks:

Early season in the young garden

If the soil has been dug and planted with annuals, your plot will harbour weed seed as well as the young plants. It is essential to be diligent and keep weeds under control or they will take all the nutrients from the soil intended for young plants.

Early season in the mature garden

It is important to cut back plants to produce new growth. This not only protects the plant but also creates lots of fresh leaf growth which can be used in cooking, the home, or for medicinal purposes.

Late season in the young garden

Mulch well between perennial herbs. This not only inhibits weeds, but also protects the roots of young plants through winter.

Late season in the mature garden

Remember to start feeding the birds so that they stay in the garden for the season. If the weather is excessively wet, cut back hardy herbaceous top-growth to prevent it from rotting.

▲ **When frost is forecast**, wrap up tender plants that are too large to be brought indoors, using horticultural fleece.

▲ **In spring**, check plants for damage by pests such as vine weevil. If damage is extensive, introduce a predator to restore the balance.

▲ **Late autumn** is the season to cut back herbs like thyme so that they will burst into new growth the following spring.

▲ **Late summer** is the time for trimming box. It will then keep its shape through winter and spring before the summer growing season.

Early season in the young garden

Spring in a young garden is exciting because you can start to see the results of your propagation and planning work. Having prepared the ground (see page 22), it is very difficult to remain patient and not to rush out and start sowing on the first day of good weather, but you need to wait for the soil to warm through. There is a saying that "if you can sit on the soil without feeling the cold it is time to plant". Alternatively, wait for weeds to start appearing, a sure sign that the soil is warming up and that it is time to

Planting out annuals and salad herbs

If you live in an area prone to hard frosts or damp soil, sow seeds under protection; they will need hardening off before they are planted outside. Start by taking them outside during the day for a week then, if no frost is forecast, start leaving them outside at night. As a general rule, plant seedlings 5cm (2in) apart. Water in well and, for the first week, cover them at night with horticultural fleece to encourage them to root.

Some annual herbs to plant from seed:
Borago officinalis (borage); *Calendula officinalis* (pot marigold); *Carum carvi* (caraway); *Coriandrum sativum* (coriander); *Diplotaxis muralis* (wild rocket); *Ocimum basilicum* (sweet basil); *Origanum majorana* (sweet marjoram); *Satureja hortensis* (summer savory).

Shelter for young plants

When young plants are becoming established, they need protection from birds and high winds. Make a shelter from twigs to act as a wind break and protective cage, which will allow water and sunlight to reach the seedlings. If you have trouble with birds eating large plants, string up lines that hum in the wind to scare them off. These are available through organic gardening catalogues.

Some herbs that need protection from birds:
Anethum graveolens (dill); *Anthriscus cerefolium* (chervil); *Carum carvi* (caraway); *Chenopodium giganteum* (tree spinach); *Cichorium intybus* (chicory); *Coriandrum sativum* (coriander); *Foeniculum vulgare* (fennel); *Origanum majorana* (sweet marjoram); *Petroselinum crispum* (parsley).

plant. When planting, stand on a plank to spread your weight evenly so as not to compress newly dug soil. Use the side of the hoe to carve a straight shallow drill in the soil where you wish to plant. When sowing dark-coloured seed, line the drill with sharp sand prior to sowing to make the seed visible and easier to sow thinly. After sowing, check for signs of pests and disease. Young herbs are tender morsels for slugs, snails, greenfly, and other pests that frequent the garden in spring.

Staking young plants

If you want to encourage a herb plant like bay to grow into a standard tree shape, the young plants will need staking and training. This is also the case if you want to make a rosemary hedge or intend to grow herbs on an exposed site, to keep them upright in strong winds. Stake young plants with pea sticks or bamboo. If possible, support the plant without fastening it to the stake or the stem may bend towards the pole; simply place the stake parallel to the plant stem. On exposed sites, a ring of pea sticks around the herb will protect it from wind and keep it vertical.

Herbs to support:
Laurus nobilis (bay); *Luma chequen* (luma); *Myrtus communis* (myrtle); *Rosmarinus officinalis* (rosemary).

Weed control

Weeding techniques:
HOEING — for best results, keep the hoe tool sharp, and hoe dry soil on a sunny day, cutting off the weeds where the stem joins the root. (Weed seedlings wilt in sunshine and do not take root again.) Make sure you collect all the weeds when you have finished.

FLAME GUN, THERMAL WEED KILLER — a thrilling way to kill perennial weeds is to torch them. This also sterilizes the soil.

SLASHING AND CUTTING — a good short-term solution is to cut down the weed plants. Repeat cutting is effective because it weakens and slows down the growth of stubborn weeds.

Early season in the mature garden

As the soil starts to warm up early in the year in an established herb garden, all your favourite hardy perennials like chives will reappear. This is the time to start weeding. When the ground is clear, apply a layer of mulch (see page 23) to "top up" the nutrient content of the soil after winter so providing feed for established plants. Also mulch beds that you intend to leave free of plants, to suppress weeds. In areas where you want to sow annual herbs, dig in well-rotted compost or mature leaf mould (see pages 36–37).

Trimming to shape

In spring, when all chance of hard frosts has passed, trim box plants and rosemary, especially if you are growing either plant as a hedge feature. When growing bay tree standards, cut off the growing tips in spring. This will encourage bay to put out sideshoots and fill out. If you have been picking thyme through the winter for cooking, it is a good idea to give it a light trim to reshape it, and to encourage it to produce new growth in the spring.

Herbs that need trimming:

Buxus sempervirens (box); *Eriocephalus africanus* (South African wild rosemary); *Laurus nobilis* (bay); *Luma chequen* (luma); *Myrtus communis* (myrtle); *Rosmarinus officinalis* (rosemary); *Thymus vulgaris* (thyme).

Removing pests

Early season pests include:

CATERPILLARS – check plants where you have seen butterflies. Pick off eggs and caterpillars by hand. Encourage blue tits and wasps; both are good predators.

CUTWORM – these brownish-white larvae of a nocturnal moth feed at night on seedlings, roots, and corms. Remove larvae by hand or turn the soil and expose the cutworm for birds to feed on.

SLUGS – remove by hand or from spring to late summer, introduce a biological control like the parasitic nematode *Heterorhabditis megidis*.

VINE WEEVIL – these pests attack species of primula and houseleek (*Sempervivum* species). Remove by hand or use the same biological control as for slugs.

In cold and wet geographical regions, spring rather than autumn is the best time to cut back sun-loving, silver-foliage plants like artemisia, because autumn pruning will let water penetrate the plant and kill it off. Spring is also the time of year to reorganize the location of plants in an established garden. Dig up plants that have become invasive, and free up space around tall herbaceous herbs like cardoons. Create more space around biennial herbs such as angelica in the year that they are going to flower.

Pruning

In spring, some herb plants may need pruning to remove dead branches and to cut out dead growth. Spring is the best time of year to prune because you can see what needs doing more clearly when there is little leaf canopy. It is also a good time to prune and reshape Mediterranean herb plants like myrtle and olive that favour dry conditions. Avoid pruning these in autumn; the wound caused by pruning may not heal before cold and wet winter weather sets in, encouraging infection.

Herbs to prune in spring:

Aloysia triphylla (lemon verbena); *Artemisia abrotanum* (southernwood); *Lavandula angustifolia* (lavender); *Olea europaea* (olive); *Rosmarinus officinalis* (rosemary); *Santolina chamaecyparissus* (cotton lavender).

Feeding

Some herbs are best fed in spring, to set them up for the year. This is particularly the case with salad herbs and fruit-producing herbs, as you will be harvesting them regularly and feeding will produce plenty of lush leaf growth. Take care to get the balance right; over-feeding will lead to weak growth, making plants susceptible to pest damage. Spring feeding is also a good idea for tender herbs that have been lifted in autumn and planted out again in spring, to kick-start spring growth.

Plants that benefit from spring feeding:

Allium fistulosum (Welsh onion); *Aloysia triphylla* (lemon verbena); *Buxus sempervirens* (box); *Levisticum officinale* (lovage); *Olea europaea* (olive); *Pelargonium* species (scented pelargoniums).

Late season in the young garden

By late summer, plants in a young herb garden will have started to meld together to create a harmonious whole. There will be some herbs that have exceeded expectations and thrived in your chosen planting position, while for others growth may have been disappointing. Plants that have romped away can be cut back drastically, but if you are concerned that your pruning is too savage, plant some of these vigorous herbs in pots to overwinter in a cold frame as insurance against loss. For the poor performers, lift and

Mulching

Apply extra mulch to a young garden in autumn to keep weed seeds at bay but also to keep the roots of young plants free from frost damage in their first season. Mulches allow water to permeate the soil more easily and reduce the likelihood of the young plants sitting in water. To prevent the plant stem from rotting, do not lay mulch right up close to the herb. There are many different forms of mulch (see pages 36–37) and one may be better suited to your soil and plant than another.

Herbs that benefit from late-season mulching:
Aloysia triphylla (lemon verbena); *Cedronella canariensis* (balm of Gilead); *Ginkgo biloba* (ginkgo); *Humulus lupulus* (common hop); *Juniperus communis* (juniper); *Laurus nobilis* (bay).

Removing seed heads

Deadheading or removing seed heads can prolong flowering of herbs such as pot marigold and nasturtium up until the first frosts. It is important to remove the flowers of feverfew and borage; if they self-seed, you could have swathes of white and blue flowers the following season, which can be very frustrating when trying to establish a mixed herb garden. Another reason for removing the seed heads, especially from annuals, is to save them for drying and sowing the following season.

Herbs that become invasive if they self-seed:
Anethum graveolens (dill); *Angelica archangelica* (angelica); *Digitalis purpurea* (foxglove); *Lysimachia vulgaris* (yellow loosestrife); *Oenothera biennis* (evening primrose); *Portulaca oleracea* (purslane).

check their roots for signs of growth during the season. Pot them up and put them into a cold frame for the winter, and move them to a new site the following year. Late season is also the time to protect young herbs, especially trees such as olives and ginkgos, that are about to experience their first winter in the soil. Small trees should be covered with a cloche which is open at both ends for good air circulation. Larger trees can be wrapped in horticultural fleece when frosts are forecast.

Cutting back

At the end of the season, some young plants need more drastic cutting back than others, either of flowers and flowering stems, flowers and new growth (to prevent flowering stems falling back in on themselves and rotting out the plant centre), or all top-growth.

Young herbs to cut back in late season:
Flowers and flowering stems: *Lavandula* species (lavenders); *Salvia* species (sages); *Thymus* species (thymes).
Flowers and new growth: *Scutellaria lateriflora* (skullcap virginia); *Symphytum officinale* (comfrey); *Tanacetum balsamita* (alecost); *Tanacetum cinerariifolium* (pyrethrum).
Top-growth: *Melissa officinalis* (lemon balm); *Origanum vulgare* (oregano).

Lifting tender plants

As the winter months approach, check the weather forecasts and be ready to lift all tender herbs before the first frost. As soon as the night-time temperature dips below 4°C (39°F), lift the herbs, cut them back, pot up, and water them in. Place in a frost-free environment (without central heating) for winter. They will need little water, but check that the substrate is not shrinking away from the sides of the pot. Replant in the garden the following spring, once all threat of frost has passed.

Some tender herbs to lift:
Aloe vera (aloe); *Cymbopogon citratus* (lemon grass); *Elettaria cardamomum* (cardamom); *Lavandula stoechas* 'Kew Red' (lavender 'Kew Red'); *Pelargonium* species (scented pelargoniums).

Late season in the mature garden

The hope is that you will have had a bountiful harvest from your herb garden and your shelves will be groaning with produce to use in the kitchen during the winter months. Now is the time to put your garden to bed for the winter, so that it will perform as well, if not better, the following year. Dig up the older herbs that are past their best and no longer looking beautiful or producing leaves full of flavour. This is better done now than left to the spring because you can place the old plants on the compost heap, dig over the bare

Removing debris from plant crowns

In autumn, I recommend cutting back and clearing the debris from around herbaceous herbs rather than letting the leaves and stems die back naturally. In cold, damp climates, clearance will prevent the crown from rotting away over winter, and you will have a much healthier plant the following spring.

Herbs that benefit from crown clearance:
Scutellaria lateriflora (skullcap virginia); *Tanacetum balsamita* (alecost); *Teucrium scorodonia* (woodsage).

Cutting back hard

In early autumn, if you cut back all the season's growth of herbs like oregano, you will see a compact rosette of new growth appearing, encouraged by the warmth remaining in the soil. This growth will ensure light pickings of fresh leaves for cooking throughout the winter months. Cutting back hard can also prevent the spread of disease such as rust, to which mints are prone, and maintain a herb plant's shape.

Herbs that benefit from cutting back hard:
Hyssopus officinalis (hyssop); *Melissa officinalis* (lemon balm); *Mentha* species (mints); *Nepeta cataria* (catnip); *Origanum vulgare* (oregano); *Origanum* x *onites* (French marjoram); *Persicaria odorata* (Vietnamese coriander); *Teucrium scorodonia* 'Crispum' (curly woodsage).

soil and add in some well-rotted manure. By spring the ground will be ready for planting a young herb in the same place, which will grow well in its first season. At this time of year, choose a few herbs to shelter from the cold weather so that you can continue to have fresh herbs for cooking through the winter; thyme, sage, and rosemary are good candidates. Either cover the plants in the soil with a cloche or pot up some of the plants and bring them into the greenhouse, conservatory, or kitchen.

Encouraging birds and wildlife

I have been extolling the virtues of keeping your herb garden tidy in order to minimize disease and maintain productivity. That said, you need to create space for both pest and predator to hibernate during the winter, encouraging them to stay and so maintaining the ecobalance.

Bird boxes made with untreated wood should have small entry holes and be placed so that cats and squirrels cannot reach in.

Stacks of wood or logs will shelter hedgehogs and beetles.

Mulches left undisturbed in a mound during the winter are ideal shelter for frogs, toads, shrews, and spiders.

Mulching the crown

After mature hardy herbaceous herbs like sweet cicely (shown here) have been cut back in autumn, they will benefit from having the area of soil around the crown mulched with compost, but avoid well-rotted manure as this is too rich in nutrients. This layer of mulch will encourage the mature plant to produce lush new growth the following spring and come back healthy and vigorous.

Herbs that benefit from mulching:
Levisticum officinale (lovage); *Myrrhis odorata* (sweet cicely); *Phytolacca americana* (pokeroot); *Scutellaria lateriflora* (skullcap virginia).

Harvesting techniques

An abundant harvest is the reward for having spent time nurturing your herbs. To enjoy the best flavour and medicinal benefit the plants have to offer, it is important to pick the leaves, flowers, seeds or berries and roots or bulbs carefully and in the best possible conditions. For annual herbs, harvesting times vary according to the plant part you wish to obtain. For biennial herbs, good leaf harvests are achieved in the first year, while roots should be left alone until the second year to mature. For evergreen herbs, the first season is spent patiently feeding and shaping the plant to ensure that it puts on healthy growth.

When to harvest

Although evergreen leaf trimmings can prove adequate for adding flavour to cooking or making a tisane, larger harvests are only an option in the second and third year. But it is well worth the wait because the leaf flavour of evergreen herbs like bay then remains consistent over the year, so that they can be harvested at any time.

Herbaceous herbs, like French tarragon, can only be picked fresh in their own specific growing season. If they are being harvested for culinary use, however, the harvesting period is actually even narrower because the best leaf texture and flavour is generated by the new growth.

Harvesting the leaf of flowering herbs, such as chives and oregano, should be done either side of flowering. During flowering, the energy of the plant is diverted into producing flowers and the leaves become tougher in texture and have less flavour. By cutting perennial herbs back hard after flowering, and giving the plant a feed, you will encourage a second flush of tender young leaves for harvesting.

If you are harvesting herbs for their medicinal properties, you will want to be able to extract the best quality essential oil the plant leaf or root has to offer – this is best from young leaves, just as they start to mature, or mature roots, while succulent young roots are better for cooking. More detailed information on harvesting is provided on the following pages and in my Top 100 (see pages 74–215).

Harvesting times

Knowing when to harvest the various parts of your plants ensures that you will be able to use each herb at its best, whether for medicinal or culinary purposes. The following pages give more detail on techniques – see below for a quick reference guide to harvesting times.

Leaf – from herbaceous and annual herbs. Pick these fresh as soon as the leaf is large enough, and continue to harvest throughout the growing season. Harvest evergreen leaves all year round.

Flower – from early summer and in some cases until the first frosts in autumn. The flower is best picked when the bud is just about to open out fully.

Seed – in late summer after the plant has flowered.

Berry – in early autumn after flowering and when the berry is ripe (usually signalled by a change in colour).

Root – in autumn. For culinary use, harvest the root just before the plant's top-growth dies back. For medicinal use, wait until the plant has died back but before it has used up its root store to grow again.

Bulb – harvest in late summer. Wait until the plant's top-growth has died back in autumn so that the bulb has a rich store of nutrients.

▲ **Fennel seeds** (*Foeniculum vulgare*) can be collected from the flowerhead for drying in late summer, after flowering.

▲ **Echinacea flower** (*Echinacea purpurea*) is harvested before the seedheads are fully formed. In autumn, mature roots are dug up for medicinal use.

▲ **Pokeroot berries** (*Phytolacca americana*) are toxic, and turn deep purple when the seed is ready for harvest, from late summer to late autumn.

▲ **Sweet cicely seeds** (*Myrrhis odorata*) are brown and shiny when ripe, and should be harvested in late summer.

Harvesting leaves

Fresh herb leaves can be picked throughout the growing season for use in cooking. For best flavour, harvest just before flowering – for soft-leaved herbs like parsley, harvest before flowering but after the plants have been well fed, as the leaves respond to feeding, becoming lusher and sweeter. Pick leaves in dry weather, before the heat of the midday sun, or the oils that give flavour will evaporate. All herb leaves can be dried or frozen, but drying is preferable; it intensifies the flavour, while freezing diminishes it.

Gathering leaves
Pick in the morning after dew has evaporated, but before the heat of the day. Choose lush, healthy leaves. Harvest fresh leaves in small quantities to avoid waste, and keep different herb flavours separate so as not to taint them. Evergreen leaves can be harvested all year and are best used fresh.

Harvesting

1 Pick healthy leaves
For perennial herbs like thyme and oregano, the leaf flavour is strong so you will only need a few leaves. It is best not to pick more than a third of available leaves at any time, as perennial herb leaves grow back slowly. When picking annual herbs, especially salad leaves, you can take more leaves because they are grown to be cropped regularly and the leaf flavour is milder. Pick quickly as their soft leaves are more likely to wilt. For all herb leaves, choose the healthiest-looking as they are the ones with the most beneficial properties. Try not to bruise them as you pick, as this will damage their structure and impair flavour.

Drying

2 Spread leaves out
The object of successful drying is to eliminate the leaf's water content and at the same time retain the oil that gives flavour. Dry herb leaves separately from each other; small ones will dry faster, and strongly scented herbs may taint more subtle ones. Spread leaves on muslin stretched over a wooden frame. Place in a dark, warm, dry, well-ventilated room. Turn the leaves over several times during the first week as they need air to reach every surface in order to dry.

Preserving

3 Store in jars
When the leaves are dry enough to crumble, they are ready to be stored. They will quickly lose their flavour and colour if not stored properly. Put them into a dark glass jar with a screw top; label with the herb name and date. Check the container for the first few days; if moisture forms on the lid, the herbs are not dry. Return them to the drying rack. The shelf life for dried herbs is about a year. They are usually three to four times more potent in flavour than fresh herbs so smaller amounts are needed.

Harvesting flowers

Herb flowers usually have only one flowering season a year, so it is important to get the timing right and harvest them at their best. Whichever flowers you harvest, always pick them just as they break open to maintain the best colour, fragrance, and taste. There are a number of ways of preserving them, but the best method for preserving flowers for use in winter is to dry them. Many herb flowers dry well, from lavender to cornflowers, and flowers like chamomile are popular in tisanes (see page 221).

Gathering flowers

Pick in the morning as soon as the dew has dried. Gently shake the flowerheads to remove any insects. Pick the flower either in bud or just when it is starting to open. Pick in small bunches to enable air to circulate and prevent the buds from rotting. Once cut, keep out of direct sunlight.

Harvesting

1 Select flower buds
Herb flowers are best harvested just after the flower buds appear but before they open fully. At this stage in their development, they offer their most intense oil concentration and flavour. Younger flowerheads are also more beneficial; once overblown their qualities are reduced. Flowers will continue to open during the drying process.

Drying

2 Warm and dry
Once cut, keep flowers out of sunlight. This is important to maintain good colour, fragrance, and taste. You can dry individual flowers on a muslin frame, or cut whole stems and tie them in small bunches. Dry bunches with the flowerheads hanging down in an area where warm, dry air circulates. When dried, the flower should feel stiff and dry.

Storing

3 Airtight jars
Dried single flowers can be stored in dark airtight jars for use in tisanes. Flowers dried in hanging bunches should only be picked off their stems and stored in jars if they are going to be used for medicinal or culinary uses. Once exposed to the air and light, their properties deteriorate. Alternatively, use dried herb bunches in the home (see page 236).

Harvesting seeds

It is important to know when seeds are ripe for harvesting. For example, borage seeds turn black when ripe and fall to the ground. Fennel seeds turn light brown and should be harvested as the seeds become loose and start breaking free of the seedhead. If you are unsure, gently tap the plant. If seed falls off, it is time. Always harvest on a still, sunny day, once any morning dew has dried. Take a paper bag or a seed tray lined with newspaper to the plant to avoid dropping and spreading seed in the garden.

Gathering seeds
Collect seeds as they start to fall or float away from the seed head. Always use paper not plastic bags to collect seeds to avoid a build-up of condensation, which may rot the seed. Use separate bags or trays to collect different seeds, and take a plant label with you to identify the seed afterwards.

Collecting

1 Ready to gather
Angelica seed (shown here) is ripe for harvest when it falls into the hand with a gentle tap of the seed head. Use a paper bag to collect a small number of seeds or line a cardboard box with newspaper, cut the head from the plant and put it into the box.

Drying

2 Allow to dry out
Clean the seed by removing it from the stems and stalks. Small seeds require a lot of cleaning, while others are easy to extract from the dry seed pods by simply shaking them vigorously. Once extracted, spread the seed out thinly on muslin or kitchen towel. Place in a dry, airy room and leave the seed for a few days to dry out.

Storing

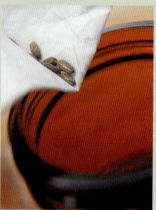

3 Ready for sowing
Check the quality of seeds before storing, and discard any that are damaged or half-eaten. Store them in a dark glass jar, cardboard box, or paper envelope, clearly labelled. Write on the month and year that the seeds were collected, so you can check that the seed is still viable when you come to sow it.

Harvesting berries

When berries start to form, autumn is well on the way. Seeds encased in berries are best collected fresh. Drier, pithier berries can be left on the bush to shrivel slightly, making it easier to extract the seed, but there is a risk that they may be eaten by wildlife. Another proven method is to place the berries in a bowl of water for several days. Use a pestle and mortar to mash them to a pulp and return to clean water. The pulp and dead seed rise to the surface, while viable, heavy seeds settle at the bottom.

Gathering berries
Pick fresh berries when ripe and soft. Pick dry berries just as they start to shrivel. Berry seeds from either fresh or dry berries are best sown as soon as they are extracted rather than dried and sown the following season. Wear protective gloves when picking toxic berries like pokeroot.

Wet berries

Dry berries

1 Separating seed from pulp
There are several methods of removing the pulp from fresh berries. You can place the berries in a sieve under running tap water and rub off the pulp. Alternatively, wrap the berries in a piece of muslin, hold the cloth under running tap water, and squeeze the berries. Wring out the muslin, then open out the cloth and the seeds will have separated from the pulp. For toxic berries like pokeroot (shown here) that also have a dark juice that can stain the hands, wear gloves when extracting seed.

2 Extracting the seed
Having exposed the seed, you will need to lift it away from the pulp and place it on a clean piece of kitchen towel. For best results, sow the moist seed immediately in substrate, and winter in a cold frame. If you are not ready to sow the seed straightaway, keep the seeds damp (but not wet) by storing them in a refrigerator, buried in a tray of vermiculite (see page 44) until the following spring.

Harvesting dry berries
These myrtle berries were left on the bush over winter before harvesting. To extract the seed, open the berry with your fingertips rather than a knife so as not to damage it. Gently rub between your thumb and forefinger and the seeds will fall out. For successful germination sow immediately, or keep for one month, stored damp in the refrigerator in a tray of vermiculite (see page 44).

Harvesting roots

When harvesting herb roots, it is best to dig them up at the end of the growing season, when the plant's top-growth is starting to die back and the maximum amount of nutrition has been stored in the root system. Obviously it is best not to wait for the top-growth to die back completely, or you may not be able to identify or locate your plant in the garden. In my Top 100, the herbs whose roots I use most are echinacea and Joe Pye weed for medicinal purposes, and liquorice and horseradish for cooking.

Gathering roots
Dig up roots in autumn before the plant's top-growth has died back fully. Wash roots well; do not soak or the flavour will leach out, and they will tend to absorb water and rot. If harvesting several different roots at the same time, label them and keep separate so as not to impair their individual flavour.

Collecting

Washing

Grating

1 Harvesting
The first light autumn frost is the signal for plants to start building up energy reserves in their root system to help them survive the long winter months. It is also the time to harvest roots. Dig early in the morning or last thing at night, because at these times the plant's energy remains in the root system; on warm days it rises up to the top-growth. Take care not to bruise the roots when you are lifting them.

2 Clean the roots
Rinse the roots under cold running water to wash off soil and dirt before you preserve them. If necessary, use a soft vegetable brush to gently clean off stubborn dirt without damaging them. If roots are caked in mud, perform the first wash outdoors with the garden hose so as not block the kitchen sink with soil.

3 Use or store
Horseradish is my favourite culinary root (see page 90). To use fresh, peel off the tough outer layers once washed, and grate the flesh. To prepare the root for drying, peel it and then slice into sections. Arrange the slices on a muslin frame until dry. Store the dried root slices in a clearly labelled dark glass jar.

Harvesting bulbs

The only herb bulb that I include in this book is garlic (see page 81). The most reliable indicator for harvesting is when the first leaves start to yellow. Sometimes garlic puts out a false seed stalk topped by small bulbils; these are edible and taste just like garlic, and are ready for harvest earlier than the bulb. Some people suggest that the true garlic bulbs will be larger if these seed stalks are removed. To do this, wait until the seedheads form a coil, and then cut them off as close to the ground as possible.

Gathering bulbs

The garlic in supermarkets is not a named species, nor has it necessarily been grown in the UK. However, when planted, it will produce a small crop. For a more reliable crop, buy seed garlic bulbs from a reputable organic source; these will have been acclimatized to the UK's damper growing conditions.

Gathering

Drying

Storing

1 Harvesting
The best time to harvest garlic bulbs is midsummer, as the top-growth starts to die back and the soil is dry so that the bulbs come away clean. Lift the garlic bulbs carefully – damaged bulbs can only be stored for short periods of time before they become diseased. Do not delay the harvest, for the following reasons: it makes garlic bulbs harder to clean because the outer leaves start to decay in wet soil; the skins stain as the bulbs mature, and late-harvested garlic does not store as well and may rot.

2 Leave to air
This stage is critical. In warm, dry climates, garlic can be dried outside. In unreliable or damp climates, it is best to dry it under shelter. Make sure that there is good air circulation and that the bulbs are out of direct sunlight. Depending on conditions, drying will take 14–25 days, after which roots can be trimmed back and the top-growth cut off just above where the bulb forms. If plaiting bulbs together, leave a few strands of dried leaves (as shown here).

3 Cool and dry
A garlic bulb is ready to store when the skin feels papery and rustles when handled. Either plait the dried garlic into ropes, or hang individual bulbs in net sacks to store. Place in an area with good ventilation, which has a temperature above freezing but no higher than 4°C (39°F), otherwise the garlic cloves will sprout green shoots. If the air circulation is poor or the air humid, the garlic bulbs may start to turn mouldy and rot.

TOP 100 HERBS

Reasons for choice

Over the past decade, as we have become more familiar with the negative effects of processed foods and prescription medicines, herbs as both healing foods and natural remedies have increased in significance as the key to good health. When I first started growing herbs organically over twenty years ago I was thought eccentric, but now these ideas have been integrated into the mainstream with more and more people becoming aware of the health benefits that come with choosing foods that are grown free from pesticides and other harmful chemicals.

Organic and natural

Choosing my Top 100 herbs for this book was difficult, as I have a passion for all these useful plants, including those from far-flung outposts of the world. There are so many dimensions to herbs: not only are they used in the kitchen or medicinally, but they also work as companion plants in the organic garden, helping other plants to grow successfully – or they can form the basis of natural beauty products and household cleaners to help create a toxin-free home. Once grown successfully, the herbs in this section can be pressed into service in the many culinary, medicinal, and household recipes found later in this book.

Start by growing just a few herbs for yourself, and discover a world of uses for them, in the kitchen and around the home.

Everyday and exotic

One of the main criteria for the herbs that feature here was that they had to be grown on the farm, although I have included a tropical plant, the curry tree (*Murraya koenigii*), because I have managed to raise a cherished specimen in a warm greenhouse. I have tried to stick to everyday species, such as sage, thyme, mint, and garlic, that have a role in the kitchen or an indispensable use as a herbal remedy. I describe how to grow each one using my tried-and-tested organic methods. I have also included herbs like shiso (*Perilla* species), which are common in the East but need to have their profile raised in the West. I especially like the purple variety (*Perilla frutescens* var. *purpurascens*), which is not only wonderful in cooking but looks stunning in the garden.

I have also included herbs that can be used in home remedies. For example, I have chosen *Echinacea* species for their immune-boosting properties, and lemon balm (*Melissa officinalis*) for its powers of healing and preventing cold sores. However, although I have described medicinal uses for more serious complaints, I would always consult a fully trained herbalist or a doctor before using herbs medicinally, especially when taking them internally (see page 232).

Finally, I have chosen some herbs for their perfume, such as lemon verbena (*Aloysia triphylla*) with its refreshing lemon fragrance, and *Pelargonium* 'Attar of Roses' with its sweet rose perfume. Once you start growing and using herbs, I defy you not to become hooked.

◄◄ **Golden thyme** (*Thymus pulegioides* 'Aureus'). Medicinal and culinary herb, excellent with roasted vegetables.

◄ **Lettuce leaf basil** (*Ocimum basilicum* 'Napolitano'). Wonderful for pesto sauce or for tearing over a tomato salad.

◄◄ **Pink rosemary** (*Rosmarinus officinalis* 'Roseus'). Great for barbecues, rinsing dark hair, or settling the stomach.

◄ **Angelica** (*Angelica archangelica*). This herb is a magnificent structural plant for the large herb garden.

◄◄ **Sweet woodruff** (*Galium odoratum*). A lovely little traditional herb that is very useful in the home.

◄ **Fringed lavender** (*Lavandula dentata*). A highly aromatic lavender, lovely grown in containers.

Achillea

Yarrow ASTERACEAE

Yarrow has naturalized all over the world: it can be found growing in waste land, fields, and pastures. Gardeners who prefer the immaculate lawn find it a totally obnoxious weed, whereas I find it useful in the organic garden. It makes a good compost accelerator (see page 37) and copper fertilizer. Historically, the plant name "Achillea" is taken from Greek mythology, where the great hero, Achilles, used yarrow leaves to heal his wounded warriors. Today it is still sought after by the army, and those partaking in country pursuits, as a useful first aid remedy to staunch blood flow.

▲ ***Achillea ageratum***
ENGLISH MACE
A hardy perennial, with a height of 30–45cm (12–18in) and a spread of 30cm (12in), with aromatic leaves that are finely serrated, oval, and bright green. Clusters of small white flowers with cream centres appear in summer.

How to grow

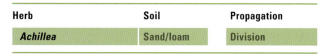

Herb	Soil	Propagation
Achillea	Sand/loam	Division

PROPAGATION In autumn, sow seeds into a container and winter in a cold frame. Germination is erratic. In spring, plant out young plants 20–30cm (8–12in) apart. Since yarrow can be invasive, I do not advise sowing seeds directly into the ground. To control its spread, divide mature plants in spring or early autumn.

SITE Once established, yarrow will survive in most soils. It is drought-tolerant.

MAINTENANCE This plant is prone to self-seeding. Cut back after flowering to prevent it from setting seed.

HARVESTING Cut the leaves and flowerheads for drying when it comes into flower, or to use fresh.

How to use

Yarrow is known as a "plant doctor" and when it is planted near unhealthy plants, secretions from its roots actively help the ailing plant by triggering its disease resistance. Yarrow leaves can be infused to make a copper fertilizer to prevent fungi and cure downy mildew, and a few leaves added to the compost heap will speed up decomposition. Before using leaves for medicinal or culinary purposes, wash them well, then pat dry with kitchen towel. Add young leaves to salads. Yarrow is well-known for staunching the flow of blood. Simply crush the leaves to release the tannins, then apply to the wound to stop the bleeding. An infusion made from the flowers is a good remedy for fevers. The flowers can also be used in dried-flower arrangements.

▼ ***Achillea millefolium***
YARROW, WOUNDWORT, MILFOIL
This hardy perennial has a height of 30–90cm (12–36in) and a spread of 60cm (24in), and produces small white-pink flowers grouped in flat clusters in summer until autumn.

Flower colour can vary from greyish-white to pale pink. It is very long-lasting

Leaf is aromatic and very finely divided like a feather. It has a light flavour

Stem is pale grey-green, very tough and slightly ridged. It is covered in soft, fine woolly hair when young

Agastache

Anise hyssop LAMIACEAE

Renowned for its beautiful flower spikes that attract butterflies, this comparatively new addition to the European herb garden looks stunning in a flower border. A native of North America, its medicinal healing properties were well-known to the North American Indians. In the kitchen, the young leaves and flowers offer a mild anise, minty flavour and taste good with fish and chicken dishes. This plant should not be confused with the Mediterranean *Hyssopus officinalis* (see page 129), which also has the common name "hyssop".

How to grow

Herb	Soil	Propagation
Agastache	Sand	Seed

PROPAGATION Sow seeds in early spring under protection at 20°C (68°F); germination takes seven to ten days. Alternatively, sow seeds in late spring into prepared open ground (see page 47), when the air temperature at night does not fall below 10°C (50°F), and germination takes two to three weeks. The plant will flower in the first year. Softwood cuttings can be taken in early summer. When the cuttings have rooted, pot them and place in a cold frame or cold greenhouse over winter.

SITE Plant in a warm, sunny site in any well-drained soil. Anise hyssop can withstand dry conditions, though it is less tolerant of clay soil, where it should be grown as an annual so its roots do not rot. When grown in a container, make sure that the pot size can accommodate the mature plant. Use a standard loam-based substrate with added grit for drainage.

MAINTENANCE Once established, this plant needs little maintenance. In the spring of the third season it is advisable to dig it up and divide it (see page 53) to maintain its health and shape. Feed with a small amount of organic fertilizer such as comfrey or seaweed before replanting.

HARVESTING Pick the leaves to use fresh in cooking or to conserve in oil or vinegar (see pages 222–223) before the plant flowers in summer. Pick the flower spikes as they open. Remove the florets before use.

How to use

The plant is used to treat coughs and wheezing. The fresh leaves and edible flowers can be used in leaf and fruit salads, or to make a refreshing infusion.

▼ *Agastache foeniculum* (Pursh) Kuntze
ANISE HYSSOP, GIANT HYSSOP, BLUE GIANT HYSSOP
A hardy herbaceous perennial, grown as an annual in cool or damp climates, with a height of 70cm (28in) and a spread of 30cm (12in). Erect long spikes of violet-blue flowers appear in summer. The leaves are oval, toothed, and mid-green with a mild anise, minty flavour.

Alchemilla

Lady's mantle ROSACEAE

This is one of the most attractive herbs in the garden, and I love to see the dewdrops form on the pale green lacy leaves. Native to Europe and the UK, it has a special importance for women and its attributes are said to include preserving a woman's youth and protecting her from dark forces. It was dedicated to the Virgin Mary and named "Our Lady's mantle" as the leaf shape was thought to resemble Our Lady's cloak. This versatile plant is used to treat hormonal problems in people and animals, and produces a vibrant green dye for wool.

CAUTION Do not use in pregnancy and seek professional advice on treating menstrual problems.

How to grow

Herb	Soil	Propagation
Alchemilla	Loam	Division

PROPAGATION Self-seeds easily, or can be sown in pots in a cold frame; germination takes four to six weeks, but this method is not always successful. Alternatively, sow into prepared ground in early spring; germination takes six to eight weeks, but again this can be erratic. Thin the seedlings to 30cm (12in) apart. Established plants can be divided in spring or autumn (see page 53).

SITE Lady's mantle will grow in sun or partial shade in all but excessively wet soils.

MAINTENANCE This plant is prone to self-seeding, which can cause it to spread prolifically. To prevent seed dispersal, cut off the flowerheads as soon as they die back. In autumn, cut out old growth. In spring, tidy up around established plants. In containers, use a soil-based substrate and site in partial shade. Repot each autumn. Containers can be wintered outside but avoid waterlogging or the roots will rot.

HARVESTING From spring until early summer, cut very young leaves to use fresh in cooking and mature leaves for use in herbal medicine. The roots can also be used in herbal medicine and should be dug up in the second year. To make the plant dye, harvest mature leaves before flowering.

How to use

An infusion of leaves helps alleviate menopausal discomfort, and can be used to treat thrush and children's diarrhoea. Young leaves have a mild, dry, bitter taste and can be added to salads.

▼ *Alchemilla xanthochlora* syn. *A. vulgaris*
LADY'S MANTLE
A hardy herbaceous perennial, with a height of 45cm (18in) and a spread of 50cm (20in). This species is very similar to *A. mollis,* but is thought to have more potent medicinal healing properties.

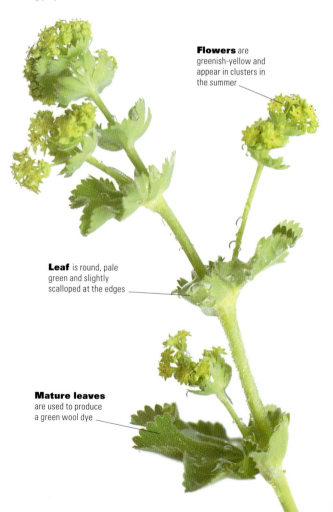

Flowers are greenish-yellow and appear in clusters in the summer

Leaf is round, pale green and slightly scalloped at the edges

Mature leaves are used to produce a green wool dye

Allium
Onion family ALLIACEAE

This popular and important medicinal herb family is grown throughout the world. Alliums have marvellous health-giving properties, and people believed that the stronger the smell, the more effective the healing powers of the plants. In the Middle Ages, people hung bunches of onions outside their front doors to absorb infections, the plague, and deter pests. The juice was used as a strong disinfectant and to heal gunshot wounds. Alliums make good companion plants in the organic garden; they help prevent leaf curl in trees, especially peaches, and planted next to roses, they ward off black spot.

How to grow

Herb	Soil	Propagation
Allium	Loam	Seed/division

PROPAGATION In early spring, sow seeds under cover at 20°C (68°F); germination takes 10–20 days. Alternatively, sow seeds in late spring into prepared ground, when the air temperature at night is above 7°C (45°F); germination takes two to three weeks. Thin seedlings to 25cm (9in) apart and divide established clumps every three years in spring.

SITE Plant in a well-drained fertile soil. Keep well-watered throughout the growing season. In autumn, mulch plants with well-rotted manure.

MAINTENANCE Onions are prone to disease. Keep the soil fertile and take care not to damage the roots or leaves when clearing around the plants in spring as the scent will attract the onion fly. Also, when thinning seedlings remove all wilted ones and any seedlings not required. Take care not to damage the bulbs when hoeing or digging the site, or neck or bulb rot may occur.

HARVESTING Dig up bulbs from early summer until early autumn. Cut fresh leaves from late spring until early autumn. Leaves do not dry well but can be frozen.

How to use

The fresh onion juice is antibiotic, diuretic, expectorant, and antispasmodic, and useful in the treatment of coughs, colds, bronchitis, and gastroenteritis. Eating onion, especially garlic, helps lower blood pressure. Use bulbs raw in salads or add to pasta dishes, stews, and casseroles. Use fresh leaves in salads.

◀ *Allium cepa*
Proliferum Group
TREE ONION, EGYPTIAN ONION, LAZY MAN'S ONION

A hardy perennial, with a height of up to 1.5m (5ft) and a spread of 60cm (24in). Small flowers appear in the second summer, followed by edible bulbs at the top of the stem. In autumn or spring, propagate from the small stem bulbs.

Flowers are creamy-white, globe-shaped, and edible

Stem is long, hollow, and cylindrical and can easily bend in high winds or dry conditions

▶ *Allium fistulosum*
WELSH ONION, JAPANESE LEEK

A hardy perennial evergreen, with a height and spread of 50cm (20in). Large creamy-white, globe-shaped flowers appear early in the second summer. The leaves can be used in salads. The name Welsh comes from "walsch" meaning "foreign".

Allium
Chive family ALLIACEAE

This herb is the only member of the onion family growing wild in Asia, Europe, Australia, and North America. Records of its medicinal use date back to 3000 BC, and historically it was used as an antidote to poison and to staunch the flow of blood. I find chives indispensable in the kitchen: the leaves add a mild onion flavour to salads, and I like to mix them with sour cream to liven up plain baked potatoes. There is an old saying "chives next to roses creates posies" because the herb is believed to inhibit black spot. A decoction made from the leaves is also thought to prevent scab infection in animals.

How to grow

Herbs	Soil	Propagation
Allium	Loam	Seed

PROPAGATION See page 81 for details.

SITE Plant in rich, moist soil in a sunny position. Keep well-watered throughout the growing season. In the autumn, mulch with well-rotted manure. Both chives and garlic chives grow well in containers. Use a soil-based substrate.

MAINTENANCE To encourage new, lush growth, cut back after flowering and feed with comfrey liquid feed (see page 39). Chives can suffer from a rust virus. If this occurs, cut back diseased growth and burn it. Or, if your plant is well away from buildings or fences, cover the plant with straw and set it alight; this will burn the top growth and sterilize the soil. The plant should not be composted, as the virus will live on in the compost and transfer to the ground. In autumn, on cool, wet days, downy mildew can be a problem. If this is the case, cut back all the remaining growth, dig the plant up, divide it, and replant in a new, prepared site.

HARVESTING Cut fresh leaves during the growing season. Use fresh or preserve in a herb butter (see pages 224–225). Use fresh flowers in early summer. Divide the flowerhead into individual bulbils.

How to use

An excellent culinary herb. The leaves stimulate the appetite and aid digestion. They are also mildly antiseptic.

▲ ***Allium ursinum***
WILD GARLIC, RAMSONS

A hardy perennial, with a height of up to 45cm (18in) and a spread of 60cm (24in). Clusters of star-shaped flowers appear in late spring; the mid-green leaves are elliptical. Plant in moist, fertile soil in semi-shade. Sow the seeds and divide the rhizome in autumn. Flowers and leaves are edible; eat the leaves before flowering. The leaves may be boiled, and the resulting liquid used as a disinfectant wipe.

◀ *Allium tuberosum*
GARLIC CHIVES, CHINESE CHIVES
A hardy perennial, with a height and spread of 30cm (12in). Clusters of white, star-shaped flowers appear in summer. The mid-green leaves are flat, solid, thin, and lance-shaped and have a mild, sweet, garlic flavour.

Flowers are pink or purple and globe-shaped. Edible, they have a mild onion flavour, which is great in salads

Stem flavour is inferior to that of the leaf

Leaf is hollow and cylindrical. It can be cut into rings with scissors and used in salads

▶ *Allium schoenoprasum*
CHIVES
A hardy perennial, with a height and spread of 30cm (12in). The purple, globe-shaped flowers are composed of individual bulbils, and flower all summer. Leaves are green, cylindrical, and hollow, and have a mild aroma and flavour similar to onion.

Aloe

Aloe ALOEACEAE

This tropical plant is an indispensable part of my natural first aid kit, as it produces a soothing gel to treat burns. I always keep a pot growing on my kitchen windowsill so I can act quickly if I burn myself when cooking – I am notoriously clumsy. It has been identified in wall paintings of the ancient Egyptians, and it is said that Cleopatra was the first to use it as a beauty treatment. As a child, I remember having "bitter aloes" put on my fingers to stop me sucking them – it didn't work. Do not take fresh aloe internally without seeking professional advice.

CAUTION The leaves are a potent laxative, and should not be taken by pregnant women or young children

How to grow

Herb	Soil	Propagation
Aloe	Sand	Softwood cuttings

PROPAGATION Sow seeds on the soil surface, under protection at 21°C (70°F). Germination is erratic, taking anything from four months to up to two years. It is easier to propagate by division; simply remove the off-shoots that form at the base of a mature plant. Replant the off-shoots in a coarse loam substrate a day later to give them time to dry out slightly.

SITE In tropical or subtropical climates only, plant outside in full to partial shade in a free-draining soil. In cooler climates, grow it in a container as a house plant. Use a soil-based substrate with extra grit. Although the foliage looks like a succulent, it is more closely related to the lily family and needs water in the growing season.

MAINTENANCE If grown as a pot plant, feed monthly throughout the growing season with a liquid fertilizer like liquid seaweed. In winter, keep watering to a minimum, but do not allow the substrate to dry out.

HARVESTING Cut fresh leaves throughout the growing season and store in an airtight container in a refrigerator. Plants over two years old have stronger medicinal properties.

How to use

Break the leaf to extract the soothing gel. Apply the gel to wounds and minor burns. It will form a protective seal over the wound and help the skin to regenerate (see page 238). It can also be used to treat eczema and fungal infections like ringworm and thrush. Used internally, under professional medical supervision, it soothes peptic ulcers and irritable bowel syndrome.

Foliage is succulent, grey-green with spiny edges

Foliage when young may have a lightly spotted appearance

Foliage is fleshy when broken to release its gel, and will heal over within days

▶ *Aloe vera* syn. *A. barbadensis*
ALOE
This half-hardy perennial grows at a minimum temperature of 10°C (50°F) and has a height and spread, when grown outside, of 60cm (2ft). Yellow or orange bell-shaped flowers appear on mature plants only.

Aloysia
Lemon verbena VERBENACEAE

The uplifting lemon scent of this South American herb can transport you to another world. It was first imported into Europe in the 18th century by the Spaniards, and was used to make perfume until cheaper essential oils like lemon grass were substituted. The leaves were also used to perfume and sweeten the water in the fingerbowls offered at banquets. Medicinally, a tea made from three to five leaves of lemon verbena will aid sleep if drunk at bedtime; the herb also helps digestion, and is a mild sedative and calmative.

How to grow

Herb	Soil	Propagation
Aloysia	Sand	Softwood cuttings

PROPAGATION In spring, sow seeds under protection at 15°C (60°F); germination takes 10–20 days. When seedlings are large enough to handle, prick out into 9cm (3½in) pots, using a soil-based substrate with extra grit. Continue to grow in pots, under cover, for a minimum of two years before planting out. I do not advise sowing seed directly into the soil. In early summer, take softwood cuttings from new growth (see page 50).

SITE This herb only tolerates outdoor temperatures above 4°C (40°F), below which protection is needed. Plant in a light, free-draining soil in a warm sunny site (against a warm sunny wall is perfect). It grows well in containers using a soil-based substrate with extra grit. Place the container in a warm, light, and airy spot, and water well during the growing season.

MAINTENANCE In spring, trim back stems to a point where new growth is developing. (Some years, new growth does not appear until late spring or early summer.) In late summer after harvesting the leaves, lightly prune the plant to remove dead flowerheads and to reshape it.

HARVESTING The best time to pick leaves is when the plant goes into flower. Dry the fresh leaves (see page 68) and store them in a dark glass jar. They will keep their scent for at least three years. Harvest fresh flowers and use them as required.

How to use

Add leaves to flavour vinegars (see pages 222–223), fruit puddings, jellies, and cakes. Regular, long-term medicinal use of the herb may cause indigestion or upset stomach.

▶ *Aloysia triphylla*
LEMON VERBENA, LIPPIA, VERVAIN
A half-hardy, deciduous shrub, with a height of up to 3m (10ft), and a spread of up to 2.5m (8ft). The flowers have a light lemon flavour; the leaves have a stronger fragrance and taste.

Flowers are white with a hint of lilac and slightly lemon-scented

Stem is pale beige in colour and ridged

Leaves are very fragrant, lance-shaped, rough to the touch, and arranged in groups of three around the stem

Angelica

Angelica APIACEAE

A native of continental Europe, this herb can be found on river banks and in other damp sites. Take care not to confuse it with poisonous hemlock (*Conium maculatum*), which has white flowers, purple spots on the stem, and leaves that produce a foul smell when crushed. The origin of the species name, *Angelica archangelica*, derives from the story of a monk who, when praying for a cure to the plague, was visited by St Michael the Archangel and shown this herb. Angelica has antibacterial and antifungal properties, and is also one of the flavourings in alcoholic drinks such as gin.

CAUTION All angelica species may cause skin photosensitivity or dermatitis when touched. Do not take medicinally if you are suffering from diabetes.

How to grow

Herb	Soil	Propagation
Angelica	Loam	Seed

PROPAGATION Sow fresh seeds immediately because they only remain viable for three months after harvesting. In early autumn, sow in the ground or into seed plug trays (see page 43) that are placed outside, exposed to all weathers. Seedlings are hardy and do not need protection from frost. Mature plants do not transplant well.

SITE Plant in deep moist soil, making sure that the roots will be in shade and the flowers in sun. This is a good architectural plant which gives structure to a herb garden. It is not an ideal pot plant because of its height – up to 2.5m (8ft).

MAINTENANCE Make sure that seedlings and plants do not dry out. Keep well-watered in hot summers. Collect seeds for sowing in late summer. Cut the seedheads off before they drop onto the soil, or you will be inundated with seedlings. In exposed sites, stake long stems to prevent them from breaking.

HARVESTING In late spring or early summer, pick young, soft leaves to use fresh. Cut the stems of second-year growth in late spring before the flowerheads form to use fresh or preserve as a candy. Collect ripe seeds in early autumn.

How to use

Angelica is used to treat indigestion, anaemia, coughs, and colds; a tea made from the young leaves helps alleviate nervous headaches. Stems of second-year growth can be candied or cooked with stewed fruit. Young leaves can be chopped up and added to salads, soups, and stir fry dishes. The seeds are used in Moroccan cooking.

▲ *Angelica sylvestris* 'Vicar's Mead'
ANGELICA VICAR'S MEAD
A hardy, short-lived perennial with a height up to 2m (6ft) and a spread of 85cm (2½ft) in its second year. It produces domed umbels of lightly-scented, pale mauve-white flowers in late summer of the second season and has large, deeply-divided, maroon leaves.

Flower is sweetly scented and has a warm, mildly aniseed flavour

▶ *Angelica archangelica*
ANGELICA

A hardy, monocarpic herb, which dies after setting seed and has a height of up to 2.5m (8ft) and a spread of 1m (3ft) in its second year. It produces round umbels of sweetly-scented flowers in late spring to early summer of the second season, and has large, deeply-divided, bright green leaves around the base of the plant, smaller around the stem.

Stem is hollow and lightly ribbed. It is the second-year's growth that is used to make candied angelica

Angelica plants give height and structure to a herb garden.

Leaf is large, deeply divided and bright green. It has a dry flavour with a slightly bitter tang and a hint of aniseed.

Anethum
Dill APIACEAE

Originating in the Middle East, dill can now be found throughout the world, and has naturalized in Europe, North and South America, Asia, and Scandinavia. There is evidence that it has been in use for over 5,000 years, and it is mentioned in the Bible as a means of paying taxes. In the Middle Ages, dill was used as a protection against witchcraft. Today it is well known as the active ingredient of gripe water, which is used to calm infants with colic or flatulence, and an infusion of dill seeds will relieve stomach ache and digestive problems in adults.

Seeds have a sharper flavour than the leaves. Use fresh, dried, or roasted in vegetable dishes, soups, and breads.

How to grow

Herb	Soil	Propagation
Anethum	Loam	Seed

PROPAGATION In early spring, sow seeds under cover at 15°C (60°F); germination takes five to twenty days. Or sow seeds in late spring into prepared, open ground, when the air temperature at night stays above 7°C (45°F); germination takes two to three weeks. Thin seedlings to 25cm (9in) apart. In my experience, sowing the seeds directly into open ground is the best method because this plant does not respond well to transplanting. Sow in small amounts at a time to provide a constant supply of leaves.

SITE Dill favours a well-drained soil and a sunny position sheltered from high winds. Do not plant dill near fennel because they can cross-pollinate, producing an inferior plant. Dill can be grown in large containers, but bear in mind that it dislikes being transplanted. Place the container in a sheltered position in full sun. It does not seem to grow well on kitchen windowsills.

MAINTENANCE After cutting, fertilize with comfrey liquid feed (see page 39) to promote new growth. In winter, dig up any remaining plants. Check that all the seeds have been removed to prevent self-seeding of this invasive plant, and then feed the remaining stalks to the compost heap.

HARVESTING In summer, cut back the leaves or the whole plant when it reaches about 30cm (1ft) high. Use the leaves fresh or dry. Preserve in butter or vinegars (see pages 222–225). Harvest seed when it turns brown, dry well, and store in a dark glass jar (see page 70).

How to use

This herb is used to treat dyspepsia, flatulence, and stomach ache in adults — try a tea made with a teaspoon of dill seeds to ease these symptoms effectively.

▲ *Anethum graveolens*
DILL, DILLWEED

A hardy annual, with a height of up to 1.5m (5ft), and a spread of 30cm (12in). The small flowers appear in summer, followed by aromatic seeds in late summer. The flower is good with fish dishes; it has a sweeter flavour than the leaf, with a hint of mint. The leaves have a mild, warm flavour, distinguishing them from fennel's aniseed taste.

Anthriscus

Chervil APIACEAE

This herb, native to the Middle East and the Caucasus, has been cultivated throughout Europe, North America, and Australia where, in some areas, it has naturalized. It is advisable not to collect chervil from the wild as it is similar in appearance to other plants of the same family, like hemlock, which is deadly poisonous. Chervil was a popular Lenten herb and was eaten on Maundy Thursday for its blood-cleansing and restorative properties. Medicinally the leaves are very high in vitamin C, magnesium, iron, and carotene. A tea made from the leaves can stimulate digestion.

How to grow

Herb	Soil	Propagation
Anthriscus	Loam	Seed

PROPAGATION Seeds are viable for one year. Sow in early spring under cover at 15°C (60°F); germination takes five to ten days. Or sow seeds in late spring into prepared open ground, when the air temperature at night stays above 7°C (45°F); germination takes two to three weeks. Thin seedlings to 25cm (9in) apart. Chervil plants do not like being transplanted and will bolt and run to seed.

SITE Plant in a well-prepared site in a light but not too dry soil, in partial shade. Too much sun in summer will make chervil plants bolt and go to flower; they will also discolour and lose flavour. Chervil can be grown as a container plant in a large pot. Place outside in partial shade, and water regularly. This herb does not grow very well on kitchen windowsills.

MAINTENANCE For fresh winter leaves, sow seeds in late summer. Cover with a cloche or horticultural fleece (see page 47) when the weather is wet or the temperature drops below -2°C (30°F).

HARVESTING The leaves can be picked for fresh use six to eight weeks after sowing. Always start with the outside leaves of the plant, leaving the new young shoots to develop.

How to use

This useful culinary herb is one of the four ingredients of "fines herbes", which include parsley, chives, and tarragon. In winter, late-sown chervil makes a good substitute for parsley. Use fresh leaves in salads, soups, chicken, fish, egg dishes, and sauces.

▲ *Anthriscus cerefolium*
CHERVIL

A hardy biennial, grown as an annual, with a height of up to 60cm (24in) and a spread of 30cm (12in). Clusters of tiny white flowers appear from spring until summer. It has light green leaves that can develop a purple tinge in early autumn. The leaf flavour is sweet and slightly aniseed, and resembles a mixture of parsley and sweet cicely.

Armoracia

Horseradish BRASSICACEAE

This robust herb, native of western Asia, has naturalized in many countries and is found on waste ground and roadsides in the UK, North America, and New Zealand. Its common name, "horse", is often used to mean a large, strong, or coarse plant. It has many excellent culinary and medicinal properties, and played a major part in my childhood, as I watched my mother grate the fresh root to make horseradish sauce to accompany the Sunday roast. You should avoid continuous dosage of horseradish if you are pregnant or suffering from kidney problems.

Root is high in vitamin C, calcium, sodium, and magnesium. It also has antibiotic properties.

How to grow

Herb	Soil	Propagation
Armoracia	Loam	Root cuttings

PROPAGATION This plant is very easy to propagate from root cuttings, taken from spring up until late autumn (see page 52). Either place the cuttings directly into a prepared site, 5cm (2in) deep and 30cm (12in) apart, or start the root cuttings off in individual pots, planting them out when the roots are established.

SITE Horseradish is invasive and difficult to eradicate from the garden once established. It will tolerate all but the driest of soils. Plant in a light, well-dug, rich, moist soil in a sunny position, or dappled shade. To contain the roots and keep the plant under control, grow it in a dustbin. Make drainage holes in the container, and fill with rich soil. Place in partial shade.

MAINTENANCE In the autumn of the third season, after harvest, established clumps benefit from being divided and replanted in a well-prepared soil that has been fed with well-rotted manure before replanting.

HARVESTING Pick young fresh leaves in spring and early summer. Dig up the root at any time between spring and early autumn to use fresh. The strongest flavoured root is produced in autumn. Preserve the prepared root in vinegar.

How to use

In Europe, the fresh raw root is used as a condiment, but it loses all flavour when cooked. Medicinally, the root is a powerful circulatory stimulant with antibiotic properties. Horseradish is a good companion plant for root crops, helping build disease resistance. A spray made from an infusion of the leaves helps to prevent brown rot when applied to apple trees.

CAUTION Do not use if your thyroid function is weak, or if you are taking thyroxine.

Leaf when crushed has a pungent aroma similar to the root

▶ *Armoracia rusticana*
HORSERADISH
This hardy perennial has a height of up to 90cm (35in), with an infinite spread. Tiny white flowers appear in early spring, though not every year. It has large, mid-green leaves which have a crinkled texture. Its long, thick tap root can reach up to 60cm (2ft) in length.

Arnica

Arnica ASTERACEAE

This plant is a native of the Rocky mountains in North America and the Selkirk mountains of British Columbia, Canada. Its name most probably derives from the Greek word "arnakis" meaning "lamb's skin", because of the soft texture of the leaves. It has many medicinal uses, and is particularly effective for treating bruises and sprains. The flowers of the species *Arnica chamissonis* are commonly used to make the first-aid remedy. The rhizomes of *A. montana* can also be harvested for the same purpose, which has contributed to this species becoming an endangered plant in Europe.

How to grow

Herb	Soil	Propagation
Arnica	Sand	Seed

PROPAGATION In autumn, sow fresh seeds into a loam-based substrate and place in a cold frame. Germination takes three to four weeks. If no germination occurs, place the container outside so the seeds are exposed to all weathers; germination can then take a further five to seven months or up to two years. A more reliable method of propagation is to grow new plants from root cuttings taken from the rhizomes in the spring.

SITE Plant in sun or partial shade in an acid or alkaline sandy soil that is rich in humus. Arnica is well-suited to rock gardens or medicinal herb gardens and grows well in containers. Use an ericaceous potting substrate. Arnica has creeping roots. In autumn, repot container-grown plants to protect the roots from excessive wet.

MAINTENANCE Deadhead flowers to prolong flowering. In the autumn, collect fresh seeds for sowing immediately to ensure quick germination.

HARVESTING In summer, pick the flowers just before they are fully open for medicinal use. Pick leaves for drying in summer.

How to use

In homeopathy, arnica is used to treat symptoms of shock and injury. Arnica cream soothes chilblains, but should not be used if the skin is broken. A tincture can be used to treat angina, but only under supervision from a qualified practitioner.

Flowers are lightly scented in summer and very attractive to bees

Stem can be hairy or smooth depending on planting situation and time of year. It is usually smoother towards the end of the growing season

Leaf is lightly ribbed, lance-shaped, and slightly velvety to the touch

▶ *Arnica chamissonis*
ARNICA, MOUNTAIN TOBACCO, NORTH AMERICAN ARNICA
A hardy herbaceous perennial, with a height of up to 60cm (2ft) and a spread of 15cm (6in). Throughout the summer, it produces medium-sized, single, daisy-like, golden-yellow flowers. *Arnica chamissonis* is similar in appearance to *A. montana* – an endangered species.

Artemisia

Artemisia ASTERACEAE

The great culinary herb *Artemisia dracunculus* was used excessively by Catherine of Aragon and was cited as a reason for divorce by Henry VIII. Native to southern Europe, true French tarragon has a light aniseed flavour, with a hint of warmth. It is not the same as Russian tarragon, *A. dracunculoides*, which has a more robust habit, a paler, larger leaf, and a pungent, slightly bitter anise flavour. Medicinally, French tarragon was traditionally used to heal snake bites and remove poisonous venom. A tea made from tarragon leaves can help relieve insomnia and constipation, and aid digestion.

How to grow

Herb	Soil	Propagation
Artemisia	Sand	Seed

PROPAGATION In spring, sow fresh seeds but do not cover with compost or perlite. Place under protection at 20°C (68°F). Germination takes ten to twenty days. Take softwood cuttings from lush new growth in early summer. Divide established plants in spring every three to four years. Replant in a well-prepared site.

SITE Plant in a well-drained, light soil in a sunny position. Do not grow wormwood near culinary herbs as it can impair their flavour. Both wormwood and southernwood can be grown in large containers – use a well-draining loam substrate and protect the plants from excessive wet and cold in winter.

MAINTENANCE Cut back wormwood stems to 15cm (6in) in autumn. Cut back southernwood to 30cm (12in). In climates where the temperature drops below -2°C (30°F) in autumn, wait until the spring to cut stems back. In winter, protect the plants when the night temperature falls below -5°C (23°F).

HARVESTING In summer, pick the herb's leaves for drying, and collect the flowers just as they open.

How to use

Wormwood is best used as a moth repellent (see page 237). Try hanging bunches of wormwood leaves in a chicken coop to deter fleas, lice, and flies (see page 246). The leaves and roots produce a natural yellow plant dye for textiles.

▲ *Artemisia abrotanum*
SOUTHERNWOOD, LAD'S LOVE
A hardy, semi-evergreen shrub, with a height and spread of up to 1m (3ft). Tiny, dull yellow flowers form dense panicles in late summer, though they are rarely present in cool climates. It has aromatic, very finely-cut, grey-green leaves. The leaves make one of the best natural moth repellents and a good mosquito repellent when rubbed on the skin.

▲ *Artemisia annua*
SWEET ANNIE, SWEET WORMWOOD
A frost-hardy annual, with a height of
up to 3m (9ft) and a spread of up to
1.5m (4½ft). It has tiny yellow flowers
clustered in loose panicles in summer
and aromatic, bright green leaves.
It is a very important medicinal herb
that is used as an antimalarial agent,
as well as a natural herbicide.

Leaf is covered in fine
hairs – a characteristic
of the *Artemisia* genus

Stem in early
spring is lush
and green, but
as the season
progresses,
it turns woodier

▲ *Artemisia dracunculus*
FRENCH TARRAGON
A hardy herbaceous perennial, with a height of 90cm (3ft)
and a spread of 45cm (18in). Sprays of tiny yellow flowers
appear in summer in warm climates, though rarely in cool
climates. It has aromatic, long, narrow, and smooth green
leaves, which when crushed release a warm aroma.

Borago

Borage BORAGINACEAE

This very pretty flowering herb originated in the Mediterranean, where it can be found growing on wasteland. It has now spread and naturalized in North America and northern Europe. Historically, it was given to young Roman soldiers for courage and comfort, and borage flowers were given to the Crusaders – floated in stirrup cups – for the same reason. I am not sure about courage, but it raises the spirits to see these pretty summer flowers. It has several culinary and medicinal uses, but eaten excessively it can cause liver damage. The fresh leaves may cause contact dermatitis.

CAUTION Borage can cause liver damage if eaten in excess. Always consult a fully qualified herbalist.

How to grow

Herb	Soil	Propagation
Borago	Sand	Seed

PROPAGATION In early spring, sow seeds into pots under protection at 20°C (68°F). Germination takes five to fourteen days. Alternatively, sow seeds in late spring into prepared open ground, when the air temperature at night does not drop below 7°C (45°F). Germination takes two to three weeks. Thin seedlings to 45cm (18in) apart. Once pot-grown seedlings are large enough to handle, plant them out into their final position; borage plants produce a long tap root and do not like being disturbed.

SITE Borage tolerates most soils including clay but prefers well-drained, light, poor soil in a sunny position. If the soil is too rich it may grow tall and weak and need staking. For this reason, it does not make a good container-grown plant.

MAINTENANCE Borage self-seeds easily, especially in light soils. Once the petals of the flowers drop, the seeds will appear. Collect those seeds that you want to propagate for next year's plants, and carefully remove any others.

HARVESTING Pick fresh flowers just as they open fully. The best way to preserve the flowers is by freezing them with water in ice cube trays (see page 221). Pick fresh, young leaves of *Borago officinalis* throughout the season.

How to use

Medicinally, the oil made from borage seeds is high in polyunsaturated fats. It is used to treat eczema, pre-menstrual complaints, and rheumatic problems. The fresh leaves of *B. officinalis* taste good added to salads, soups, and with cream cheese or yoghurt.

◄ ***Borago pygmaea***
PROSTRATE BORAGE, CORSICAN BORAGE
A hardy perennial, with a height and spread of 45cm (18in). It has small, star-shaped, bright blue flowers that fade to pink with age and very bristly, oval, dark green leaves, which grow in basal rosettes. Only the flowers of this species are edible.

▲ ***Borago officinalis***
BORAGE, STAR FLOWER
A hardy annual, with a height and spread of 60cm (24in). Loose racemes of blue star-shaped flowers with black stamens appear in early summer until the first frosts. The mid-green leaves are bristly, oval or oblong in shape, and succulent.

Bulbine

African bulbine ASPHODELACEAE

This attractive herb looks spectacular growing in drifts in its native habitat in the Western Cape of South Africa, which is where I was lucky enough to see it growing. It can also be found in the desert grasslands of the Northern and Eastern Capes; from here it has spread, becoming naturalized in Texas and many other warm, dry states of the USA where it flourishes in the dry conditions. It was traditionally used by the Zulu to cure rashes, to stop bleeding, and as an antidote to poison, but also to treat their livestock. Today, it is still used medicinally in South Africa by the Sangoma healers.

How to grow

Herb	Soil	Propagation
Bulbine	Sand	Cuttings/division

PROPAGATION Sow fresh seed in late spring under protection at 20°C (68°F). Germination takes 10–20 days. Take cuttings, including the aerial roots, in early spring from container-raised plants, or late spring from garden-raised plants. In early summer, divide established garden plants using two forks back-to-back (see page 53), or by hand for pot-raised plants.

SITE This herb is a drought-loving plant that will survive a light frost. It can be planted out in cold climates in the early summer, and then lifted before the frosts. Plant in a well-drained, fertile soil that has been fed lightly with rotted manure the previous spring. Position in full sun or semi-shade, protected from cold winds. Alternatively, it will happily grow in a container. Plant in a loam-based potting compost mixed in equal parts with horticultural sand.

MAINTENANCE In warm, arid climates this is a low-maintenance plant. In cold and cool climates, protect when temperatures drop below 0°C (32°F). In winter, cut back the watering to a minimum, but do not allow the plant to dry out.

HARVESTING Leaves can be picked for use throughout the year.

How to use

The leaves are filled with a clear gel similar in appearance and consistency to aloe vera. This gel can be used directly on minor burns, wounds, cuts, abrasions, stings, and rashes. It can also be used to treat eczema, cracked lips, and herpes. The medicinal properties of this herb are currently under research, with the leaf gel being used to aid the healing of post-operative scars.

▲ *Bulbine frutescens*
AFRICAN BULBINE, BURN JELLY PLANT, SNAKE FLOWER, CAT'S TAIL
A frost-tender, evergreen perennial, with a height of 60cm (2ft), and a spread of 1m (3ft). Attractive, star-shaped, yellow or orange single flowers appear sequentially throughout the summer. The leaves vary in length and are mid-green, cylindrical, narrow, and succulent.

Buxus

Box BUXACEAE

This ancient shrub was once widespread throughout Europe, eastern Asia, and North Africa. It was much in demand for its timber, which is close-grained and does not warp in adverse conditions, making it the ideal wood for navigational instruments and printing blocks. Nowadays, box is better known as a traditional knot garden hedge, whose clipped leaves have a pungent smell. All parts of the plant are poisonous, especially the leaves and seeds, and animals such as goats, cows, and sheep have died from eating the leaves.

How to grow

Herb	Soil	Propagation
Buxus	Loam	Softwood cuttings

PROPAGATION Take cuttings from new growth in spring and propagate in the shade. Rooting takes three to four months, but with warm 21°C (70°F) shady conditions, it takes only six to eight weeks. Keep the cuttings moist but not over-wet. Alternatively, take semi-ripe cuttings in late summer and place in shade. Rooting should occur in eight to twelve weeks.

SITE Box favours an alkaline chalk or limestone soil, but it will adapt to all but water-logged conditions, in sun or partial shade. It grows well in containers. Use a soil-based substrate and feed with liquid fertilizer like seaweed or comfrey in the growing season. *Buxus sempervirens* makes a good hedge. Prepare a trench with well-rotted manure and plant 37–45cm (15–18in) apart.

MAINTENANCE Cut box hedges in late spring, after the chance of frost has past, and again in early autumn. Slow-growing varieties only need trimming once, in summer. In autumn, feed with well-rotted manure or a layer of fresh comfrey leaves (see page 37). If plants develop box blight, they will die back and leaves will become crisp and brown. Dig up infected plants and burn. Feed any remaining plants weekly with liquid comfrey (see page 39) – this can help to build up resistance.

HARVESTING Cut sprigs from spring until late autumn to use in floral arrangements.

How to use

Box is used medicinally by homeopaths as a tincture to treat rheumatism and urinary tract infections – this should only be done under supervision. Box wood is used by cabinet makers and wood turners to make furniture and chess pieces.

◀ ***Buxus sempervirens*
'Latifolia Maculata'** AGM
VARIEGATED GOLDEN BOX
A hardy evergreen shrub, good for hedging, with a height and spread of up to 1m (3ft). It has oval, shiny green leaves splashed with gold. All new growth is very golden in the spring.

Leaf is glossy on the upper surface, dull on the underside. It turns orange-brown when deficient in minerals

▶ ***Buxus sempervirens***
BOX, COMMON BOX
A hardy evergreen shrub, varying from bush to tree, with a height of up to 9m (27ft) and a spread of up to 5m (15ft). This plant is ideal for hedging, and is slow-growing and long-lived, with tiny pale green flowers in early summer.

Calendula
Pot marigold ASTERACEAE

This well-known herb has been widely used in Arab and Indian cultures as a medicine, food colourant, and cosmetic. In medieval times, the flowers were considered an emblem of love; if marigolds appeared in your dreams, they were an omen of good things to come. Just looking at the sunny orange flowers was thought to cheer the spirits, which, in my opinion, they still do today. Excellent companion plants in the organic garden, pot marigolds (*Calendula officinalis*) deter asparagus beetles and tomato horn worms, but are not to be confused with *Tagetes* species (see page 200).

How to grow

Herb	Soil	Propagation
Calendula	Loam	Seed

PROPAGATION In early spring, sow seeds under protection at 20°C (68°F); germination takes five to fourteen days. Or sow seeds in late spring into prepared open ground when the air temperature does not fall below 5°C (41°F) at night.

SITE Plant in any soil, except poor draining, waterlogged soil, in a sunny position. *Calendula* plants grow well in containers and combine well with other herbs.

MAINTENANCE To encourage continuous flowering, deadhead regularly. In light soils, pot marigold will self-seed abundantly – otherwise it is manageable. Beware of slug attack, and remove the pests from young plants. In late summer and early autumn, leaves may contract powdery mildew. Destroy the affected leaves to prevent the disease from spreading.

HARVESTING Pick fresh flowers as they open in early summer. Harvest young leaves to use fresh in salads.

How to use

The flower petals are used to make a natural gold-coloured food dye for butter, scones, and omelettes. Add young leaves to salads – the term "pot" marigold refers to its use in the cooking pot. Medicinally, marigold is known as a remedy for skin complaints; it is effective for most minor skin problems, cuts, grazes, wounds, inflamed skin including minor burns, sunburn, and fungal conditions like athlete's foot, thrush, and ringworm. It also helps to alleviate nappy rash. The sap from the plant stem has the reputation for removing warts, corns, and calluses.

▲ *Calendula officinalis*
POT MARIGOLD, MARIGOLD
A hardy annual, with a height and spread of up to 60cm (24in). Large orange or yellow, daisy-like, single or double flowers appear from spring until the first frosts. The light-green, lance-shaped leaves are lightly aromatic. The flowers are sensitive to temperature variation and dampness – open flowers forecast a fine day ahead.

Calomeria

Incense plant ASTERACEAE

I was given my first incense plant by a passionate plant collector. It has become rare in the UK, for it is no longer grown in parks or large private estates. It is a most fantastic plant for scent – in flower it will perfume the whole glasshouse and surrounding area – though in full flower, its perfume can cause breathing difficulties. Historically the plant arrived in England from Australia with the plant collector Sir Joseph Banks who gave some seed to Lady Hume (hence its former name, *Humea elegans*). The leaves and bracts can cause skin irritation and burns.

CAUTION The fresh leaves and bracts can cause skin irritation and burns. The perfume can cause breathing difficulties when in full flower.

How to grow

Herb	Soil	Propagation
Calomeria	Loam	Seed

PROPAGATION To achieve a very high germination rate, I suggest placing the dry seeds in a pillow case and tumble drying them on a high heat for ten to fifteen minutes. In late autumn, sow the seeds onto the surface of the substrate. Do not cover. Place in a light, well-aired, frost-free position. Germination takes 16–20 weeks. When the seedlings are large enough to handle, plant in a pot and grow until 30cm (12in) tall. Then pot up one size at a time, or plant out when the night temperature does not fall below 5°C (41°F). Take care not to transfer the plant to a larger pot size, or plant it outdoors too early, or you may cause it to "damp off". This Madagascan plant is difficult to propagate in a cool climate.

SITE Plant in a well-drained soil in a sunny position. Choose a site where people will not brush against this plant, as it may burn their skin. It also grows well in a container, using a soil-based substrate. Feed the young plant regularly from the appearance of the first bract.

MAINTENANCE This plant is very popular with whitefly when grown as a container plant. At the first sign of this pest on the leaf (look out for slight curling), treat with a proprietary horticultural soap according to the manufacturer's instructions.

HARVESTING Pick the coral bracts for drying as soon as the flowers appear. The best indication, as the flowers are minute, is when the bracts turn from deep bronze to a light coral colour.

How to use

The dried flowers look wonderful in fresh or dried floral arrangements. Their incredible incense scent lasts for a long time when the bracts are dried, adding another dimension to dried floral displays. The individual bracts add colour and scent to pot-pourri (see page 237).

▲ *Calomeria amaranthoides* syn. *Humea elegans*
INCENSE PLANT, PLUME BUSH
A half-hardy biennial, with a height of up to 1.8m (6ft) and a spread of up to 90cm (3ft). Aromatic, delicate, coral bracts surround small, cream daisy-like flowers and cascade from thin branches in summer. The mid-green leaves are large and oblong in shape, and aromatic.

Capparis

Caper CAPPARACEAE

This trailing, evergreen shrub, with its beautiful flowers, originated in the Middle East and can now be seen growing wild throughout the Mediterranean. I have seen it in the crumbling walls of an ancient ruin, near the seashore, and even in the rubble beside a newly built hotel. The Greek name, *kapparis*, is said to originate from the Persian *kabar*, hence "caper". The first recorded use of capers for medicinal purposes was by the Sumerians in 2000 BC, to relieve flatulence. Today, the small flowering buds and the berries, which form after flowering, are used in dishes throughout the Mediterranean.

CAUTION *Capparis spinosa* has incredibly sharp spikes, so wear gloves when handling this plant.

How to grow

Herb	Soil	Propagation
Capparis	Sand	Softwood cuttings

PROPAGATION Caper seeds are minuscule. When sown fresh under cover in cool climates at 10°C (50°F) they germinate quickly; however, they do take a long time to grow into transplantable seedlings. Dry seed is dormant and needs to be soaked in hot water at 40°C (105°F) for a day, then put in the refrigerator for two to three months. After refrigeration, soak the seeds again in warm water overnight prior to sowing. Cuttings are the best and most reliable method, taken from the new spring growth.

SITE Plant in a well-drained soil in a hot, sunny location with little or no water. It hates damp cold wet winters so, if you live in northern Europe, you will need to grow it in a container and place the container in a sheltered position for the winter. The caper bush is salt- and wind-tolerant, making it ideal for coastal gardens.

MAINTENANCE Flowers are borne on first-year branches, so cut plants back annually in the autumn. Capers can tolerate the cold to -7°C (18°F); however, the growing tips can be damaged even in light frost so cut these off in the following spring.

HARVESTING The flower buds are picked early in the morning for pickling and salting. The berries are picked when they are fully swollen and then pickled. As for the leaves, pick only young, succulent ones.

How to use

Fresh young caper buds, fresh caper berries, and fresh young leaves are either preserved in brine or pickled before eating. The pickled or salted buds are often served with pasta, pizzas, and in many sauces; one of the best known being tartar sauce, which is served with fish. The caper berry is served as a mezze and sometimes as a substitute for olives as a garnish. Caper leaves are used in salads or with fish dishes.

▲ ***Capparis spinosa* var. *inermis***
SPINELESS CAPER
An evergreen shrub, with a height of up to 1.5m (5ft) and a spread of up to 1.5m (5ft). Masses of edible green buds followed by solitary, white, four-petalled flowers with long, pink-purple stamens appear from early summer until autumn. It has oval, mid-green leaves with a hint of brown.

Carum

Caraway APIACEAE

I find it reassuring that this small biennial herb has survived and is still grown today for use in the kitchen and as a medicinal herb. Records show that it was used in the Stone Age, and it has been found in Egyptian tombs and at the ancient caravan stops along the Silk Road trade route. In Elizabethan feasts, eating caraway seeds became a traditional way to finish the banquet and the herb was also reputed to ward off witches and to prevent lovers from straying. I like using the seeds and leaves in the kitchen for their flavour, and I love to grow the herb for its delicately pretty flowers.

Seeds have a strong, distinctive flavour and are often considered a spice.

How to grow

Herb	Soil	Propagation
Carum	Sand	Seed

PROPAGATION Sow fresh caraway seeds in early autumn into prepared ground, when the air temperature does not fall below 7°C (45°F) at night; germination takes two to three weeks. Alternatively, sow fresh seeds in early spring under protection at 15°C (60°F); germination will take five to ten days. Plant out as soon as possible, with minimal root disturbance. It is important to use fresh seed because it only remains viable for one year.

SITE Plant in a fertile, well-drained soil, in a sunny position. Thin to 20cm (8in) apart. Caraway is not suited to container growing.

MAINTENANCE In autumn, clear weeds from around first-year plants. When the seeds have been harvested in the second autumn, dig over the area well. If planting out young plants in spring, cover the plants with horticultural fleece to protect them from carrot root fly; rotating the crop will also reduce the risk of an attack.

HARVESTING Leaves can be picked fresh for use from the first-year crop; they have a mild parsley-like flavour. The seeds can be picked to use fresh from the second-year crop in early summer, or for drying as soon as they turn brown and start to drop from the flowerhead.

How to use

The young leaves have a mild aniseed flavour and taste good in salads and soups. Use seeds sparingly or they may dominate other flavours. A small dish of seeds at the end of a spicy meal both sweetens the breath and aids digestion. Medicinally, caraway is an antispasmodic, diuretic, and expectorant. It is a mild remedy and is suitable for children, especially in cough remedies or to relieve colic.

▲ *Carum carvi*
CARAWAY, KÜMMEL

A hardy biennial, with a height of 20cm (8in) in the first season, growing to 60cm (24in) in the second year with a spread of 30cm (12in). Tiny clusters of flowers grow in the early summer of the second season. It has feathery, bright green leaves that look similar to the leaves of carrots.

Cedronella

Balm of Gilead LAMIACEAE

Known as "Balm of Gilead", *Cedronella canariensis* is native to the Canary Islands. It has a strong eucalyptus scent similar to other plants with "balsam" as part of their name (such as *Populus balsamifera* or *Commiphora opobalsamum*), which may be the explanation for why they share the same common name. When passing a plant, take the chance to rub some of the leaves between your hands and then sniff their head-clearing scent. Allow the plants to form seedheads to hear the seeds rattling in the breeze. This lovely aromatic herb also has the reputation of being an aphrodisiac.

How to grow

Herb	Soil	Propagation
Cedronella	Loam	Softwood cuttings

PROPAGATION Sow seeds in spring under protection at 20°C (68°F); germination takes 14–20 days, but can be erratic. Take softwood cuttings in early summer. When the cuttings have rooted, pot up, and winter in a greenhouse or cold frame. Plant out the following spring at 1m (3ft) intervals.

SITE Plant in a warm sunny site against a south-facing wall in well-drained soil. In cool climates, when the night temperature falls below -2°C (29°F), cover the plant with horticultural fleece, or bring it into a cool greenhouse or conservatory. In cold climates, it grows well as a container plant. Use a soil-based substrate. Trim the container plant to maintain its shape and to prevent it from becoming too tall.

MAINTENANCE Cut back after flowering to keep the plant's shape and encourage new growth. Protect from hard frost. When grown as a container plant, the leaves can be prone to whitefly. Treat by introducing a predator or with horticultural soap, according to the manufacturer's instructions.

HARVESTING Pick leaves for drying before the plant flowers. Harvest the flowers for drying as soon as they appear. Pick the seed heads when the flower petals have dropped. When dried, they look good in flower arrangements.

▶ *Cedronella canariensis* syn. *C. triphylla*
BALM OF GILEAD, CANARY BALM
A half-hardy herbaceous perennial, with a height of 1m (3ft) and a spread of 60cm (2ft). Pink to pale mauve, two-lipped flowers appear in summer, followed by black seedheads. The leaves are three-lobed and tooth-edged.

How to use

Balm of Gilead leaves can be used in hot water to make an infusion to clear the head or blocked nasal passages. An infusion of the leaves added to bath water has an invigorating effect. The leaves can be rubbed directly onto the skin as a mosquito repellent. Dried leaves can be added to pot-pourri (see page 236).

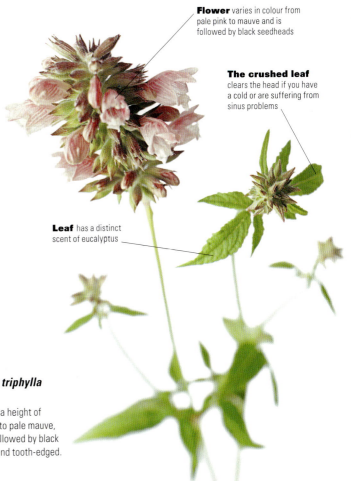

Flower varies in colour from pale pink to mauve and is followed by black seedheads

The crushed leaf clears the head if you have a cold or are suffering from sinus problems

Leaf has a distinct scent of eucalyptus

Centaurea

Cornflower ASTERACEAE

This European wild flower almost became extinct in the UK in the 1970s as a result of the introduction of chemical weed controls in farming. The French eyewash "Eau de Casselunettes" was made from cornflowers, because of their eye-brightening properties. Juice extracted from the petals makes a blue ink, and a watercolour painting pigment. I adore the stunning blue flowers of this herb. They have little scent but dry very well and can be added to pot-pourri for their attractive appearance. The bright blue blooms also attract bees into the garden, which helps with pollination.

The beautiful flowers of this herb are a striking shade of blue.

How to grow

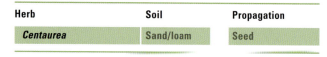

Herb	Soil	Propagation
Centaurea	Sand/loam	Seed

PROPAGATION For best results, sow seeds in open ground, when the air temperature does not fall below 10°C (50°F) at night. Germination will take 14–21 days.

SITE Plant in a well-drained soil in a sunny position. If you wish to create a natural cornflower meadow effect, clear all grasses and weeds and allow a 30cm (12in) square area for each plant. Sow five seeds per patch but thin out once established, leaving two plants per area. In autumn, allow the plants to die back and self-seed naturally. Cornflowers can be grown in large containers using a soil-based substrate. Tie the fragile stems together for support and to minimize damage from high winds or heavy rain.

MAINTENANCE To produce straight stems for drying or flower arranging, you will need to support cornflower stems with pea sticks or, if the plants have been sown in a row, with netting.

HARVESTING Cornflowers mature and fade within a few days of flowering. Pick the flowers when they are half open, and before the centre stamens become visible. When drying flowers, tie bunches of ten stems together and dry them fast, otherwise the colour will fade and their petals will disintegrate.

How to use

The petals of the flower are edible: they can be used to great effect scattered over salads, either whether, vegetable, or rice. A water distilled from cornflower petals was traditionally used as a remedy for weak eyes – the famous French eyewash "Eau de Casselunettes" used to be made from them. The dried flowers look lovely added to pot-pourri.

▼ *Centaurea cyanus*

CORNFLOWER, BLUE BOTTLE, BACHELOR'S BUTTONS

A hardy annual, with a height of 60cm (24in) and a spread of 15cm (6in). Single and double, blue daisy-like flowers in summer. The grey-green leaves are lance-shaped. The lower leaves are often toothed and covered in fine hairs. There are hybrids with the same habit which have pink, white or purple flowers.

Flower is such a striking colour that "cornflower blue" has become the commonly used term for this shade of blue. They have very little scent

Flower bud is covered in tiny hairs

Stem is narrow but surprisingly tough – in the days of harvesting by hand it was known to make a sickle blunt

Centella

Gotu kola APIACEAE

This is an important medicinal herb, native to subtropical and tropical India, Pakistan, Sri Lanka, and South Africa, where it can be found growing in swampy areas including paddy fields. It was traditionally used to help wound healing and slow the progress of leprosy. In India, it is a key herb in Ayurvedic medicine where it has been used for over 3,000 years, but it did not become important in western medicine until the 1800s. Throughout Asia it is not only a medicinal herb, but is also eaten in salads or as a vegetable, where it is believed to stimulate the appetite and aid digestion.

> **CAUTION** Excessive use of this herb taken internally or externally can cause itching, headaches, and even unconsciousness. Avoid if you are pregnant or nursing, using tranquillizers or sedatives, or have an overactive thyroid.

How to grow

Herb	Soil	Propagation
Centella	Loam	Division

PROPAGATION Gotu kola is easily grown from cuttings. Take the cutting at the point where the leaf joins the stem, from spring until late summer, or propagate it by division (see page 53) in summer. It rarely sets seed in cold climates.

SITE In tropical or subtropical climates, it will grow outdoors all year round. In cooler and cold climates it will tolerate temperatures down to 10°C (50°F) before it needs protection. It will grow in a container. Plant in a soil-based substrate in partial shade.

MAINTENANCE Protect from cold rain, frost, and snow. Repot every season and do not allow the compost to dry out in the growing season. In warm summer weather, place the container outside. Container-grown plants are prone to red spider mite. Introduce *Phytoseiulus persimilis* – its natural predator – or treat the whole plant, stem included, with a proprietary horticultural soap according to the manufacturer's instructions.

HARVESTING Throughout the growing season, pick the young succulent leaves and stems for use in salads, and the more mature leaves for cooking as a vegetable. To extract the juice, boil the leaves, then pound them into a paste for use on skin infections.

How to use

A rejuvenating, diuretic herb that clears toxins and reduces inflammation. It is used in the treatment of rheumatism and rheumatoid arthritis. In India the fresh leaves are given to children for dysentery. It is also used there to help concentration and also to treat leprosy. As a beauty aid, it stimulates the production of collagen and helps improve the tone of veins near the surface of the skin. The leaves are used in Sri Lanka and India as a vegetable.

▲ *Centella asiatica*
GOTU KOLA, PENNYWORT, SPADELEAF
A creeping, tender perennial plant, with a height of 8cm (3½in) and an indefinite spread. Tiny magenta flowers appear in summer, under the leaves. Although edible, the leaves are slightly dry and tough in texture, and have a bitter-sweet flavour.

Chamaemelum

Chamomile ASTERACEAE

Chamomile species can be a bit confusing because a number of different plants share the same common name. There is dyers' chamomile (*Anthemis tinctoria*) which produces bright yellow through to olive natural dye colours for textiles; wild chamomile (*Matricaria recutita*) which is principally used in medicine; and there is chamomile (*Chamaemelum nobile*), which is one of our favourite old garden herbs. The delicate flowers are used fresh or dried to make a calming herbal tea that can be taken for insomnia and digestive disorders.

How to grow

Herb	Soil	Propagation
Chamomile	Sand/loam	Seeds/cuttings

PROPAGATION Chamomile has very fine seeds which may wash away when sown in the ground, so it is best started in early spring under protection at 18°C (65°F); germination takes 14–20 days. Take cuttings in spring and autumn from the offsets. Divide established plants in spring, replanting in a well-prepared site.

SITE Although chamomile adapts to most soils, except wet, it favours well-drained soil in a sunny position. All *Chamaemelum* species grow well in containers in a soil-based substrate.

MAINTENANCE Cut back after flowering to encourage new growth and to prevent the plant from becoming straggly. If you are making a chamomile lawn, do not let the plants dry out in summer. Roll once a week through the growing season.

HARVESTING Pick the flowers just as they open, ideally in the early morning, on a dry day. Either use fresh or for drying.

How to use

Renowned for its sedative properties, a tea made from the fresh or dry flowers relieves insomnia, digestive disorders, travel sickness, and hyperactivity in children. Use a chamomile infusion as a gargle for mouth ulcers or as an eye wash. This infusion can also be applied to the skin to soothe burns. A hair rinse made with chamomile flowers lightens fair hair. Chamomile is known as the "physician's plant" – because when planted next to sick plants it helps them revive. A spray made from the leaves and flowers helps prevent "damping off" of seedlings. Fresh chamomile leaves can also be added to the compost heap to help activate the process of decomposition (see page 37).

◀ *Chamaemelum nobile* **'Treneague'**
LAWN CHAMOMILE
A hardy, non-flowering, evergreen perennial, with a height of 6cm (2in) and a spread of 15cm (6in). If grown as a lawn, roll once a week in the growing season to encourage the stems to root into the ground. Lawn chamomile can only be propagated from cuttings.

▲ *Chamaemelum nobile* **'Flore Pleno'**
DOUBLE-FLOWERED CHAMOMILE
A hardy evergreen perennial, with a height of 8cm (3in) and a spread of 30cm (12in). It produces small, double daisy-like flowers throughout the summer and dense, aromatic, finely-divided foliage. It can provide good ground cover for lawn areas and between paving stones. Harvest the flowerheads just as they open in summer and use fresh.

Flower is daisy-like with a yellow centre and a light scent

Stem of the flower has individual leaves spaced along its length

Leaf is finely divided and very aromatic when crushed

◄ *Chamaemelum nobile*
CHAMOMILE, ROMAN CHAMOMILE

A hardy evergreen perennial, with a height of 10cm (4in) in the green and 30cm (12in) when in flower, and a spread of 45cm (18in). It produces large, single, white daisy-like flowers throughout the summer months. The finely-divided foliage is green and sweet-smelling when crushed underfoot or between the fingertips.

Chenopodium

Goosefoot CHENOPODIACEAE

When I first came across Good King Henry I was intrigued by its unusual name and wanted to find out more – it is one of the reasons why I became a herb farmer – so I have a special affection for this plant. I wondered whether there was a "Bad Henry" and how this herb that looked like spinach could be used in cooking. I have since discovered that this unassuming plant is rich in vitamins and that "Bad Henry" is, in fact, *Mercurialis perennis* (dog mercury), a poisonous woodland plant. As a form of spinach, Good King Henry and tree spinach are both returning to favour in today's kitchen.

How to grow

Herb	Soil	Propagation
Chenopodium	Loam	Seed

PROPAGATION Sow seeds in early spring, under cover at 18°C (65°F); germination takes 14–20 days. Alternatively, sow seeds in late spring, when the air temperature at night does not fall below 7°C (45°F). Sow seeds into prepared open ground, in 1cm (½in) drills. Leave 45cm (18in) between rows, and cover the seed with 6mm (¼in) soil. Germination takes two to three weeks. Thin seedlings to 30cm (12in) apart. In spring, divide established plants of perennial species only. Replant into a prepared site that has been fed with well-rotted manure.

SITE For a good leaf crop, plant in a soil that has been fed the previous autumn with rotted manure. It will tolerate most soil conditions except waterlogged soils but favours free-draining soil and a sunny position. It will grow well in containers in a loam-based substrate.

MAINTENANCE Keep well-watered in the summer months. Feed the soil in the autumn with well-rotted manure. Renew perennial species every three to four years. Collect seeds or cut back in late summer to early autumn to prevent self-seeding.

HARVESTING Pick leaves to use fresh in spring until late summer. Pick seeds in late summer, just as they ripen. Dry and store seeds for later use (see page 70).

How to use

The young leaves are rich in iron, calcium, and vitamins B1 and C, and can be added to salads. Treat mature leaves like spinach. Steam the flowers and eat like asparagus. Ground seeds can be used as flour, or made into a tea, which can have a mild laxative effect.

◄ *Chenopodium bonus-henricus*
GOOD KING HENRY
A hardy herbaceous perennial, with a height of 60cm (24in) and a spread of 45cm (10in). It produces tiny greenish-yellow flowers in summer and has large, mid-green leaves. The plant is also used to fatten poultry and as a remedy for coughs in sheep.

▼ *Chenopodium giganteum*
TREE SPINACH, GIANT GOOSEFOOT
A hardy annual, with a height of up to 2m (6ft) and a spread of 45cm (18in). Tiny greenish flowers appear in summer; the leaves are arrow-shaped. The young leaves are a wonderful magenta colour that fades to green with age.

Leaf is typical of *Chenopodium* species. It is arrow-shaped with serrated edges

Young leaves at centre are magenta in colour

Stem becomes coarse with age

Cichorium

Chicory ASTERACEAE

Chicory was first used by the ancient Egyptians as a medicinal herb, vegetable, and salad plant. In the Napoleonic era, roasted chicory roots were found to make an ideal coffee substitute, and can still be found in French coffee today. It can be seen growing wild throughout Europe, Australia, and America. The leaves of chicory have a mild, bitter flavour and are excellent in salads. In winter, chicons are produced by forcing the roots in warmth and darkness, which blanches the new growth; these are often called "endives". The edible flowers are pretty and can add visual interest to a salad or rice bowl.

CAUTION Medicinally, chicory should be used with care as excessive use impairs the function of the retina.

How to grow

Herb	Soil	Propagation
Cichorium	Loam	Seed

PROPAGATION Sow seeds in spring under cover at 15°C (60°F); germination takes five to ten days. Or sow seeds in summer into prepared open ground; germination takes two to three weeks. Thin seedlings to 10–30cm (4–12in) apart, closer together for leaves, further apart for flowers as it needs space to run to flower.

SITE Chicory prefers a light, alkaline soil, though it will adapt to all but heavy clay soils. Plant in a sunny site. This tall plant is not suited to growing in containers.

MAINTENANCE In autumn, cut down the flowering stems and collect seeds for next year's sowing. Dig in well-rotted manure. If you want substantial roots, do not allow the plant to flower. To force the plant to produce leaves in winter, dig up some of the roots in late autumn, and cut off the plant tops to just above ground level. Plant the roots in a box filled with loam-based substrate so that the crowns sit at soil level. Water well and keep the plants in the dark with the temperature above 10°C (50°F). In four to six weeks, the root will produce 15–20cm (6–8in) long chicons (blanched leaves).

HARVESTING The leaves can be picked to use fresh from late spring onwards. Pick flowers from two-year-old plants throughout the summer. Chicons (forced roots) can be picked throughout the late autumn and winter. These should be used quickly, as once they are introduced to the daylight the foliage can become limp.

How to use

We need to learn to appreciate bitter foods like chicory as they are very beneficial to the digestive system. Add leaves to salads fresh, or blanch quickly as this will reduce the bitter flavour. Medicinally, a tea made from the leaves is a gentle tonic that increases the flow of bile.

▲ *Cichorium intybus*
CHICORY, SUCCORY
A hardy perennial, with a height of 1m (3ft) and a spread of 30cm (1ft). In the second season, the chicory plant produces clear, blue, single flowers from summer until early autumn. The oval, mid-green leaves are coarsely toothed with tiny hairs on the underside.

Coriandrum

Coriander APIACEAE

This important culinary and medicinal herb has been cultivated for over 3,000 years and is mentioned in the Old Testament. The Chinese believed it bestowed immortality, and in the Middle Ages it was an ingredient of love potions. Coriander is an interesting culinary plant because its seeds and leaves have two distinctly different flavours, and the whole plant is edible. The seed is warm and aromatic with a hint of orange, while the leaf is pungent and oily, with a hint of earth in its distinctive taste. *Coriandrum sativum* has wonderful leaf flavour and is a good species to grow for cooking.

Seeds are aromatic with a mild orange flavour. Use whole or crushed.

How to grow

Herb	Soil	Propagation
Coriandrum	Loam	Seed

PROPAGATION Sow seeds in early spring under protection at 18°C (65°F); germination takes five to ten days. Or sow seeds in late spring into prepared open ground, when the air temperature at night remains above 7°C (45°F); germination takes two to three weeks. Thin seedlings to 5cm (2in) intervals for a leaf crop, or 23cm (9in) apart for a seed crop (seed plants need more space). In my opinion, sowing the seeds direct into the open ground gives the best crop. Coriander does not like to be transplanted and may bolt and run to seed. Sow in small amounts at weekly intervals to give a constant supply of leaves.

SITE Plant in a light, well-drained soil in a sunny position. This plant dislikes damp and humid conditions. *Coriandrum sativum* 'Leisure' is the one variety of coriander that grows well in containers. It produces a good amount of leaves, and is slow to run to seed.

MAINTENANCE As the coriander seeds ripen, plants become top-heavy; support the stems with stakes. Once the seed is harvested, pull up the plant and dig over the plot.

HARVESTING From late spring until late summer, cut the fresh leaves and eat as required – they do not store well. Pick flowers to use fresh throughout the summer. Harvest seeds from summer onwards.

How to use

The leaves taste earthy and aromatic, and should be added at the end of cooking to preserve the flavour, while the seeds have a warm, spicy flavour with a hint of orange. Medicinally, coriander stimulates digestion.

▼ *Coriandrum sativum*
CORIANDER

An annual, with a height of 60cm (24in) and a spread of 23cm (9in). It bears white flowers in summer followed by round seeds. The first and lower leaves are broad and scalloped, with a strong scent and flavour; the upper leaves are finely cut with a pungent taste.

Flowers are white and appear in the summer

Leaf of the first growth, before flowering, is the one used in cooking. It is pungent and oily, with a hint of earth

Stem is weak and needs staking when seeds begin to form

Crithmum

Sea fennel APIACEAE

This seaside herb, found growing on cliffs and rocks and at the water's edge, is a native of the coasts of the Atlantic, Mediterranean, and the Black Sea, where it has been dedicated to St Peter, the patron saint of fishermen. It has been used as a vegetable for centuries. I first saw it growing wild on a seaside holiday with my children. Having crushed the salty, succulent leaves between my fingertips, I was sure it was a herb and was delighted to find that I could use it in cooking. I now grow it successfully away from its natural habitat.

How to grow

Herb	Soil	Propagation
Crithmum	Sand	Seed

PROPAGATION Sow fresh seeds in autumn under protection at 10°C (50°F); germination takes two to three weeks. If there is no germination within that period, place the container in a refrigerator for four weeks to stratify the seeds, then return to a protected environment; germination should occur within four to six weeks. During winter, keep seedlings in a frost-free environment and plant out the following spring. Propagate established plants by division (see page 53) in spring. Replant in a well-prepared site.

SITE Sea fennel favours a well-drained site with extra grit added to the soil. Plant in a sunny position and protect from cold winds. Protect from hard frosts and temperatures below -5°C (23°F). Do not mulch or feed with well-rotted manure. This plant grows well in containers in a soil-based substrate mixed equally with grit.

MAINTENANCE In spring, divide established plants. From late summer until early autumn collect the ripe seed for sowing immediately into pots or prepared module trays. Winter in a cold frame or greenhouse.

HARVESTING Pick the young stems, the young succulent leaves, and the green seed pods in early summer to use fresh in the kitchen, or for use in pickling. Please note that this herb is not marsh samphire or glasswort (*Salicornia europaea*), with which it is often confused.

How to use

This plant is rich in sulphates, iodine compounds, and pectin. Medicinally, it relieves flatulence, eases digestion, and is a diuretic. There is research into its uses for treating obesity. The leaves can be eaten in salads, cooked in butter, or used to make sauces and a pickle which is very aromatic. The leaves also have a high vitamin C content, and contain a fragrant oil which is rich in eugenol and other fragrant substances that are widely used in modern perfumery and medicine.

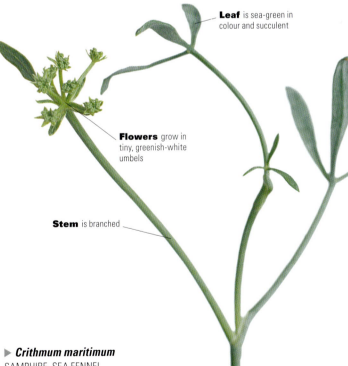

Leaf is sea-green in colour and succulent

Flowers grow in tiny, greenish-white umbels

Stem is branched

▶ ***Crithmum maritimum***
SAMPHIRE, SEA FENNEL
A hardy perennial, with a height and spread of up to 30cm (12in). Tiny white-green flowers grow in flat umbels in summer. Its succulent leaves have a strong, salty flavour.

Curcuma

Turmeric ZINGIBERACEAE

This tropical herb is regarded as one of the most valuable to mankind. The early Assyrian herbal records show that it has been in use for over 2,500 years. It most probably originated from India where it is used not only in the kitchen, but also as an important herbal remedy with curative and cleansing properties. It is considered sacred by Hindus and Buddhists and is widely used in Indian wedding ceremonies, particularly in North India. Recent research indicates that the rhizome is potentially beneficial in treating many illnesses, including cancer, high cholesterol, and dyspeptic conditions.

CAUTION If the roots are cut, their yellow sap will stain fingers or cloth indelibly.

How to grow

Herb	Soil	Propagation
Curcuma	Peat/loam	Root cuttings

PROPAGATION Take root cuttings from fresh roots with a growing node; the best supply outside the tropics is from Asian and Caribbean shops. Fill a shallow container, not much larger than the root, with seed compost mixed in equal parts with horticultural grit. Add the root, tooth-bud facing up, and cover with compost, leaving the bud just showing. Place in a plastic bag, seal, and store under protection at 20°C (68°F) for three to four weeks. Once the shoots emerge, remove the plastic bag, maintain warmth, and protect the cuttings from direct sunlight.

SITE Outside the tropics this herb will adapt to being container-grown, and will produce a good supply of leaves but not much root. Use a loam-based potting compost, mixed in equal parts with horticultural grit. Keep warm, at a minimum night temperature of 18°C (64°F). Protect from direct midday sun as the leaves will scorch.

MAINTENANCE In spring, divide the rhizomes and pot up into a container just big enough to hold them. Do not over-pot, as this can cause the rhizome to rot in cool climates. In autumn, reduce the watering of container plants and keep in a frost-free greenhouse.

HARVESTING Harvest the rhizome in late summer or early autumn. The leaves can be used as a flavouring; pick them as required throughout the growing season. The rhizome is dried and powdered to make the well-known ground spice.

How to use

In Malaysia the young rhizomes are eaten fresh in ulam, a Malay salad. The powdered rhizome is an essential ingredient in Asian cuisine; it is used in virtually every Indian meat, vegetable, and lentil dish. The leaves of the turmeric plant are used fresh to wrap fish or sweets before steaming. Medicinally, it is a very good first-aid remedy and can be used to treat gastric disorders. Turmeric has been used as a yellow dye for centuries; it is used to colour medicine, confectionery, paints, varnishes and fabrics.

▲ *Curcuma longa*
TURMERIC, INDIAN SAFFRON, HALDI, HARIDRA, KUNYIT

A tropical/subtropical, herbaceous perennial, with a height of 1m (3ft) and an indefinite spread. The yellow and white flowers, with pink tinges at the tips of the petals, appear in spring on a single stem surrounded by pale green bracts. The long, mid-green, oval leaves are aromatic. The root is a large rhizome.

Cymbopogon

Lemon grass POACEAE

This important culinary and medicinal herb grows in tropical regions and is used extensively in Asia, India, and Thailand. I have been lucky enough to see it growing and flowering naturally in the Caribbean, where it is used primarily for reducing fevers. In Malaysia, it is used extensively as a flavouring agent, as well as in perfumery and aromatherapy. This useful plant has a strong lemon flavour and can be grown successfully outside in temperate climates, although it rarely flowers in cooler regions or when cultivated. It is now grown commercially for its widely used essential oil.

Stems are cut at ground level; they have an intense lemon flavour, and are used in cooking and medicine.

How to grow

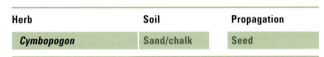

Herb	Soil	Propagation
Cymbopogon	Sand/chalk	Seed

PROPAGATION Sow seeds in spring under cover at 20°C (68°F). Germination takes 15–25 days. Pot in a loam-based substrate, and grow on until well established. In warm climates, plant out in the garden; in cooler regions, lemon grass can be grown as a container plant. In spring, propagate established plants by division. Keep at least two crowns per clump. Replant into the ground or into containers, according to the climate.

SITE In regions where temperatures at night do not fall below 8°C (48°F), the summer days are hot and wet, and the winters warm and dry, lemon grass will grow outside in any soil. In cool climates, grow as a pot plant in soil- or loam-based substrate.

MAINTENANCE When light levels drop, this plant goes dormant. In autumn, move into a frost-free site with a temperature of no less than 5°C (40°F). Reduce watering to a minimum. In early spring, as the plant starts to produce shoots, increase the heat and light and cut back all dead growth and stalks to 5cm (2in). Repot the lemon grass plants if necessary and liquid feed once a week.

HARVESTING The best-flavoured lemon grass leaves are obtained from the lower 10cm (4in) of the plant. Pick them throughout the growing season to use fresh or dry. The lower white section of the plant's stem also has a concentrated lemon flavour, and is harvested during the summer months.

How to use

A tea made from fresh leaves is a stomach and gut relaxant. The essential oil is antiseptic and deodorizing, and is used in perfume and in poultices to ease pain and arthritis, and as an insect repellent.

▶ *Cymbopogon citratus*
LEMON GRASS, FEVER GRASS
A half-hardy perennial, evergreen in warm climates, with a height of 1.5m (5ft) and a spread of 1m (3ft). It has lemon-scented, linear leaves that grow up to 90cm (3ft) in length, and robust, cane-like stems.

Leaves are sharp and rough to the touch, with a lemon scent when crushed between the fingers

Cynara

Cardoon ASTERACEAE

This large, attractive herb has been in cultivation for thousands of years as a vegetable and as a gentle laxative. *Cynara cardunculus* is currently popular as an ornamental plant for adding structure and height to the garden. In Australia, where it is classed as a weed, its potential is being researched as winter fodder for livestock, a vegetable oil (extracted from the seed), and as an environmentally friendly energy source. The flower buds and blanched leaves, roots, and stalks, are the edible parts, but I consider the taste inferior to the more familiar globe artichoke, *Cynara scolymus*.

How to grow

Herb	Soil	Propagation
Cynara	Loam	Seed

PROPAGATION Sow seeds in early spring under cover at 18°C (65°F); germination takes five to ten days. Or sow seeds in late spring into prepared open ground, when the air temperature at night does not fall below 7°C (45°F); germination takes two to three weeks. Alternatively, in spring or autumn, take the suckers (sideshoots) off the main stem and set them in pots filled with loam-based substrate. When they have taken root, plant out (when all threat of frost has passed).

SITE Plant in a sunny site in a well-drained, deep, fertile soil that has been fed the previous autumn with well-rotted manure. Space the young plants at 90-cm (36-in) intervals.

MAINTENANCE When grown in hot, dry conditions, cardoon leaves and stalks become pithy and tough and the flower bud hardens, making all parts inedible. To prevent this, maintain a good supply of water throughout the growing season. In autumn, feed the soil around established cardoon plants with well-rotted manure.

HARVESTING To produce edible blanched artichoke leaves, tie the mature outer leaves together, and wrap up the whole plant in sacking to shield it from the light. Leave for four to five weeks. Then, unwrap and harvest the blanched leaves around the heart. Pick flower buds before the outer green bracts start to open. Collect seeds in early autumn as the flowers drop. When harvesting, wear gloves and beware of prickles.

How to use

Cardoon is a detoxifier that helps the liver regenerate and stimulates the gall bladder. The leaves, ribs and stalks can be blanched and used as a winter vegetable.

▲ *Cynara cardunculus*
CARDOON
A perennial, evergreen in warm climates, with a height of 2m (6ft) and a spread of 1.2m (4ft). The flowers are very attractive to bees and butterflies, and the seeds that follow are also a good food source for garden birds.

Digitalis

Foxglove SCROPHULARIACEAE

This herb is native to Europe, Australia, New Zealand, and North America, where in some states it is classed as a weed. The common name, "foxglove", is said to have derived from the Anglo-Saxon "foxglue" or "foxmusic" after the shape of a musical instrument of that period. It became very important medicinally in the late 1700s when William Withering developed the use of *Digitalis* in the treatment of heart disease. Despite the high toxicity of the plant and its seed, infusions made from the leaves of foxgloves were often used in traditional country medicine to treat common ailments.

How to grow

Herb	Soil	Propagation
Digitalis	Clay/loam	Seed

PROPAGATION Sow fresh seeds in autumn. As the seed is very fine, mix it with flour to make the dark seeds more visible as you sow them. Do not cover the seed. Place the seed tray outdoors or in a cold frame. Germination takes five to seven weeks.

SITE Foxgloves adapt to most conditions, except for dry, exposed sites. They prefer partial shade in a moist but well-drained acid soil, enriched with leafmould. They also grow well in containers, in a soil-based substrate. Place the container in partial shade and shelter the plant from high winds as they grow very tall in the second year.

MAINTENANCE Water well in dry weather. During the first winter, protect the plants if the temperature at night falls below -10°C (14°F). Use leafmould to enrich the soil around established plants (see page 37). In the second season, remove the main flowering spike (after flowering) to increase the size of the others. Foxgloves self-seed, so pick out seedlings if you want to keep plants under control. Pot up a few seedlings as insurance against hard winters. Thin out plants if overcrowded. Wear gloves because just touching the plant may cause rashes, headaches, and nausea.

HARVESTING In the summer, the pharmaceutical industry harvests the leaves from second-year growth for the extraction of glycosides. This should only be done by a trained professional.

How to use

This herb is an important medicinal plant for treating heart failure. However, it should never be used by the amateur, nor used for self-medication. It should only be administered by a professional.

CAUTION The whole plant, including the seeds, is highly poisonous.

Flower is purple or white with irregularly shaped purple spots in the throat

▶ ***Digitalis purpurea***
FOXGLOVE, FAIRY GLOVES
A hardy biennial, with a height of up to 1.8m (6ft), and a spread of 60cm (2ft). Plants first flower in the spring of the second season; flowers are tubular and purple or white, with purple spots on the throat. The green leaves are large, textured, and lance-shaped.

Flowerbud is sealed at end

Stem is round and green with a velvet texture

Diplotaxis

Wild rocket BRASSICACEAE

A form of this herb can be found growing wild throughout Europe, Asia, and North and South America. For hundreds of years it has been collected in the wild and sold in markets, and both the leaves and seeds of rocket were used as flavouring by the Romans. Today, rocket is increasingly popular as a fresh salad herb and adds a distinctive peppery, beefy flavour; it has a much stronger taste than its close relative, salad rocket, *Eruca vesicaria* subsp. *sativa*, and can be distinguished by its more deeply-divided leaf shape and the colour of its flower, which is yellow not beige.

How to grow

Herb	Soil	Propagation
Diplotaxis	Sand	Seed

PROPAGATION Sow seeds in early spring under protection at 18°C (65°F); germination takes five to ten days. For best results, sow seeds in late spring when the air temperature at night does not fall below 7°C (45°F). Sow into prepared open ground; germination takes two to three weeks. Thin plants to 20cm (8in) apart.

SITE This herb will grow anywhere, taking off like a "rocket" – hence its name. It has adapted to the poorest of sites, growing in crevices and walls, but poor sites produce tough and bitter-tasting leaves. To produce a lush, tender leaf crop, grow rocket in light shade in a well-prepared, well-fed soil. It is not ideal as a container plant because it produces a long tap root.

MAINTENANCE For a good leaf crop, sow annually in spring. Later in the year, cover young plants with horticultural fleece to extend the picking season until the temperature falls below -1°C (30°F). The following spring, dig up old plants and sow a new crop. This herb is prone to flea beetle attack. To prevent attack, you can cover the young crop with horticultural fleece from mid-spring onwards.

HARVESTING The leaves can be picked from early spring until the first hard frosts, for using fresh, or for making pesto (see page 227). The flowers can be picked just as they open for adding to salads.

▶ **Diplotaxis muralis**
WILD ROCKET, RUCOLA
A perennial, often grown as an annual, with a height of 30cm (12in) and a spread of 15cm (6in). Yellow, four-petalled flowers appear in summer. The green, deeply divided aromatic leaves form a rosette as the plant matures.

How to use

Rocket is a digestive stimulant and is high in sulphur, which is good for healthy skin, hair, and nails. The leaves are delicious in salads. Dress the leaves with salt, lemon, oil, and vinegar, or simply serve rocket leaves with a little fresh Parmesan cheese.

Flower is bright yellow with four petals. It has little scent

Leaves become more deeply divided and pungent as the plant matures

Stem is narrow and edible when young, adding crunch to a fresh green salad

Echinacea

Echinacea ASTERACEAE

This marvellous North American herb suggests that we should hold folk medicine in higher regard. For many years Native Americans have known that echinacea increases resistance to infection, but it is only in the past decade that modern research has confirmed these properties. Now demand for echinacea almost exceeds supply. *Echinacea angustifolia*, *E. pallida*, and *E. purpurea* all have similar medicinal properties, and are becoming increasingly rare in the wild due to over-collection; today, only cultivated herb plants grown by reputable sources should be purchased.

How to grow

Herb	Soil	Propagation
Echinacea	Sand	Seed

PROPAGATION In early spring, sow seeds into a container under cover at 18°C (65°F). If germination does not occur within 28 days, place outside for a further 21 days, then re-cover the container, and place out of direct sunlight. Germination should occur within a further 20 days. When the seedlings are large enough to handle, plant into a prepared site, 30cm (12in) apart. In winter, divide established plants while they are still dormant, or take root cuttings in late winter or early spring. When the roots take, plant out into a prepared site in the garden.

SITE Plant in a sunny site in a rich, free-draining soil. Excessive wet causes roots to rot. (*E. purpurea* is not as sensitive to wet soils as other species.) Echinacea will grow well in a large container. Use a soil-based substrate and repot each winter.

MAINTENANCE After flowering, cut back the plant and collect the seeds. In spring, lightly mulch established plants with well-rotted manure. Spring growth in mature plants and young plants attracts snails. Check plants and remove snails on a daily basis.

HARVESTING Pick flowers and leaves during flowering before the seedheads (cones) are fully formed. When the petals are dead, pick the seedheads and dry them. In autumn, harvest roots and rhizomes from four-year-old plants.

How to use

Echinacea raises the body's resistance to infection by stimulating the immune system. It is very effective in preventing colds and flu. A decoction of juice extracted from flowers can also be used to treat minor wounds, burns, and boils, and as a gargle for throat infections.

▲ *Echinacea angustifolia*
NARROW-LEAFED ECHINACEA, BLACK SAMPSON
A hardy herbaceous perennial with a height of 60cm (24in) and a spread of 30cm (12in). An endangered species in its natural habitat.

▲ *Echinacea pallida*
ECHINACEA, CONEFLOWER
A hardy herbaceous perennial with a height of 80cm (33in) and a spread of 45cm (18in). *E. pallida* is not as medicinally effective as other species, but is a very attractive plant.

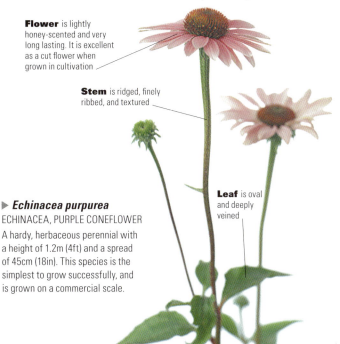

Flower is lightly honey-scented and very long lasting. It is excellent as a cut flower when grown in cultivation

Stem is ridged, finely ribbed, and textured

Leaf is oval and deeply veined

▶ *Echinacea purpurea*
ECHINACEA, PURPLE CONEFLOWER
A hardy, herbaceous perennial with a height of 1.2m (4ft) and a spread of 45cm (18in). This species is the simplest to grow successfully, and is grown on a commercial scale.

Elettaria

Cardamom ZINGIBERACEAE

This tropical plant was originally found growing wild in the Ghat Mountains on the Malabar Coast of south-west India, in an area known as the Cardamom Hills. Today, it is cultivated for its lemon-flavoured seeds in India, Sri Lanka, Guatemala, and Tanzania. Aromatic cardamom seeds are used to flavour sweet and savoury foods, and drinks such as coffee and wine. In cool temperate climates, cardamom plants will grow successfully in a conservatory or greenhouse. They will not flower or produce seed pods in these conditions, but, in my opinion, their beautiful leaves more than make up for it.

Pods contain approximately 12–18 black seeds. The seeds have a warm, spicy, lemon flavour.

How to grow

Herb	Soil	Propagation
Elettaria	Sand	Division

PROPAGATION In late autumn, sow fresh cardamom seeds under protection at 24°C (75°F). An additional light source may be needed to encourage germination. Germination takes 14–21 days. Seed-raised plants will take five years to flower. It is much easier to propagate plants by the division of rhizomes in spring. In warm climates, they will take three years to flower.

SITE Plant in a rich, moist soil in partial shade, where temperatures do not fall below 10°C (50°F). It will only produce flowers and fruit under tropical conditions. In subtropical or cool regions, it is best grown as a foliage plant in a container using a loam-based substrate. Place in a warm conservatory or greenhouse in partial shade; full sun will make the leaves turn yellow.

MAINTENANCE In hot climates, cardamom can be invasive. In spring, dig up its creeping rhizomes to control it. In spring, repot container-grown plants. Feed container-grown plants regularly from spring until early autumn with liquid seaweed or comfrey.

HARVESTING In hot climates, seeds are harvested by hand, which makes them an expensive crop to produce. In cool climates, pick the leaves to use fresh as required.

How to use

Seeds, extracted from the pod and chewed, freshen the breath and aid digestion. Some varieties have green and others brown pods. The bright green pods are best for culinary use. Use the leaves to add flavour to steamed fish, chicken, and vegetable dishes by lining the steamer with leaves.

Leaf is highly aromatic when crushed or steamed

Stem is smooth and ridged. The leaves unfurl from the growing tip

▶ *Elettaria cardamomum*
CARDAMOM

A tropical evergreen perennial, with a height of up to 3m (10ft) and an indefinite spread. Orchid-like white flowers with a striped purple-pink lower lip are followed in tropical climates by 15–20 aromatic seeds. The smooth, lance-shaped, dark green leaves have a silky, paler underside. They are highly aromatic when crushed or heated.

Eriocephalus
Wild rosemary ASTERACEAE

I have been growing this plant in the UK for over ten years but for a long time was unaware of its herbal properties – I only knew that the leaves smelt lovely, and that, in winter, it produced attractive flowers followed by fascinating fluffy white seeds. When my neighbours brought back a medicinal plant book from South Africa, I discovered that this plant grew wild in the Western Cape, and that it was an important medicinal and culinary herb. Its colloquial name, "kapokbos", derives from the Afrikaans word for snow, which is "kapok" and refers to the appearance of the snow-like seeds.

How to grow

Herb	Soil	Propagation
Eriocephalus	Sand	Softwood cuttings

PROPAGATION Sow fresh seeds in spring under protection at 20°C (68°F). Germination takes ten to fifteen days. In cool climates, place young plants in a frost-free environment over winter. In late spring, take softwood cuttings from the growing tips. In cool climates, grow the young plants under protection for the first year.

SITE This plant grows wild on granite and clay slopes and by the sea. In the garden, it prefers full sun and a well-drained soil. In warm climates, it can be grown as a hedge or clipped into ball shapes. In temperatures below 8°C (45°F), it grows well as a container plant in a loam-based substrate.

MAINTENANCE Prune after flowering in late spring to encourage bushy growth. Protect from frosts and, more importantly, from damp, wet conditions.

HARVESTING Pick the leaves to use fresh, or to dry for later use, after flowering from spring until early autumn. Pick aromatic branches as required, and harvest seeds when they become fluffy.

How to use

Wild rosemary has been used to treat coughs and colds, flatulence and colic. It is also used as a diuretic. For relaxation, add an infusion of leaves to the bath. Make a foot bath of leaves to relieve swollen legs or to stimulate the onset of menstruation. An infusion of the leaves and twigs is used to control dandruff and to stimulate hair growth. In cooking, the leaves are used in meat dishes and vegetable stews. Dried leaves can be added to pot-pourri (see page 236).

▲ *Eriocephalus africanus*
WILD ROSEMARY, SNOWBUSH, KAPOKBOS
A half-hardy evergreen shrub, with a height and spread of 1m (3ft). Clusters of small white flowers with magenta centres are produced in winter. The small, silver-haired, slightly succulent leaves grow in tufts along the branch and reflect sunlight, so reducing leaf temperature.

Seed is covered in fluffy white hairs, which look like snow

Eupatorium

Joe Pye weed ASTERACEAE

Eupatorium is native to North America, and can be found growing on low, moist ground, wooded slopes, savannahs, and alongside streams. This herb is said to have taken its name from a Native American, Joe Pye, who reputedly used it to cure fevers and typhus. It is still considered an aphrodisiac by some Native American tribes, and today is used by modern herbalists to treat cystitis, and other urinary conditions. In the garden it looks most attractive planted in drifts either at the back of a border, or around a pond, where it will attract masses of butterflies in late summer.

CAUTION This herb has liver-toxic and carcinogenic properties, and should only be administered by a professional.

How to grow

Herb	Soil	Propagation
Eupatorium	Loam	Seed

PROPAGATION In autumn, sow fresh seeds in pots and place them in a cold frame. If no germination occurs within 28 days, place the container outside to expose it to all weathers, especially frost. After 21 days, move it back to the cold frame. After germination, keep seedlings in a cold frame over winter before planting out the following spring into a well-prepared site. Take root cuttings in spring. Divide established plants in autumn and replant into a well-prepared site.

SITE Plant in moist, fertile soil in full sun or light shade. This plant is not ideal for growing in containers because it grows too big, too quickly.

MAINTENANCE In late spring, pinch back the stems to make a shorter, bushier plant. In autumn, prevent self-seeding by cutting back as soon as the seeds have set.

HARVESTING For use as a dye, cut the flowering stems in spring, just as the buds begin to open. In the autumn, lift the roots for drying.

How to use

Medicinally, the roots are the most potent part of the plant. As the common name "gravel root" indicates, it helps treat bladder stones (gravel) and urinary problems. An infusion of flowers makes a diuretic tea to alleviate fluid retention. A tea made from the fresh leaves is used to bring down high fevers, and to treat rheumatism. To make a fly repellent, crush dried leaves and burn them. The flowers and seeds yield a pink or red textile dye.

▼ *Eupatorium purpureum*
JOE PYE WEED, QUEEN OF THE MEADOW, GRAVEL ROOT, PURPLE BONESET

A hardy herbaceous perennial, with a height of up to 3m (10ft) and a spread of up to 1m (3ft). Fragrant pale pink to pale purple flowers in large, domed clusters appear in summer until early autumn, followed by attractive seed heads. Leaves are oval, dark green, large, and finely toothed.

Flowers have a light vanilla scent

Stem is sturdy, hollow, and purple in colour when mature

Leaves grow in whorls around the stem

Filipendula

Meadowsweet ROSACEAE

When I first moved to my farm, I was given a housewarming present of meadowsweet vinegar, made from the flowers which grow wild along the lanes in this part of the UK. Traditionally, this herb was strewn on the floor with rushes to give the room the scent of sweet almonds, but in the 19th century, meadowsweet's reputation grew when salicylic acid was isolated from the stem sap. This was later synthesized as acetylsalicylic acid, and forms the basis of what we know today as aspirin. Meadowsweet is not recommended for anyone who is sensitive to this painkiller.

How to grow

Herb	Soil	Propagation
Filipendula	Loam	Division

PROPAGATION Sow seeds into a container in early spring and place in a cold frame. Germination usually takes one to three months, but can be erratic. Divide established meadowsweet plants in early autumn. Replant 30cm (12in) apart.

SITE Plant in moisture-retentive soil in sun or partial shade. Meadowsweet is a good plant for growing in clay soils and close to or in water. It grows well in containers, in a soil-based substrate. Place the container in partial shade and do not let it dry out.

MAINTENANCE To encourage new leaf growth, cut back after flowering in late summer. Meadowsweet is prone to mildew. If this occurs, cut off the diseased leaves. If it is very serious, cut the plant down to the ground, and destroy all the contaminated leaves.

HARVESTING Pick young leaves to use fresh or to dry before flowering. Harvest the flowers just as they open to use fresh or to dry. Dig up the roots of three-year-old plants to dry or use fresh.

How to use

Both the leaves and flowers are edible. The flowers have a mild almond flavour and can be added to stewed fruits, jellies, and jams. They are also good for flavouring meads and beers, and make an interesting wine. Young spring leaves have a dry flavour and can be added to salad or soups. The flowers make a good tea, which is ideal for those suffering from aches or pains. The roots of the plant make a black textile dye.

▶ *Filipendula ulmaria*
MFADOWSWEET, BRIDEWORT
A hardy herbaceous perennial with a height of 60–120cm (2–4ft) and a spread of 60cm (2ft). It produces clusters of frothy, almond-scented, creamy-white flowers in summer, and has aromatic, darkish-green, pinnate, serrated, deeply-veined leaves.

Flower was known as bridewort because it was strewn along the aisle for brides to walk on

Leaves smell like winter greens when crushed

Stem produces a sap containing salicylic acid

Foeniculum

Fennel APIACEAE

This beautiful aromatic herb has been in cultivation for thousands of years. The Greeks ate fennel to suppress hunger, and in the Middle Ages it was used to deter insects. Today, nearly all parts of the fennel plant are used for culinary purposes: the leaves for salads, the fennel stems on barbecues to add flavour to meat and fish, and the seeds ground into a powdered spice for use with lamb, pork, and vegetables. Care should be taken, however, as taken in large doses, oil made from fennel seed can cause convulsions and disturb the nervous system.

Seeds are very aromatic. You can chew them to freshen the breath.

How to grow

Herb	Soil	Propagation
Foeniculum	Sand	Seed

PROPAGATION Sow seeds in spring under protection at 20°C (68°F); germination takes seven to ten days. Continue to grow under protection until all threat of frost has past. Or sow seeds in late spring into prepared open ground when the air temperature at night remains above 5°C (41°F); germination takes 14–20 days. If you have light soil, divide established plants in spring.

SITE Plant in a warm, sunny site in well-drained, fertile soil. If grown in poor soil or arid conditions, fennel will taste bitter. Also, do not plant fennel near dill or coriander – the former may cross-pollinate with fennel, and the latter alters the flavour. Fennel grows well in containers in a loam-based substrate.

MAINTENANCE Harvest the seeds and then cut back the plant to promote new leaf growth. Replace fennel plants every three to four years to maintain a good flavour. In autumn, when the plant has died back, mulch the soil around the plant with well-rotted manure. In winter, protect the fennel plant from wet conditions because it is susceptible to mildew and/or rot.

HARVESTING Pick leaves to use fresh in summer prior to flowering. Pick flowers to use fresh as they open. Harvest seeds just as they change colour from green to brown and dry well.

How to use

The seeds of the fennel plant have the best medicinal properties. An infusion of fennel seeds eases flatulence and colic in young children and prevents heartburn and indigestion in adults. A mild infusion can be used as an eye wash.

◀ *Foeniculum vulgare* **'Purpureum'**

BRONZE FENNEL

A hardy herbaceous perennial with a height of 1.5–2.1m (4–7ft) and a spread of 45cm (18in). Large umbels of small yellow flowers appear in summer, followed by aromatic seeds. This fennel looks striking in a mixed border as well as in the herb garden.

Flower has a light sweet aniseed flavour and a slight crunch

Leaf is made up of a collection of small thread-like segments that make it appear soft and feathery

▶ *Foeniculum vulgare* FENNEL

A hardy herbaceous perennial with a height of 1.5–2.1m (4–7 ft) and a spread of 45cm (18in). This herb is often confused with *Foeniculum vulgare* var. *dulce* (Florence fennel), which produces a bulb and is grown as a vegetable.

Stem is hollow and ridged when mature

Fragaria

Wild strawberry ROSACEAE

This herb grows in the cool temperate climates of Europe, Northern Asia, Australia, and North America. For me, picking wild strawberries on walks in the forest, bringing them home carefully, and then eating them the following morning with my cereal is a vivid childhood memory. The strawberry fruit was dedicated by the ancient Romans to Venus and in medieval times to the Virgin Mary – possibly because of its medicinal properties as a diuretic and an astringent, or maybe just because it is so heavenly to eat. Some people, however, are allergic to strawberries.

Fruit is edible, small and scarlet, and smells and tastes sweet.

How to grow

Herb	Soil	Propagation
Fragaria	Loam	Division

PROPAGATION In late summer, pick fresh fruit and leave to dry on muslin. Rub the seeds off the dried fruit and sow fresh in early autumn, on the surface of the substrate. Place in a cold frame but do not cover; germination takes six to ten weeks. Alternatively, sow in spring, on the surface. Do not cover. Place under protection at 20°C (68°F). As soon as the seeds have germinated, remove them from heat and grow on under protection at 15°C (60°F). Plant out when large enough to handle and there is no chance of frost. Established plants produce runners. As each runner has a small root system, plant where required into a prepared site in the garden.

SITE Plant in sun or partial shade in a fertile soil that does not dry out in summer. This herb is good for ground cover and grows well in containers in a soil- or loam-based substrate.

MAINTENANCE Feed regularly with liquid comfrey fertilizer throughout the fruiting season. Cut back runners if the plant becomes too invasive. As insurance against an extreme winter, pot up a few runners in the autumn.

HARVESTING Pick leaves to use fresh or to dry in late spring before the fruit sets. Pick ripe fruit from summer until early autumn. Harvest the fruit to dry for seed collecting in early summer.

How to use

Medicinally, the leaves are mildly astringent and can be made into a gargle for sore throats. The fruit is a diuretic. They are a useful addition to the diet for those suffering from rheumatic gout. The fresh fruit can help remove tooth discolouration.

Flower has five white petals, and a yellow centre and stamen

Leaves have a musky scent and flavour

▶ *Fragaria vesca*
WILD STRAWBERRY

A hardy perennial, with a height of 15–30cm (6–12in) and a spread of 18cm (7in), or an indefinite spread if you include the runners. Flowers with yellow centres followed by small, scarlet, sweet fruit appear in the summer. The leaves taste good mixed with other herbs in a salad or as a tea.

Galega

Goat's rue PAPILIONACEAE

Indigenous to central and southern Europe and western Asia, this herb has naturalized across Europe and in New Zealand, as well as in western Pakistan, where it is the host to the caterpillar of many forms of the *Coleophora vicinella* moth. It has also spread to the USA, where it has been classed as a noxious weed. It has been used for hundreds of years to treat plagues and infections, and was historically recommended as a cure for snake bites. The name "galega" comes from the Greek word gala, meaning "milk", because of its reputation for increasing lactation in nursing mothers and animals.

CAUTION Only to be used under professional supervision when treating diabetes.

How to grow

Herb	Soil	Propagation
Galega	Loam	Seed/division

PROPAGATION In early spring, sow seeds into prepared seed or plug module trays; germination takes 10–20 days without extra heat. Alternatively, in mid-spring, sow directly into a prepared site in the garden, thinning to 75cm (30in) apart. Divide established plants in the second or third year either by using two forks, back-to-back, or by digging up the whole plant. Once divided, replant in a well-prepared site.

SITE This fully hardy herb will grow in most soils. It prefers a deep soil that does not dry out in summer and allows the roots to become well established. If the plant becomes invasive or outgrows its position, cut it back hard; this will keep it under control and encourage flowering at a lower height, which can look very effective.

MAINTENANCE This can be a sprawling plant, so cut back hard in early summer to keep it under control and maximize the flowers, and again after the first flowering to promote a second flush.

HARVESTING All the aerial parts of the plant are harvested in summer just before flowering, then dried for medicinal use.

How to use

Used medicinally, goat's rue reduces blood sugar levels and is a useful diuretic, and is also used to increase lactation in nursing mothers. The leaves and stem are used as an animal food supplement to increase milk yield. Goat's rue can also be grown as a green manure, and it is an excellent bee plant.

▲ *Galega officinalis*
GOAT'S RUE, FRENCH LILAC
A hardy, herbaceous perennial, with a height of 1–1.5m (3–5ft) and a spread of up to 1m (3ft). Attractive clusters of white or mauve flowers in summer are followed by long seed pods. Its leaflets are compound, divided, and lance-shaped.

Galium

Sweet woodruff RUBIACEAE

Formerly known as *Asperula odorata*, this herb is a native of Europe and was introduced into North America and Asia, where it became naturalized. Sweet woodruff is ideal for ground cover, under deciduous trees, and by hedges or on banks, and is one of the few herbs to grow well in dappled shade. It has a pretty, star-shaped flower and attractive foliage. The leaves can be picked in early spring, dried, and used like lavender to scent fresh laundry – their scent is reminiscent of freshly mown hay with a hint of vanilla. Historically, the dried leaves were used as a stuffing for beds.

How to grow

Herb	Soil	Propagation
Galium	Loam	Root cuttings

PROPAGATION This plant happily self-seeds in the wild but in controlled conditions it may be a challenge to grow from seed. In autumn, sow fresh seeds into a pot and cover with coarse horticultural sand. Place outside. Germination takes one to six months. Alternatively, it may be easier to propagate established plants by division or take root cuttings in spring (see pages 52–53). Once divided or rooted, plant in a prepared site 30cm (12in) apart.

SITE Plant in a moist, fertile soil in partial shade. (Sweet woodruff will adapt to most soils, but will need extra water in hot or dry conditions.) It can be mildly invasive if grown in its optimum conditions. It will adapt to containers but allow enough room for seasonal growth or the roots may rot in wet conditions.

MAINTENANCE In hot, dry conditions this herb may suffer from seasonal die-back, causing the leaves to turn yellow. Cut it back, and it will revive with watering and the cooler temperatures of late summer. If the plant becomes invasive, dig it up before the flowers have set.

HARVESTING Pick the leaves and flowers together in early spring. Its scent of freshly mown hay is strongest after the plant has been dried.

How to use

Fresh leaves are used as flavouring agents in alcoholic and non-alcoholic drinks. Dried leaves are placed between clothes, towels, and sheets as a fabric freshener. As a medicinal plant, woodruff has been used as an antispasmodic and a diuretic.

Leaves, when crushed, smell like sweet, freshly mown hay

▶ *Galium odoratum*
SWEET WOODRUFF
A hardy, herbaceous perennial with a height of 15cm (6 in) and a spread of 30cm (12in) or more. Small, white, star-shaped flowers appear from spring until early summer. The leaves are narrow and lance-shaped. Six to eight leaves grow around each stem in a complete circle.

Stem is trailing. It often forms roots at the nodes, which increase the spread of the plant

Ginkgo

Ginkgo GINKGOACEAE

This fascinating tree is thought to be one of the oldest trees on the planet; it is regarded as the ancestor of all conifers, and is one of the most well-researched herbs in the world. In Chinese medicine, it is regarded as the herb for the elderly, because of its powerful effects on the circulatory system. The nuts are used to treat asthma, bronchial congestion, and coughs. The name "ginkgo" is derived from the Japanese word *ginkyo*, meaning "silver apricot", which refers to the fruit. "Biloba" translates as "two-lobed", referring to the split in the middle of the fan-shaped leaves.

CAUTION If taken in excess, ginkgo can cause a toxic reaction.

How to grow

Herb	Soil	Propagation
Ginkgo	Loam	Seed

PROPAGATION In autumn, remove the pith from around the seed and wash in a mild detergent to remove the protective coating around the seed. Sow one seed per pot. Cover with coarse grit and place in a cold frame. Germination takes four to six months or longer. Grow on in a pot for a further five years before planting out. Take cuttings from new growth in summer. When rooted, grow on as a container plant for at least five years before planting in the final growing position. Fruits will only be produced in a warm climate when a male and female tree are planted near one another.

SITE Plant in full sun to partial sun in a light, fertile, deep soil. It is adaptable and tolerates air pollution. Young specimens grow well in containers in a loam-based substrate.

MAINTENANCE Little maintenance is needed for trees in the open ground. If growing as a container plant, remove the leaves from around the plant in autumn after leaf fall. Repot each year in the spring.

HARVESTING Pick fresh leaves as they turn from green to yellow in autumn, and dry. The small plums are picked when ripe. The kernel (nut) is extracted and dried in autumn.

How to use

The seeds are a culinary delicacy, and should be cooked before eating. They can be roasted or used in soups and stir fries, and are often served at wedding feasts. They are available in Eastern supermarkets where they are often called "white nuts". Medicinally, an infusion of the leaves is used to improve the memory and circulation, and to ease tinnitus. The leaves are being researched as a treatment for Alzheimer's.

Leaf blade is sometimes whole, but often has a characteristic slit in the centre. The veins are slightly raised

▲ *Ginkgo biloba*
GINKGO, MAIDENHAIR TREE
A hardy deciduous tree, with a height of 40m (130ft) and a spread of 20m (70ft). It is dioecious, which means that it bears male and female flowers on different trees in early summer. The flowers are followed by small fruit on the female tree. The leaves are fan-shaped.

Glycyrrhiza

Liquorice PAPILIONACEAE

One of the most popular and widely consumed herbs in the world, liquorice is native to southern Europe, Asia, and the Mediterranean and is commercially cultivated in Russia, Spain, Iran, and India. It has been used medicinally for over 3,000 years. The ancient Egyptians and the Greeks recognized its benefits in treating coughs and lung disease. It was introduced into the UK in the 16th century but is now no longer grown as a commercial crop. I used to eat liquorice strings as a child and just loved the flavour; I still find it a fascinating old herb today.

Root is dried before use as a flavouring for confectionery (known as liquorice sticks) or as a medicine.

How to grow

Herb	Soil	Propagation
Glycyrrhiza	Loam	Seed

CAUTION Do not take liquorice medicinally if pregnant, or if suffering from kidney disease.

PROPAGATION Seeds collected in cool climates tend not to be viable. Sow seeds in spring under protection at 20°C (68°F). Germination takes 10–14 days but can be erratic. Grow on for two years in a container before planting out in the open ground. Divide established plants in autumn after the plant has died back. Make sure that there is a growing bud visible in each division, replanting into a well-prepared site.

SITE Plant in a fertile, deep, well-cultivated soil in a sunny position. Plant pot-grown plants or divided roots, at a depth of 15cm (6in), and place 1m (3ft) apart. Liquorice is not well suited to growing in containers unless they are very deep, like a dustbin.

MAINTENANCE To produce a good crop of roots, mulch the soil in autumn with well-rotted manure. In spring, cut back old leaf growth.

HARVESTING In early winter, dig up the roots of established three- or four-year-old plants for drying. As this plant is slow-growing, dig up one-third of the root now and leave the rest to harvest in subsequent years. Fill in with well-rotted manure to encourage root growth.

How to use

Liquorice root is used to flavour black treacle, and beers such as Guinness. Medicinally, it is one of the most prescribed herbs in China. It is used to treat the spleen, liver, and kidney. The Japanese use a liquorice preparation to treat hepatitis. In western medicine, it is used to alleviate sore throats, coughs, and bronchitis.

Leaf is composed of between 9 and 17 oval leaflets

▶ ***Glycyrrhiza glabra***
LIQUORICE
A hardy herbaceous perennial, with a height of 1.2m (4ft) and a spread of 1m (3ft). Short spikes of pea-like white flowers tinged with mauve-purple appear in late summer followed by long pods. The large green leaves are divided into oval leaflets.

Hesperis

Sweet rocket BRASSICACEAE

The scent of this herb, wafted on the warm evening air, is of violets with a hint of warm cloves. This evening-scented plant's name, *Hesperis,* is the Greek word for "evening". In the language of flowers it is said to represent deceit, since it gives out a lovely perfume in the evening but none in the day. It has naturalized in Europe, where it hosts caterpillars from several different butterfly species including the Orange Tip (*Anthocharis cardamines*) and Small White (*Pieris rapae*). Unfortunately, sweet rocket has been classed as a weed in some US states because of its ability to self-seed.

How to grow

Herb	Soil	Propagation
Hesperis	Loam	Seed/division

PROPAGATION Sow seed in autumn in prepared seed or plug trays. Winter the young plants in a cold greenhouse. By sowing early, you can sometimes have plants flowering in the first season. Alternatively, sow direct into the garden in early summer. Thin after germination to 30cm (12in) apart and, when well established, to the final planting distance of 45cm (18in). Divide established plants in late spring (see p.53) either by using two forks back-to-back, or by hand. Replant into a prepared site.

SITE Plant in full sun or light shade, in a well-drained fertile soil, in the middle or towards the back of the border. This herb looks most attractive when planted in large clumps, rather than as single plants. A word of warning: sweet rocket can be invasive in light soils.

MAINTENANCE Cut back hard in midsummer, after flowering, to promote a second flowering flush. This will also prevent the plants sprawling over the garden and self-seeding.

HARVESTING Pick young leaves before the plant flowers in early summer. Pick the flowers throughout the summer – preferably in the morning, just as they open.

How to use

The young leaves have a bitter flavour and can be added to salads; they work well with potatoes and pasta. The flowers are edible, and can be added to fruit and savoury salads; they also crystallize well, making an attractive garnish for cakes and puddings. Sweet rocket is a member of the mustard family, and therefore produces a prolific amount of seed in the autumn, which provides a good source of food for wild birds.

▲ *Hesperis matronalis*
SWEET ROCKET, DAME'S ROCKET, DAMASK VIOLET, DAME'S VIOLET, DAME'S-WORT, MOTHER-OF-THE-EVENING
A short-lived hardy perennial, with a height of 60–90cm (2–3ft). It produces sweetly scented, mauve, white, pink, or purple flowers in the summer of the second year, and has green, lance-shaped leaves.

Humulus

Hop CANNABACEAE

This herb is native to the northern temperate zones, and is now cultivated commercially in northern Europe and North America. It was originally eaten as a vegetable – the young shoots are similar in taste to asparagus. In the reign of Henry VIII, hops revolutionized the brewing of beer in Britain, replacing traditional bitter herbs such as alecost (*Tanacetum balsamita*) and helping the beer to keep. Hops have been used medicinally for hundreds of years as a sedative; a pillow stuffed with dried hops cured George III's insomnia, and hop pillows are still used today.

How to grow

Herb	Soil	Propagation
Humulus	Loam	Softwood cuttings

PROPAGATION Obtain seeds from a specialist supplier to avoid hop wilt disease. Sow in autumn and cover with horticultural sand and coarse grit. Place the container outside. Germination usually takes four to six months, but may take up to one season. Take softwood cuttings from the female plants in spring or early summer – it is difficult to identify the gender of plants grown from seed until they are two to three years old (see *H. lupulus*, below right). In spring, divide root stems of established plants. Replant 1m (3ft) apart in a well-prepared soil and support.

SITE Plant in a sunny position in a soil that is rich in leafmould and has been deeply dug. Grow hops in containers in a soil-based substrate. Provide support for the plants to climb, or let them cascade over the edge of the container.

MAINTENANCE In autumn, cut back the plant to the ground, clear away any leaf or stem debris, and feed with well-rotted manure or compost. Hops are prone to hop wilt which is very contagious – dig up affected plants and burn them, and do not plant hops in that area again. Leaf miner and powdery mildew are also problems for hops – remove infected leaves and burn them.

HARVESTING In spring, pick young sideshoots to use fresh. Harvest hop flowers in early autumn. Dry well, and use quickly – the flavour fades rapidly.

How to use

Medicinally, the female flower is good for insomnia, and intestinal cramps. A pillow stuffed with female flowers aids sleep. To eat, steam or lightly boil sideshoots, and parboil the male flowers to eat in salads. Blanch young leaves to remove bitterness and use in soups and salads.

▲ *Humulus lupulus*
COMMON HOP
A hardy herbaceous perennial vine, with a height of up to 9m (20ft). It is dioecious, with male and female flowers growing on separate plants in summer. The female flower is cone-like and hidden by papery scales; the male in clusters without sepals. The leaves have three to five lobes with sharply toothed edges.

Hypericum

St John's Wort CLUSIACEAE

I love the fascinating stories associated with this herb. According to the old saying, whoever treads on St John's Wort after sunset will be swept up on the back of a magic horse! In a more practical vein, however, it has many medicinal properties. Today, it is used in the treatment of neuralgia and varicose veins, and is famous as "nature's Prozac" in the treatment of depression. However, it should not be taken by people who are chronically depressed. It is a lovely herb to grow, with stunning yellow flowers in midsummer, which are followed by prolific seed heads.

CAUTION High doses may cause photosensitivity. Do not mix with other drugs. Always check before using with your doctor or herbalist. It can poison livestock.

How to grow

Herb	Soil	Propagation
Hypericum	Sand	Seed

PROPAGATION In spring, mix the very fine seeds with sand or flour for an even sowing. Do not cover. Place under protection at 20°C (68°F) or in a cold frame. Germination takes 10–20 days with warmth; 15–30 days in a cold frame. Divide established plants in early autumn, replanting 30cm (12in) apart into a prepared site.

SITE Plant in a sunny position in well-drained chalky soil, although it will adapt to partial shade and all but waterlogged soils. If grown in a light soil it may become invasive. It will grow well in a container with a soil-based substrate. Please note that in some countries, notably Australia, this herb is subject to statutory control as a weed.

MAINTENANCE After flowering and harvest, cut the plant down to the ground to allow the green growth of the herb to form a semi-evergreen mat in winter.

HARVESTING Harvest the leaves for drying any time from early spring onwards, and before the plant begins to send up flowering spikes. Harvest the flowers in summer, on a dry morning, as they open. Remove all green parts from the flower, then dry or preserve in wheatgerm oil or olive oil.

▶ *Hypericum perforatum*
ST JOHN'S WORT
A hardy semi-evergreen perennial, with a height of 30–90cm (12–36in) and a spread of 30cm (12in). Lightly-scented yellow flowers with tiny black gland dots appear in summer. The small, green leaves are covered with tiny translucent spots which are resin glands. When crushed or on a hot day, they give off an unpleasant foxy scent.

How to use

This important medicinal herb acts as tonic for the nervous system, and as an antidepressant. An oil infused with the flowers stimulates tissue repair and is used to treat wounds, burns, and shingles. It is also good for sciatic pain, sunburn, ulcers, and varicose veins. It is used in homeopathy for pain and inflammation caused by nerve damage.

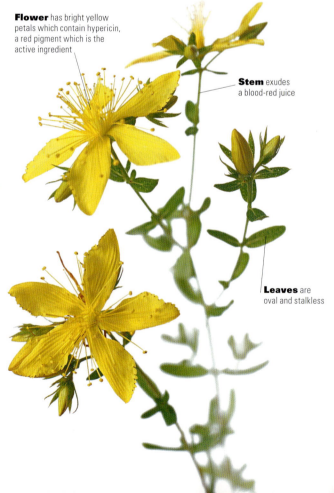

Flower has bright yellow petals which contain hypericin, a red pigment which is the active ingredient

Stem exudes a blood-red juice

Leaves are oval and stalkless

Hyssopus

Hyssop LAMIACEAE

This delightful Mediterranean herb not only looks lovely growing in the garden, but is also a great culinary and medicinal herb. It was used by the Greek physician Hippocrates (460–377BC), who recommended it for chest complaints, for which it is still used today. It was also one of the herbs taken to the New World by the colonists, for its many uses as an antiseptic, in tea, and in herbal tobacco. The wonderful blue flowers, which have a sweet anise/minty flavour, are great for attracting many pollinating insects into the garden.

CAUTION Hyssop essential oil can cause epileptic fits. Hyssop should not be taken medicinally during pregnancy.

How to grow

Herb	Soil	Propagation
Hyssopus	Sand	Seed

PROPAGATION In spring, sow seeds under protection at 20°C (68°F). Germination takes five to ten days. Take softwood cuttings in early summer from non-flowering shoots. In early autumn, only divide established plants that are less than three years old. Dig up and gently pull the plant apart to obtain pieces of stem with both roots and leaf attached. Replant into a prepared site.

SITE Plant in a sunny position in well-drained neutral to alkaline soil – good drainage is essential to the health of this plant. Hyssop makes a very pretty short-term hedge. It grows well in containers using a loam-based substrate.

MAINTENANCE A short-lived perennial, hyssop lasts for four to five years. In mild areas, cut back to 20cm (8in) in early autumn, or wait until after spring frosts, in cold areas.

HARVESTING Pick young, fresh leaves throughout the growing season. Harvest hyssop leaves for drying from non-flowering stems in summer. Pick the flowers just as they open. The flowers' scent is more intense when they are dried.

How to use

Hyssop is a good companion plant; when planted near cabbages it lures away the cabbage white butterfly. Planted near vines it attracts bees and increases pollination. In the kitchen, the leaves have a strong, bitter, minty flavour, great to use in marinades and dressings, and the flowers are delicious tossed in green salads. Medicinally, an infusion made from the leaves helps to relieve bronchial congestion and eases coughs. It is also used as a tonic for the digestive and nervous systems.

◀ *Hyssopus officinalis* **'Roseus'**
PINK HYSSOP
A hardy semi-evergreen perennial, with a height of 80cm (32in) and a spread of 90cm (36in). Dense spikes of small pale sugar-pink flowers appear from summer until early autumn. It has small, narrow, lance-shaped, aromatic green leaves.

▲ *Hyssopus officinalis*
BLUE HYSSOP
A hardy semi-evergreen perennial, with a height of 80cm (32in) and a spread of 90cm (36in). Dense spikes of small, dark blue-violet flowers appear from summer until early autumn. The small lance-shaped leaves have a slightly bitter but minty and sage-like flavour.

Inula

Elecampane ASTERACEAE

This is a magical herb and a must if you have space in the garden. I love the sunflower-like flowers in summer, which are followed by attractive seedheads which, in late autumn, are a good food source for finches. Historically, Helen of Troy was believed to be gathering this herb when she was whisked off by Paris. The Romans used to candy the roots and dye them red with cochineal; this was a favourite delicacy of the Emperor Julius Augustus. In Tudor times, sweets made from elecampane were used for coughs and chest complaints, which is still its main medicinal use today.

How to grow

Herb	Soil	Propagation
Inula	Loam	Seed

PROPAGATION In spring, sow seeds and place under protection at 20°C (68°F) or in a cold frame. Germination takes one to three weeks with heat, or three to four weeks cold. The cold method can give better results with home-collected seeds, although both can be erratic. In autumn, when the established plants have died back, propagate by division. It may be easier to remove the offshoots that grow around the parent plant as the main root can be tough. Remove carefully, maintaining the root system. Replant in a well-prepared site 1m (3ft) apart, or pot and plant out in spring.

SITE Plant in moist, fertile soil in full sun. As it grows so tall, it is not ideal for planting in containers.

MAINTENANCE In windy or exposed sites, the flowers may need staking. In hot, dry summers the plant will need extra water. In autumn, after the plant has died back, mulch with well-rotted compost or leafmould.

HARVESTING Pick flowers when fully open and dry for medicinal use, or pick just before the seeds turn brown for use in dried flower displays (if you do this later, the seeds will float everywhere). Dig up roots of two- or three-year-old plants in autumn to be used fresh in cooking or dried for medicinal use.

▶ *Inula helenium*
ELECAMPANE, ELFWORT
A hardy herbaceous perennial, with a height of 1.5–2.4m (5–8ft) and a spread of 1m (3ft). Large, bright yellow, ragged, daisy-like flowers appear in summer.

How to use

Elecampane roots were once used to flavour desserts. The flowers are used in decoctions, the roots to make syrups, powders and tinctures for treating chest complaints. Recent research has shown that elecampane is effective against bacterial and fungal infections and can expel intestinal parasites. It is also said to make a good facial wash for the complexion.

Flower is a large ragged yellow daisy, about 7cm (3in) in diameter when fully open

Stem is fibrous and covered in a fine down

Isatis

Woad LAMIACEAE

I fell in love with woad when I first grew it with my children for a school project. It is renowned as an ancient blue dye plant and is undergoing a huge revival because of the growing interest in natural plant pigments. The desirable blue colouring comes from the leaves, which are soaked in urine prior to use. It is now a popular plant with gardeners, not only for its rich, wafting, honey scent in early summer, but also for the clouds of attractive yellow flowers that seem to hover above the garden. Currently the leaves of this herb are under medicinal research as a preventative against cancer.

Root is known as "ban lang gen" in Chinese medicine, and is used to treat mumps and sore throats.

How to grow

Herb	Soil	Propagation
Isatis	Loam	Seed

PROPAGATION In autumn, sow seeds in pots and place in a cold frame. Germination takes three to four weeks. Or sow seeds in late spring direct into a well-prepared site at 30cm (12in) intervals.

SITE Plant in a sunny position in a well-drained, well-fed soil. Woad grows wild on chalky wasteland but will adapt to any soil. It is not an ideal container plant, as it looks dull for the first year, and then grows too tall in the second.

MAINTENANCE To increase leaf production and extend the life of the plant over another season, cut off the flowering stems as soon as they appear. Collect seeds before they fall; it does not self-seed naturally very well.

HARVESTING In late summer, pick the leaves of the first year's growth to dry for medicinal use or for dyeing. The dye is extracted by a process of fermentation in water and urine from fresh or dry leaves. In autumn, dig up the roots of the second year's growth and dry them. Harvest the seeds as they turn dark brown; dry well.

How to use

It is difficult to grow sufficient quantities for dyeing purposes. In Chinese medicine, they extract "qing dai" from the leaf pigment and prescribe large doses with apparently no ill effects, even though it is highly astringent and poisonous. The Chinese also use the root to treat sore throats, mumps, and meningitis. Woad is classed as a noxious weed in Australia and the US.

CAUTION Do not take internally unless under supervision.

Flower bud cluster turns into a four-petalled flower with a sweet honey perfume

Stem grows in the second year

▶ **Isatis tinctoria**
WOAD, DYER'S WOAD
A hardy biennial, with a height of 45cm (18in) in the first year, growing to 1.3cm (48in) in the second, and a spread of 45cm (18in). Clusters of small bright yellow flowers appear in the second summer, followed by pendulous black seeds. It has lance-shaped, lightly toothed, blue-green leaves.

Leaves in the second season grow more lance-shaped and blue-green in colour

Juniperus

Juniper CUPRESSACEAE

This attractive conifer can be found in many different forms growing throughout the world; from the Arctic to the Mediterranean, and from the West Himalayas to North America. This plant was first used medicinally by the Ancient Greeks, who used it to cure snake bites and protect against infectious diseases. During the bubonic plague, it was burnt in the hearth to guard against evil spirits and to fumigate homes, and during the World War II it was used to disinfect hospital wards. The berries are famous for giving the alcoholic drink gin its distinctive flavour.

Berry turns from green to blue to black as it ripens over a period of three years.

How to grow

Herb	Soil	Propagation
Juniperus	Loam	Softwood cuttings

PROPAGATION This is not the easiest tree to grow from seed, and requires patience. In early autumn, collect ripe berries and remove the seed from the pith (see page 71). Use a loam-based substrate and cover with coarse grit. Place the pot outside. Germination can take two to five years. Do not allow the seed to dry out in summer. Alternatively, take semi-hardwood cuttings from the fresh new growth in spring. With both methods, grow on for two years in a container before planting out into a prepared site.

SITE Plant in a sunny position in alkaline or neutral soil. This slow-growing plant looks attractive when grown in a container. Use a soil-based substrate. Juniper plants like being pot-bound, so do not pot on too often.

MAINTENANCE To maintain the plant shape, trim and remove any leader shoots growing out of line in late spring or early summer. Do not cut back into old growth.

HARVESTING Both male and female plants are necessary to produce berries. The berries grow on the female bush. The best flavour is from those berries grown in warm climates. Pick berries in late summer, dry them on muslin (see page 71).

How to use

The flavour of the crushed berries is warm and spicy and combines well with strong-flavoured meats and marinades. Medicinally, juniper is used internally to treat cystitis, kidney inflammation, and rheumatism. Juniper oil, which is distilled from the berries, is used in fragrances and aromatherapy oils. It also makes a good massage oil to treat aching joints and muscles.

Leaf is aromatic and needle-like

Stem is woody

▶ *Juniperus communis*
JUNIPER
A hardy evergreen conifer, with a height of 6m (20ft) and a spread of 3m (10ft). It is dioecious, bearing small male (yellow) and female (green) flowers on different trees in early summer, with berries growing on the female plant.

Laurus

Bay LAURACEAE

To the Greeks and Romans, bay was a symbol of wisdom and glory, and wreaths of laurel were once used to adorn the heads and necks of victorious athletes and leaders. A full-grown bay tree certainly has a regal shape in the garden. I love cooking with the fresh leaves, and find bay a versatile herb that goes well with savoury dishes as well as milk and rice puddings. However, do not take the essential oil made from the berries or leaves internally. In addition, an allergic reaction can occur in some people when this oil is used externally.

How to grow

Herb	Soil	Propagation
Laurus	Loam	Seed

PROPAGATION Before sowing seeds in autumn, they need scarifying (see page 45). Then place in a pot, cover with coarse horticultural sand, and keep under protection at 20°C (68°F) for one month before moving to an area with a minimum temperature at night of 13°C (55°F). Germination takes five to twelve months. Grow on in the pot for two to three years before planting out. Take cuttings from new growth in late summer. High humidity is essential for successful propagation which takes three weeks to six months. Alternatively, propagate by division in spring or autumn.

SITE In hot, dry climates, plant in well-drained soil in partial shade. In cool climates, with temperatures at night above -5°C (23°F), plant in a sheltered, sunny position in well-drained soil. In cold climates, grow in a container with a soil-based substrate. They prefer to be pot-bound. Protect in winter.

MAINTENANCE In cold climates, prune into shape in spring or prune in autumn in warm climates. Check leaves regularly for sooty mould, caused by the scale insect. To treat sooty mould, wash the leaves with horticultural soap or rub with cotton buds dipped in brandy.

HARVESTING As this is an evergreen herb, the leaf can be picked for use fresh all year round. Pick the berries in the autumn.

How to use

Bay leaves in cooking promote digestion, especially of meat. You can use the leaves fresh or dried (I prefer fresh). They are an ingredient in a bouquet garni (see page 229). A bay leaf placed in a jar of flour or rice will deter weevils.

▲ *Laurus nobilis* 'Aurea' AGM
GOLDEN BAY
A perennial evergreen with a height of up to 5m (18ft) and a spread of 2m (6ft). It needs shelter from the wind, frosts, and sun to prevent leaf scorch.

▲ *Laurus nobilis* f. *angustifolia*
WILLOW LEAF BAY
A perennial evergreen tree, with a height of up to 7m (23ft) and a spread of 2.5m (8ft). This is a hardier variety of bay than *L. nobilis* 'Aurea'.

Leaf when held to the light becomes translucent, showing all its veins

Flower is waxy in appearance, with very little scent

▶ *Laurus nobilis*
BAY, SWEET BAY
A perennial evergreen tree with a height of up to 8m (26ft) and a spread of 3m (12ft). Small, pale yellow flowers appear in spring, followed by berries that are black when ripe. When crushed, the leaves give off an aromatic scent.

Stem as it matures becomes woody

Lavandula

Hardy lavender LAMIACEAE

For many people, this is the quintessential herb: it smells good, looks good, and does you good. It was first introduced to the UK by the Romans who used it in their bathwater for its scent, to promote the healing of cuts and wounds, and as a flea and nit repellent. In France, hardy lavenders have been grown since the 17th century for their essential oil, which was, and still is, used in the perfume industry. Lavender's soothing and calming properties are well known. A tea made from lavender flowers can help you sleep, as can a bath with a few drops of the essential oil.

▼ *Lavandula* x *intermedia*
OLD ENGLISH GROUP
OLD ENGLISH LAVENDER
Hardy evergreen perennial. Height 90cm (36in) and spread 60cm (24in). Aromatic, pointed spikes of pale blue-purple flowers appear in summer. *L.* x *intermedia* is a hybrid, bred to produce a high yield of essential oil.

How to grow

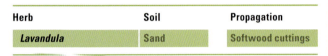

Herb	Soil	Propagation
Lavandula	Sand	Softwood cuttings

PROPAGATION In spring, sow seeds under cover at 18°C (65°F). Germination takes 18–28 days. Lavenders grown from seed rarely produce identical plants. For a lavender hedge, where symmetry is important, grow plants from softwood cuttings taken from non-flowering stems in late spring.

SITE These plants are hardy to -15°C (5°F) – it is wet conditions and high humidity that kill, not cold. Plant in a sunny position, in fertile free-draining soil. These species will adapt to most soils, except heavy and wet soils, and will tolerate semi-shade. They grow well in containers using a soil-based substrate.

MAINTENANCE Trim plants each year, either after flowering in early autumn or in spring in cold, wet climates. Do not cut into the old wood as it will not produce new growth.

HARVESTING Cut the flowers in summer, just as they open, to use fresh or to dry. Dry loose on a flat tray or make small bunches to hang up and dry. Pick leaves to use fresh or dry before flowering.

How to use

Use flowers and leaves sparingly in cooking. The flowers are used to scent sugar for making biscuits and cakes. A few leaves can add flavour to roast lamb. Lavender essential oil is used to treat burns, stings, or cuts, or can be added to the bath to calm children and relax adults. Rubbed into the temples, the oil can help ease headaches. It is also a good mosquito, midge, and fly repellent. Sprinkle a few drops on bed linen to repel mosquitoes. Place sachets of dried lavender flowers and leaves with clothes to deter moths (see p.236).

▲ *Lavandula angustifolia*
'Hidcote'
HIDCOTE LAVENDER
A hardy evergreen perennial, with a height of 55cm (22in) and a spread of 45cm (18in). An ideal lavender for hedges, it should be planted at a distance of 30cm (12in) apart.

▲ *Lavandula angustifolia*
'Twickel Purple'
A hardy evergreen perennial, with a height of 45cm (18in) and a spread of 30cm (12in). This richly scented purple lavender is a hybrid, and can only be grown from cuttings.

The classic flower for drying and using in lavender bags

Flower is a clear, pale blue-purple, clustered on a tapering, pointed spike

Leaf is long, narrow, and silver-grey-green

Lavandula
Tender lavender LAMIACEAE

These tender lavenders, which originate from North and South Africa, the Canary Islands, and Madeira, are truly worth collecting and should not be ignored because they are less hardy than other lavender species. They can make excellent summer bedding, are wonderful when grown in containers, flower all year round, and produce attractive foliage. Both *L. candicans* and *L.* x *allardii* are high in essential oil, which can be used for burns and cuts, as a sedative, and as a fly and mosquito deterrent. *L.* x *christiana* looks stunning in flower, but does not produce a useful oil.

How to grow

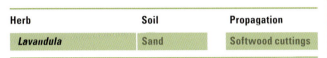

Herb	Soil	Propagation
Lavandula	Sand	Softwood cuttings

PROPAGATION Grow from cuttings taken in spring from non-flowering stems. Once rooted and well established, you can pot up but not too often as it prefers being pot-bound. Protect from frost.

SITE Tender lavenders make a fine display when grown outside from late spring to autumn. Plant in a fertile, well-draining soil, in full sun, protected from cold wind. In the UK, and other cold climates, they need to be brought in before the first frosts, ideally into a heated glasshouse or conservatory, and kept warm at around 5°C (40°F). They do not thrive in over-wet or humid conditions but are ideal for growing in containers, using a soil-based substrate.

MAINTENANCE These lavenders have a very long flowering period from spring until early autumn. I have known *L.* x *christiana* to flower all year round in a container. Keep deadheading to encourage more blooms and to prevent the plant from becoming over-woody and straggly. Cut back hard (not into the hard wood) and repot in spring. Feed container plants regularly throughout the growing season using a liquid feed. Keep the plants well-ventilated throughout the season to prevent rot.

HARVESTING Cut flowers for drying when the third part of the trident starts to flower; the best time is summer when the air is drier. Dry on open trays or by hanging in small bunches.

How to use

The dried flowers and leaves of these varieties look most attractive when added to pot-pourri or used in dried flower arrangements, and they could even be used to decorate a summer hat.

▲ *Lavandula dentata* var. *candicans*
LAVENDER CANDICANS, FRINGED LAVENDER

A tender evergreen perennial with a height of 75cm (30in) and a spread of 60cm (24in). Attractive pale purple flowers topped with pale blue-purple bracts appear in early summer.

▲ *Lavandula* x *allardii*
LAVENDER ALLARDII, GIANT LAVENDER

A tender evergreen perennial, with a height of 1.2m (48in) and a spread of 75cm (30in). Very long, pointed spikes covered in small blue and pale blue flowers appear in summer. The leaves are used to make essential oils.

Flower opens as it spirals up the flowering stem

▶ *Lavandula* x *christiana*
LAVENDER CHRISTIANA, FEATHERED LAVENDER

A tender, unscented evergreen perennial, with a height of 75cm (30in) and a spread of 60cm (24in). It is a sterile hybrid of *L. canariensis* and *L. pinnata*, often sold as the latter.

Leaf is lacy and looks more like an *Artemisia* leaf than a standard lavender

Lavandula

Colourful bract lavender LAMIACEAE

The first time I saw these lavenders with their colourful bracts, or "ears" as they are commonly called, I thought they looked wonderful, like small colourful bees or even butterflies. Each year a new variety of bract lavender is discovered, and there are flowers with not only purple but, now, deep red bracts. Traditionally, bract lavenders were grown for their essential oil, which was used to repel insects, as an antiseptic agent, and as a relaxant. *Lavandula stoechas* is found growing wild throughout the Mediterranean area and is often confused with *L. stoechas* subsp. *pedunculata*, which is a native plant of central Spain and Portugal.

How to grow

Herb	Soil	Propagation
Lavandula	Sand	Softwood cuttings

PROPAGATION See pages 134–35 for details. (Bract lavenders grown from seed produce plants with different coloured and sized bracts.) If you want identical plants, see pages 134–35 for details.

SITE Bract lavenders are hardy to -5°C (23°F), and are at greater risk from wet conditions and high humidity than cold (see page 134).

MAINTENANCE Bract lavenders have a long flowering period from late spring until early autumn. Regular deadheading encourages new young growth; the plant will bush out and not become too woody. In autumn, cut back the plant to just above the old wood. Feed it well with liquid seaweed and protect from frost. In very cold climates, cut back in spring.

HARVESTING See pages 134–35 for details.

How to use

French lavender was probably one of the first lavenders to be used for its oils. It was used to alleviate nausea and as a mild sedative. An infusion made from the flowers of all kinds of *L. stoechas* is good as a gargle, or for washing minor grazes to stop infection. Lavender water, with its mild antiseptic properties, can also be used to wipe down kitchen work surfaces. To prevent a horse from being annoyed by flies, rub some lavender water around its head and ears.

▲ *Lavandula stoechas* 'Kew Red'
LAVENDER 'KEW RED'

A tender evergreen perennial, with a height of 40cm (36in) and a spread of 30cm (12in). Unique cerise-crimson flowers clustered around small stalks topped with short pale pink bracts are borne from late spring to early autumn. It has narrow, aromatic, green leaves. This variety needs to be protected from wet winters.

◀ *Lavandula stoechas* **'Helmsdale'**

LAVENDER HELMSDALE

A frost-hardy evergreen perennial with a height of 90cm (36in) and a spread of 60cm (24in). Lovely deep burgundy-purple flowers, clustered around medium tapered stalks and topped with short burgundy bracts, appear from late spring until early autumn. Its narrow green-grey leaves are camphor-scented. This variety originated in New Zealand.

Leaf is narrow, grey-green and highly scented

Flower comprises small, dark-purple flowers topped with short, mauve-purple bracts

▶ *Lavandula stoechas*

FRENCH LAVENDER

A frost-hardy evergreen perennial, with a height of 45cm (20in) and a spread of 60cm (24in). Attractive, small, deep purple flowers are clustered around small flowering stalks, topped with short mauve-purple bracts from late spring until early autumn. Its narrow green-grey leaves are camphor-scented.

Levisticum

Lovage APIACEAE

Lovage, as its common name indicates, was used as an aphrodisiac in the 16th century. It has many other historical claims: the Ancient Greeks used it to aid digestion and relieve flatulence, whilst travellers in the Middle Ages used it as a latter day "odour eater" by lining their leather boots with the leaves. The French call it "céleri bâtard" (false celery) because its flavour and appearance are similar to that of celery. In my opinion, lovage is a forgotten culinary delight, which adds a meaty flavour to dishes and, when combined with potatoes, makes a wonderful soup.

CAUTION Do not take medicinally if pregnant or if suffering from kidney disease. Do not eat in large amounts as it may cause nausea.

How to grow

Herb	Soil	Propagation
Levisticum	Loam	Seed

PROPAGATION Sow seeds in spring or late summer under protection at 18°C (65°F). Germination takes six to ten days. Alternatively, sow seeds in early summer into prepared open ground, when the air temperature at night does not fall below 10°C (50°F). Divide established plants in spring, replanting them 60cm (24in) apart into a well-prepared site.

SITE Lovage is a large plant, so choose the position carefully, bearing in mind that it takes three to five years to mature. Plant in a rich, well-fed, well-drained soil in full sun or partial shade. It grows well in large containers in a soil-based substrate. Do not let the container dry out in summer and feed with comfrey (see p.39) in the growing season.

MAINTENANCE To keep the lovage leaves young and tender, pick them for use regularly and cut back all leaves in succession to encourage new growth. In autumn, after the plant has died back, feed well with well-rotted manure.

HARVESTING Pick the main crop of fresh young lovage leaves before flowering. Harvest the seeds as they turn brown, dry them well, and store for later use (see page 70).

How to use

Add the tender young leaves to salads, or cook as one would spinach. The root can be cooked as a vegetable, but should be peeled before use. Use crushed seeds when baking bread or in salad dressings, soups, and stews. When dried, the leaf and seed can be used in a similar way to celery salt. Medicinally, it is one of nature's antibiotics, and an infusion of the seeds helps to reduce water retention.

Seeds ripen to light brown and have a warm, meaty, celery flavour

Stem is hollow and ribbed

Leaves are green, soft, and lightly veined, but darken in colour with age. They smell of celery when crushed

▶ *Levisticum officinale*
LOVAGE

A hardy herbaceous perennial, with a height of up to 2m (6ft) and a spread of 1m (3ft). Flat clusters of tiny, pale greenish-yellow flowers appear in summer followed by brown seeds. Old leaves become tough and bitter.

Linum

Flax LINACEAE

Flax has been grown for at least 7,000 years and was one of the first crops to be cultivated. In the Stone Age, it was used to produce textile fibre and seed, and in ancient Egypt, linen cloth made from flax was used to wrap the mummies. The Greeks used it to make sails for their boats. Linen, linseed, and rope are all made from this plant. An excellent companion plant in the organic garden, flax grown among vegetables increases pollination and therefore the vegetable yield, because bees are attracted to its lovely blue flowers.

CAUTION The seeds of some strains contain toxic glycosides which become more toxic in drinking water. These cyanogenic glycosides have caused poisoning in livestock.

How to grow

Herb	Soil	Propagation
Linum	Sand	Seed

PROPAGATION Flax does not transplant well so it is best to sow it directly into a prepared site. Sow it in late spring when the air temperature at night does not fall below 9°C (48°F). Thin the young plants to 30cm (12in) apart.

SITE Plant in a fertile (rich in humus), well-draining soil, in a sunny, sheltered position. Planting this herb in large groups is not only attractive, but will also help to attract beneficial insects to the garden.

MAINTENANCE If grown as a linear crop, rather than in a group, weed around the plant constantly in early spring to prevent it being choked by weeds. After harvest, cut hard back to promote new growth.

HARVESTING Flax is ripe when stems turn yellow and the seed capsules turn brown. In wet summers the stems may remain green and the plants continue to flower long after the early seed capsules ripen. If so, harvest when the majority are ripe. For fibre, harvest as the stems turn yellow, and dry thoroughly.

How to use

The seed can be grown as a nutritious sprouting seed in seed trays, or added direct to bread, salads, or breakfast cereals. A vegetable oil is also obtained from the seed, though it needs to be refined before use. Medicinally, the oil is valuable for maintaining a healthy heart and circulation. The plant has a long history of use in the treatment of cancer and contains anti-cancer agents. It is also used to treat constipation and in poultices to treat boils and draw splinters. Seeds and oils are used as an animal fodder. The oil is used in paint production as an emulsifier.

▶ *Linum perenne*
FLAX, LINSEED
A hardy perennial, with a height of up to 1.2m (4ft) and a spread of 30–60cm (12–24in). Sky-blue flowers in summer are followed by seed capsules. Cultivars have been developed to produce high yields of linseed oil, edible seed, and fibre for textiles.

Flower is sky blue with petals that droop in the early afternoon

Stem is thin and tough

Leaves are narrow, small, linear, and lance-shaped

Luma

Luma MYRTACEAE

This wonderful aromatic tree is a native of Chile, and is a great addition to any sheltered herb garden. I have grown it very successfully in containers as an exhibit plant, and often show it off to the public in my herb display gardens at flower shows. When grown as a container plant, it only reaches 3m (10ft) tall, which is far short of the 15m (50ft) it can reach when grown as a tree. Luma's common name in Spanish, "arrayán", comes from the Arabic "ar-rayhan" or "rihan" which translates as "the aromatic one" and refers to the tree's fragrant leaf.

How to grow

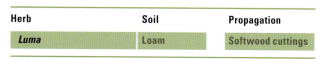

Herb	Soil	Propagation
Luma	Loam	Softwood cuttings

PROPAGATION Remove the outer pith of the berry and sow fresh seeds in spring. Place under protection at 15°C (60°F). Germination takes one to two months, but can be longer. Grow on in a container, with winter protection for a minimum of two years, before planting out into a prepared site. Take softwood cuttings from the new growth in early summer, and treat the cuttings in the same way as seedlings.

SITE Plant in well-drained soil in a sunny position. A hardy plant to -5°C (28°F) in dry, cold winters, it needs protection in wet, cold, damp winters. It is ideal for growing next to a wall, where it will be sheltered from excessive wet. This tree makes an attractive, large container plant. Use a soil-based substrate and do not allow it to dry out in summer. Keep fairly dry in winter.

MAINTENANCE In cold climates, trim branches in early autumn or spring. Prune back to the main branches in spring. Do not allow luma plants to dry out in hot summers.

HARVESTING Pick the leaves to use fresh as required. Pick the berries in autumn to use fresh or to dry.

How to use

The leaves and berries have a warm, spicy flavour and taste good in stews, soups, and marinades. The leaves are a good alternative to bay leaves. In Chile, the wood is used to make tools and charcoal. Medicinally, the seeds produce an aromatic oil that has antibiotic properties and is used in the treatment of respiratory diseases. Ferment leaves in mild olive oil for one month to make a treatment for dandruff and hair loss.

▼ *Luma chequen*
LUMA, ARRAYÁN

A hardy evergreen tree, with a height of 15m (50ft) and a spread of 6m (20ft). It produces pretty white flowers in summer, followed by dark blue-purple berries. Its aromatic leaves are slightly pointed and have a lighter underside.

Flower is slightly aromatic, with white petals and masses of delicate stamens

Stem is covered in red bark which, as it matures, flakes off to reveal white areas

Leaf is aromatic, fairly tough, and shiny on the upper surface

Lysimachia
Yellow loosestrife PRIMULACEAE

This tall, handsome European herb can be found growing in fens and wet woodland, along lake shores and on the banks of rivers. It adapts well to damp gardens or pond sites. It was named "Lysimachia" in memory of King Lysimachus of Sicily, who promoted its medicinal benefits as a wound-healing herb. When fresh young leaves were bound around a wound it was said to stem bleeding immediately. This herb is often confused with purple loosestrife (*Lythrum salicaria*, see page 142) – both thrive in similar damp habitats and are invasive – but they are not related.

CAUTION This herb is considered a pernicious weed because it is so invasive.

How to grow

Herb	Soil	Propagation
Lysimachia	Loam	Seed

PROPAGATION Sow seeds in spring and place in a cold frame. Germination takes two to four weeks. When well established, plant out into open ground 60cm (24in) apart. Divide established plants in autumn or spring. Replant into a prepared site.

SITE Plant in any garden soil that holds moisture during summer. The ideal site is close to a pond in partial shade, or plant it in a small water barrel garden. Do not allow it to take over.

MAINTENANCE An incredibly invasive plant, it not only self-seeds prolifically, but also spreads on creeping rhizomes, and has been known to swamp shorelines. In summer, cut back after flowering to prevent self-seeding. In winter and/or spring, dig up the plant and reduce the creeping rhizomes by half.

HARVESTING In spring before the plant starts to flower, pick the leaves to use fresh, to preserve in vinegar (see pages 222–223), or to dry for medicinal use later in the year. In midsummer, pick whole sprigs that include leaf and flower and dry singly or in small bunches on a muslin tray for use as a natural hair dye.

How to use

Although this herb is not used frequently by modern herbalists, it is still used in folk medicine to calm horses and cattle; tie plant stems and leaves around a horse's bridle to deter flies. It is also a good insect repellent for the home or outdoors. Burn the dried stems and leaves, and the smoke will not only deter all flying insects but also snakes. It is still used as a hair dye, highlighting blond hair and restoring greying hair to fairly blond.

▼ *Lysimachia vulgaris*
YELLOW LOOSESTRIFE, WILLOW WORT
A hardy herbaceous perennial, with a height of up to 1.5m (5ft) and a spread of 90cm (3ft). Bright yellow, five-petalled flowers, attractive to dragonflies, grow in summer if the plant is well established. The mid-green leaf is dotted with either black or orange glands, or occasionally both.

Flowers are cup-shaped and grow in pyramidal spikes at the top of the plant

Leaf is long and lance-shaped. It is soft to touch and, like the stem, covered with fine hairs

Lythrum

Purple loosestrife LYTHRACEAE

The name "lythrum" means "gore" in Greek, and was coined by a doctor who used loosestrife to heal warriors' battle wounds and stem bleeding. Later, the plant leaves were used for tanning leather because of their high tannin content. The first time I saw it growing in profusion was at the water's edge at the Wildfowl Trust at Slimbridge, in the UK, where it looked magnificent. It is highly rated by beekeepers who consider it a good plant for overwintering colonies of bees, which collect pollen from its flowers right up until late summer.

How to grow

Herb	Soil	Propagation
Lythrum	Loam	Seed

PROPAGATION The seeds are very small and prolific – a mature plant can produce over 2.7 million seeds. Before sowing, mix fresh seeds with fine sand or flour to make them easier to manage. Do not cover. Place the container outside to expose it to all weathers, including frost. Germination takes five to seven months. Pot up when the seedlings are large enough to handle. Plant into a prepared open site when the root ball is well formed. Established plants can be divided in autumn. Replant into a prepared, open site.

SITE Plant in a damp, marsh-like soil, in full sun or partial shade. It looks very attractive when grown in large clumps near water, where it attracts insects and dragonflies. It needs to be kept moist, and will only grow happily in a container if sunk into the corner of a pond.

MAINTENANCE This invasive herb needs controlling to prevent it from competing with and replacing native grasses, sedges, and other flowering plants. In autumn and spring, dig up spreading plants to maintain control. If it is out of control, introduce the beetle *Galerucella calmariensis* to strip the leaf and flower. In autumn, cut back plants before the seed sets and starts dispersing.

HARVESTING Pick leaves before flowering to use fresh or to dry for later use. Harvest the flowers in summer just before they are all fully opened to use fresh or to dry.

How to use

It was once used to treat chronic diarrhoea and dysentery, to clean wounds, and as a gargle and an eyewash. Currently, it is being researched for its healing properties relating to intestinal illnesses.

▲ *Lythrum salicaria*
PURPLE LOOSESTRIFE
A hardy herbaceous perennial, with a height of 1.2m (4ft) and a spread of 75cm (30in). Beautiful tall spires of small magenta flowers appear all summer. The flowers attract not only bees and butterflies but also dragonflies and hoverflies.

Malva

Mallow MALVACEAE

In the Middle Ages, mallow was used as a calming antidote to aphrodisiacs and love potions. Before this, the Romans ate the young shoots as a vegetable delicacy, and the root was also used as a sort of toothbrush. This herb is a native wild flower of the UK and can be found growing in various situations, from grassy meadows to along the roadside. It is very attractive to many insects, and can be grown in borders or the vegetable garden to encourage their presence. The flowers are sometimes included in other products as a natural colourant.

Root can be cut into slices and used to draw out splinters and thorns.

How to grow

Herb	Soil	Propagation
Malva	Loam	Seed

PROPAGATION Sow seeds in autumn. Place the container outside to expose it to all weathers. Germination is erratic. In early summer, when young plants are well-established, plant out into a prepared site at 60cm (24in) intervals. In late spring or summer, take cuttings from firm lower shoots.

SITE Plant in a well-drained, fertile soil in a sunny position. If the soil is damp, the plant stems will become soft and require staking in summer. *Malva moschata* is suitable for growing in containers in a soil-based substrate but has a tall, untidy habit.

MAINTENANCE Cut back stems after flowering to tidy up, promote new growth, and encourage a second flowering. In autumn, cut stems back to the lower leaves.

HARVESTING Pick young fresh leaves as required throughout the spring. Harvest fresh flowers throughout the flowering period. Dig up the roots of the second year's growth to dry for medicinal use.

How to use

The tender young leaves and flowering tips of mallow can be used in salads or steamed as a vegetable. A decoction made from the roots and leaves can be added to the bathwater to ease skin rashes, boils, and ulcers. Medicinally, this herb is thought to be inferior to marsh mallow (*Althea officinalis*), which is higher in mucilage and therefore better for coughs, but there is current research into its abilities to alleviate urinary complaints.

◄ *Malva moschata*
MUSK MALLOW
A hardy herbaceous perennial, with a height of up to 80cm (32in) and a spread of 60cm (24in). Scented pinkish, sometimes white, flowers appear from late summer to early autumn. This species has milder medicinal properties than common mallow (*Malva sylvestris*).

Leaf is lobed and downy with prominent veins on the underside

Flower petals are each thinly veined in a darker colour

► *Malva sylvestris*
COMMON MALLOW
A hardy herbaceous short-lived perennial with a height of up to 90cm (36in) and a spread of 60cm (24in). It has veined, pretty, pale purple-pink flowers throughout the summer until the first frosts. The mid-green leaves are a similar shape to ivy.

Stem is thick, rounded, and strong

Mandragora

Mandrake SOLANACEAE

There has been a resurgence of interest in mandrake due to the *Harry Potter* books and films. This herb has close links with magic ritual, and is regarded by some as evil. In folklore, it was thought fatal to dig up the plant, which would then scream piercingly and drive a person to suicide. Mandrake root was thought to have anaesthetic properties and a piece was given to patients before operations. This plant is toxic and should only be taken under professional supervision; however it bears beautiful flowers in early spring and so is beneficial as an early nectar plant: an asset in any herb garden.

CAUTION Mandrake is toxic and should only be taken under medical supervision. Avoid during pregnancy.

How to grow

Herb	Soil	Propagation
Mandragora	Sand	Seed

PROPAGATION Sow seeds in autumn in a free-draining substrate. Place in a cold frame. Germination can take from four months to two years. In autumn, take root cuttings carefully from established plants – it does not like being disturbed. In cold, wet climates grow on for two seasons in a container, protected from adverse weather, until established. In spring, plant out into a well-prepared open site.

SITE Plant in deep, well-drained, fertile soil in full sun or partial shade. It does not like chalk or gravel soils, and is prone to rot in clay or cold, wet soils. It has a long root system – up to 1.2m (4ft) – and is not well suited to container growing. Grown in pots in a soil-based substrate, plants remain small and do not set fruit.

MAINTENANCE This herb is very prone to attack from slugs, which will totally obliterate the plant. Mark the spot where it is planted; it will reappear in late summer.

HARVESTING Dig up roots in autumn when the plant is dormant. Use the root fresh for juice extraction or dried in decoctions.

How to use

Mandrake root is still widely used in homeopathy as a treatment for coughs and asthma. Modern-day witches still hold it in high regard for its supposed magical properties. Do not confuse with American mandrake (*Podophyllum peltatum*).

◄▼ *Mandragora officinarum*
MANDRAKE, SATAN'S APPLE

A hardy herbaceous perennial with a height of 5cm (2in) and a spread of 30cm (12in). Small, bell-shaped, white-blue flowers in spring, followed in late summer by aromatic, round, yellow fruits (in warm climates only). The large oval leaves have a rough, slightly prickly texture.

Leaves become darker and rougher as they mature

Marrubium

White horehound LAMIACEAE

I am fascinated by the thick silvery hairs that grow on the young stem and the underside of the young leaves of white horehound. It creates the impression that a silvery spider's web has spun them together. The Roman physician Galen used this herb to treat chest complaints, and it is still used for this purpose. Quite apart from the herb's medicinal benefits, it is well worth growing as an unusual ornamental plant. White horehound is not to be confused with black horehound (*Ballota nigra*), which has an unpleasant scent and can be used to expel intestinal worms.

CAUTION Do not take during pregnancy or if you suffer from stomach ulcers.

How to grow

Herb	Soil	Propagation
Marrubium	Sand	Seed

PROPAGATION Sow seeds in early spring and place under protection at 18°C (65°F). Germination takes one to two weeks but can be erratic. Alternatively, take softwood cuttings in summer from new growth. In cold and wet climates, grow on seedlings or cuttings in a container for the first winter. Plant out the following spring into a well prepared site. Propagate established plants by division in spring (see page 53), replanting into a prepared site.

SITE Plant in a sunny position in well-drained alkaline soil. Protect from cold winds. This plant can be grown in a container. Do not overwater and use a free-draining soil-based substrate mixed with extra grit to improve drainage further.

MAINTENANCE In spring, divide established clumps and prune new growth to maintain shape. In summer, cut back after flowering to prevent the plant from becoming straggly, and to prevent it self-seeding.

HARVESTING Gather the leaves and flowering tops in late spring, on a dry morning, just before the plant flowers; this is when the plant oils are at their richest, and are best for using fresh, for drying, or for preserving in wheatgerm or olive oil.

How to use

This useful medicinal herb treats bronchitis and whooping cough and is used in most cough mixtures to clear phlegm. The leaves and stems are boiled and used in candied products, cough drops, and syrups. Extracts of white horehound are used in traditional ale making and are brewed to make Horehound Ale in the UK. An infusion of the leaf can be used as an organic spray to deter cankerworm in fruit trees.

▶ *Marrubium vulgare*
HOREHOUND, WHITE HOREHOUND
A hardy herbaceous perennial, with a height of 45cm (18in) and a spread of 30cm (12in). Clusters of small creamy white flowers appear in summer from the second season. The aromatic, oval, green leaves are wrinkled and lightly toothed with a woolly underside.

Stem is square and covered in fine silvery hairs, making it appear woolly

Flowers grow in clusters

Leaf is wrinkled on the upper surface and woolly on the underside

Melissa

Lemon balm LAMIACEAE

In ancient times, lemon balm was planted by the front door to drive away evil spirits. Then in the Middle Ages it was used to prevent baldness, as a lucky love charm, and to help cure mad dog bites, toothache, and even neck problems. Research now shows that it can be beneficial in the treatment of cold sores by, on average, halving the healing time and reducing the chance of further outbreaks. The scent of lemon balm is a delightful asset in the garden – there is nothing nicer than going outside on a summer's evening and gently rubbing lemon balm leaves to fill the air with lemon fragrance.

Lemon balms resemble their relative, mint, but have a wonderful lemon scent.

How to grow

Herb	Soil	Propagation
Melissa	Sand	Seed/cuttings

PROPAGATION Sow seeds (*Melissa officinalis* only) in spring under cover at 20°C (68°F). Germination takes one to two weeks. Do not overwater the seedlings as they are prone to "damping off" – a fungal disease. Take softwood cuttings in early summer. Plant out when the plants are well established. Divide established plants in early autumn or early spring, replanting into a well-prepared site.

SITE This plant will grow in all soils except waterlogged ones. Melissa is invasive in light, fertile soils. The best situation is well-drained soil in a sunny position. All forms of this plant grow well in containers. Use a soil-based substrate.

MAINTENANCE To maintain a supply of fresh leaves, and to prevent the plant from becoming woody or straggly, cut it back after flowering. This will also stop self-seeding. As this plant is invasive, dig up roots as necessary. This herb is related to mint, and like mint lemon balm is prone to the rust virus (see p.148). If affected, dig up plants with the virus and burn them.

HARVESTING Pick fresh leaves before the flowers open to use fresh or to dry. This is when the highest yield of leaf oil is available.

How to use

The lemon scent of the leaves is lost in cooking. Use the leaves fresh in green or fruit salads. Medicinally, it is antiviral and antibacterial, helps lower fevers and improves digestion, as well as being a mild antidepressant. It helps heal and prevent cold sores. Rub the leaf into the skin for a good natural insect repellent. Applied in this way, it also helps to reduce skin irritation caused by insect bites.

▲ *Melissa officinalis* 'All Gold'
GOLDEN LEMON BALM

A hardy herbaceous perennial, with a height of 75cm (30in) and a spread of 45cm (18in) or more. Clusters of cream-coloured flowers appear in summer. The lemon-scented, golden-yellow leaves are oval-shaped and textured; since they are prone to scorching, plant this variety in partial shade. Cut back in summer to encourage new growth and fresh leaf colour. This variety can only be propagated successfully by softwood cuttings or root division.

▶ *Melissa officinalis*
LEMON BALM, SWEET BALM

A hardy herbaceous perennial, with a height of 75cm (30in) and a spread of 45cm (18in) or more. Clusters of small, cream-coloured flowers appear in summer. The flowers have a light lemon flavour when eaten. The leaves are lemon-scented, oval, toothed, and textured. Add leaves to stewing fruit to help reduce their tartness.

Leaves taste better raw than cooked. When crushed they have a very good lemon scent

Stem has fine hairs

Flowers grow in clusters around the stem. They have a sweet lemon flavour and are rich in nectar, making them a very good bee plant

Leaf is covered in fine hairs with toothed edges

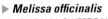

◀ *Melissa officinalis* 'Aurea'
VARIEGATED LEMON BALM

A hardy herbaceous perennial, with a height of 60cm (24in) and a spread of 30cm (12in) or more. Clusters of small, pale cream flowers appear in summer. The leaves are lemon-scented, textured, and variegated but revert to pure green in summer. This variety can only be propagated successfully from softwood cuttings or by root division.

Mentha

Classic mints LAMIACEAE

Mints are promiscuous herbs. They have successfully interbred, crossbred, and hybridized, which is wonderful for the plant collector, but difficult for me when having to decide which examples to write about. I have chosen to divide the mints up into classic mints and peppermints (see page 150). Spearmint (*Mentha spicata*) is without doubt the best-known of the classic mints. It was introduced to Europe by the Romans. It is still highly regarded and in demand as a culinary herb, as a source of leaves for refreshing mint tea, and as a useful home herbal remedy to aid digestion.

How to grow

Herb	Soil	Propagation
Mentha	Loam	Root cuttings

PROPAGATION In autumn or early spring, take root cuttings (see page 52). Spring cuttings take two weeks before new growth emerges. Softwood cuttings can be taken in late spring from new non-flowering growth. Divide mature plants in spring or autumn. Only pennyroyal grows true from seed; others set seed but are variable.

SITE The healthiest plants are those that are left to spread naturally. Plant in a rich, well-drained soil in a sunny position. It grows well in containers in a soil-based substrate. Repot each year in autumn to prevent root rot and to encourage abundant leaf the following season. Never plant two different mints together: they will intermarry and their flavours will become inferior.

MAINTENANCE Cut hard back in summer and feed with comfrey liquid feed (see p.39). Tender new growth will be ready to pick in six to eight weeks. A fungus, *Puccinia mentha,* is a common problem. Known as "mint rust", it is identified by its small rusty spots which cover the leaf, starting on the underside. The only organic way to get rid of this disease is to either dig up the plant and destroy it, or cover it with straw and set it alight. This dramatic action will sterilize the soil and burn the contaminated leaves.

HARVESTING Pick leaves before flowering, or after it has been cut back and the plant has started to regrow.

How to use

Medicinally, it relieves indigestion, nausea, flatulence, diarrhoea, and colic. Mint tea soothes colds and cold mint tea can be used as a wash to bring down a fever, or as a throat gargle.

◀ *Mentha spicata* **var.** *crispum*
CURLY MINT
A hardy herbaceous perennial with a height of up to 60cm (24in) and an indefinite spread. Small, lilac-pink flowers grow in spikes in summer. The spearmint-scented and -flavoured leaves are very crinkled – the first time I grew this plant I thought that the leaves were diseased.

▲ *Mentha pulegium* 'Upright'
PENNYROYAL UPRIGHT
A hardy, semi-evergreen perennial, with a height of 15cm (6in) and an indefinite spread. Small mauve flowers grow in clusters around the stem in summer. The small leaves are highly peppermint scented; use sparingly in cooking. It is an excellent insect repellent and gives relief from stings. It should not be taken internally, when pregnant, or when suffering from kidney disease. It can be raised easily from seed and comes true, but is best propagated from cuttings.

▲ *Mentha spicata* 'Tashkent'
MINT TASHKENT

A hardy, herbaceous perennial, with a height of up to 80cm (32in), and an indefinite spread. Small mauve flowers grow in cylindrical spikes in summer. Leaves are spearmint-scented and -flavoured, mid-green, oval shaped, and wrinkled. This variety has one of the best culinary flavours.

Flower has a lovely sweet minty flavour

▶ *Mentha spicata*
SPEARMINT, GARDEN MINT

A hardy herbaceous perennial, with a height up to 60cm (24in) and an indefinite spread. Small, purple-mauve flowers grow in cylindrical spikes in summer. The spearmint-scented and -flavoured leaves are mid-green, oval shaped, and wrinkled. Spearmint can vary in flavour and leaf colour, depending on the soil in which it is grown.

Leaf is lance-shaped with a strong spearmint scent when crushed

Leaf has distinctly serrated edge

Mentha

Peppermints LAMIACEAE

Peppermint is the quintessential herb: it attracts beneficial butterflies and hoverflies to the garden, smells lovely, aids digestion, and eases headaches. It has been used medicinally for thousands of years. The ancient Egyptians knew its medicinal properties and the Japanese have been extracting menthol oil from the leaves for at least 2,000 years. Today, peppermint oil is found in toothpaste, indigestion tablets, and confectionery. There are many different varieties available and some are more invasive than others. Variegated species tend to be weaker and therefore more easily contained.

How to grow

Herb	Soil	Propagation
Mentha	Loam	Root cuttings

PROPAGATION Peppermint is a hybrid of water mint (*Mentha aquatica*) and spearmint (*Mentha spicata*). It does not set viable seed, so is best propagated from root cuttings (see page 52) taken in spring and autumn, or from softwood cuttings taken in late spring from new non-flowering growth. Alternatively, propagate established plants by root division (see page 53) in autumn or spring.

SITE For maximum leaf flavour and oil production, plant in full sun in well-drained fertile soil. See page 148 for more details.

MAINTENANCE To maintain healthy plants, divide established plants every few years. Cut back after flowering to encourage new leaf growth, and feed with comfrey liquid feed (see page 39). New growth will be ready for picking in six to eight weeks. In winter when the plant has died back, feed with well-rotted manure. Peppermints are prone to mint rust (see page 148). If plants become invasive, dig up root runners with care – any root left behind will grow into a new plant.

HARVESTING Pick fresh leaves before flowering, or after cutting back when the plant has started to re-grow up until the first frosts.

How to use

Strongly flavoured, peppermint can overwhelm more subtle flavours but it tastes good in puddings like chocolate mousse. It is the key ingredient in remedies for indigestion and irritable bowel syndrome and is a decongestant for colds and catarrh. The oil is antiseptic and is used to treat itching skin and as a mosquito deterrent.

◀ *Mentha* x *piperita* f. *citrata*
EAU-DE-COLOGNE MINT
A hardy herbaceous perennial, with a height of up to 80cm (32in) and an indefinite spread. Small, pale purple flowers grow in spikes in summer. The eau-de-cologne-scented, peppermint-flavoured leaves are dark brown tinged with green. You can add fresh leaves to bath water for a refreshing effect.

▲ *Mentha* x *piperita* 'Logee'
LOGEE MINT
A hardy herbaceous perennial, with a height of up to 45cm (18in) and an indefinite spread. Small, pale purple flowers grow in terminal, cylindrical spikes in summer. Logee mint's leaves are green and white variegated, pointed, oval, toothed and peppermint-scented and -flavoured. This mint can be used in the same way as the standard peppermint (*Mentha* x *piperita*).

▲ *Mentha* x *piperita* f. *citrata* '**Orange**'
ORANGE MINT

A hardy, herbaceous perennial, with a height of up to 80cm (32in) and an indefinite spread. Small, pale pink-purple flowers grow in spikes in summer until autumn. It has large, rounded, oval, purple- and orange-tinged dark green leaves that have a definite orange scent. It is especially good with fresh fruit salads.

Flower is pale purple and clustered in spikes

Leaf is oval and pointed with the veins in a darker colour

Stem is square and dark plum-brown in colour

▶ *Mentha* x *piperita*
PEPPERMINT, BLACK PEPPERMINT

A hardy herbaceous perennial, with a height of up to 60cm (24in) and an indefinite spread. Small, pale purple flowers grow in terminal, cylindrical spikes in summer. The edible leaves have a strong peppermint flavour and scent; the flowers taste of sweet peppermint. The leaves are dark plum-brown tinged with green, pointed, oval, and toothed.

Meum

Meu APIACEAE

This attractive aromatic plant grows in mountain grasslands and is, in my opinion, underused in the modern herb garden, where it can look most attractive grown as a soft edging plant. It grows wild in the Scottish Highlands, and was once eaten there as a vegetable; it is a close relative of the carrot. The fresh leaves also offer a light, delicious, spicy flavour – a mixture of lovage and parsley – and are good in soup. Traditionally it is reputed to spice up a flagging love life, and has been used to treat a variety of medicinal problems: most commonly it is used as an aid to digestion.

Root is long and fibrous, with a strong spicy flavour.

How to grow

Herb	Soil	Propagation
Meum	Loam	Division

PROPAGATION First stratify the seeds (see p.45) before germination. In autumn, sow into a container and place outdoors. Germination should occur the following spring, but can be erratic. In early autumn, propagate established plants by root division. Replant into well-prepared open ground.

SITE Plant in full sun in fertile soil that holds its moisture in summer. It adapts to most soils, except waterlogged or arid ones. It can be grown in a deep container, using a soil-based substrate, but its long tap root does not respond well to being too confined. Each autumn, repot using a soil-based substrate.

MAINTENANCE To grow meu as a root vegetable, mulch with well-rotted manure in autumn. If you want a leaf crop, feed with comfrey liquid feed (see page 39) in early spring. Feed once only, or the leaves and root will grow soft and lose flavour.

HARVESTING Pick fresh either before or after flowering. The root of three-year-old plants can be dug up in early autumn and used fresh.

How to use

Fresh leaves taste similar to lovage (see page 138) but are more spicy and taste good with omelettes and cheese, and in salads and soups. If cows eat the leaves mixed with grass, it makes their milk and butter taste spicy. A member of the carrot family, meu has roots with a strong spicy flavour that is good in casseroles and soups. The roots can also be used to make a spicy wine. Medicinally, meu leaves and roots were used for curing snake bites, coughs, and flatulence. Today it is little used but it is good for digestive problems.

▼ *Meum athamanticum*
MEU, SPIGNEL

A hardy herbaceous perennial, with a height of 30cm (12in) and a spread of 20cm (8in). Umbels of small white flowers with a hint of pink at the edges appear in early summer. The bright green leaves are feathery, with a light, spicy scent.

Leaf resembles a soft, green feather

Monarda
Wild bergamot LAMIACEAE

This herb is worth growing for its flower alone, which reminds me of a flamboyant lady's hat feathers. A native of North America, wild bergamot was used by the Oswego Indians to treat colds and bronchial complaints. In the US, it is still drunk as a refreshing tea, called Oswego tea after the tribe. In 1773, following the Boston Tea Party, wild bergamot was introduced to North American settlers. It became a popular substitute for Indian tea. Although the leaves smell similar, do not confuse wild bergamot with bergamot orange (*Citrus bergamia*), which gives Earl Grey its distinctive scent and taste.

How to grow

Herb	Soil	Propagation
Monarda	Sand	Seed

PROPAGATION Sow seeds in early spring under protection at 18°C (65°F). Germination takes one to two weeks. Do not overwater the wild bergamot seedlings because they are prone to "damping off" – a fungal disease. In cool climates, take root cuttings from the creeping rhizomes in spring. Take cuttings from the growing stems in early summer. Divide established plants in autumn.

SITE There is some difference regarding site preference. *Monarda fistulosa* likes a well-drained soil and a sunny position, *M. didyma* a rich fertile soil that retains moisture in the summer and partial shade. Neither likes cold wet soil. Bergamot grows well in a large pot with some shade from the midday sun. Use a soil-based substrate.

MAINTENANCE Dig up plants over three years old, remove the dead centre and replant into a prepared site. All *Monarda* species are susceptible to mildew and rust fungus. If either appear, cut the plant back to ground level, remove contaminated parts, and burn them.

HARVESTING Pick fresh wild bergamot leaves to use as and when required. For drying, pick off the flowers and leaves from second-year plants just as they start to bloom.

▶ ***Monarda didyma***
BEE BALM BERGAMOT, RED BERGAMOT
A hardy, herbaceous, non-invasive perennial, with a height of up to 80cm (32in), and an indefinite spread. It has wonderful, large red flowers that are surrounded by red bracts throughout the summer, and mid-green, toothed, oval, strongly scented leaves that make a refreshing cup of tea.

How to use

The leaf has a strong culinary flavour that goes well with meat. The flowers have a milder, sweeter flavour. Medicinally, a decoction of leaves makes a steam inhalant to soothe bronchial complaints. Bergamot essential oil is used in aromatherapy to treat depression and to fight infection. It is also used by perfume and soap manufacturers.

Murraya

Curry tree RUTACEAE

When I first started herb farming, the only species of curry plant that was available was *Helichrysum italicum* – an evergreen shrub with silver foliage that fills the air with a curry scent. Today, the leaf from the native Sri Lankan curry tree (*Murraya koenigii*) is available as a culinary delight. In Asian cooking, the curry leaf itself is rarely eaten but is used as a flavouring in dishes before being thrown away before the dish is served. Interestingly, there is an old Indian saying which compares a curry leaf to a person who is only wanted for a particular use before being discarded.

How to grow

Herb	Soil	Propagation
Murraya	Sand	Softwood cuttings

PROPAGATION Sow seeds in spring under protection at 22°C (72°F). Germination takes two to four weeks, but can be erratic. An easier method of propagation is to lift and replant the small suckers that grow around the base of a mature shrub. Grow on the suckers in small pots. Do not plant out for at least two seasons.

SITE Plant in a fertile, light soil in full sun or partial shade. Young plants need watering once a day for the first three years. It will adapt to hot, dry climates, though the plant will be less productive and smaller. This tropical plant needs protection when temperatures fall below 13°C (55°F). In cool climates, grow as a container plant using a soil-based substrate.

MAINTENANCE In autumn, feed the curry tree with well-rotted manure. If grown in a container, feed once a week throughout the growing season with liquid comfrey (see page 39). Mature plants can be cut back in winter. Young plants are prone to aphid attack. Treat with liquid horticultural soap.

HARVESTING Pick fresh leaves as required. Dry curry leaves quickly lose their flavour.

▶ *Murraya koenigii*
CURRY TREE, KAHDI PATTA
A tropical, evergreen shrub, with a height of up to 6m (20ft) and a spread of up to 5m (15ft). Clusters of pretty, fragrant, star-shaped, white flowers appear in summer, followed by edible black berries. The large, oval, dark green leaves have a bitter, pleasant, aromatic flavour when eaten, and produce a curry aroma when brushed against or crushed.

How to use

Leaves flavour vegetable and lentil curries in southern India, and chicken and meat curries in Sri Lanka. Medicinally, curry is used to treat digestive disorders, diarrhoea, dysentery, and piles. Leaves are used as a poultice to treat burns, bruises, and skin eruptions and have weight-reducing properties. The juice of the leaf makes an eye-brightening wash.

Leaf is large, oval, and dark green

Myrrhis
Sweet cicely APIACEAE

The frothy, cream-coloured flowers are some of the earliest to appear in the herb garden, and herald the arrival of spring. Originally, the roots of this herb were boiled and chewed as a breath sweetener. The flavour is like a mix of aniseed and parsnip. *Myrrhis odorata* is closely related to *Osmorhiza longistylis*, which was used extensively by Native American tribes. Both species of sweet cicely were used as a herbal tonic for the young and elderly. In the past, the seeds were crushed and used to make a furniture polish, which was particularly good for oak.

Seeds when green have a sharp aniseed flavour, and when dark brown and ripe have a sweet aniseed taste.

How to grow

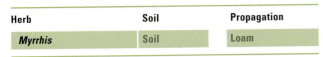

Herb	Soil	Propagation
Myrrhis	Soil	Loam

PROPAGATION These large seeds need stratifying to germinate (see page 45). In cold climates, sow the seed fresh in autumn. Use garden soil not substrate, and place the container outside. Germination occurs the following spring. Take root cuttings in autumn and spring. Divide established plants in the autumn.

SITE Plant in a soil rich in humus, in light shade. It will not grow in humid or hot climates. It is not an ideal pot plant because it has a long tap root. In light, fertile soil, contain the root to prevent it from becoming invasive; grow it in a large dustbin, using a loam-based substrate, in partial shade.

MAINTENANCE To prevent self-seeding, collect unripe green seeds to use in salads, and then cut back hard. Remove the whole tap root if you wish to prevent it from rooting.

HARVESTING Pick leaves to use fresh either side of flowering. Pick flowers just as the cluster opens and harvest seeds in the green when required. Store seeds when they have ripened to a dark brown colour. Make sure that they are dry.

▶ ***Myrrhis odorata***
SWEET CICELY
A hardy herbaceous perennial, with a height of up to 90cm (3ft) and a spread of 60cm (2ft). The scented flowers, which appear in early spring and last until early summer, are followed by long, angular seeds that ripen to black. The flowers can be made into a refreshing cordial drink.

How to use

Add leaves to soups, stews, and as a natural sweetener and flavouring for stewed fruit and fruit salads. Cook the root as a vegetable or grate raw to add to salads. The seeds, when green, add crunch to a salad. Brown seeds add aniseed flavouring to fruit. The root is used for digestive complaints, coughs, and as a tonic, and makes a good wine.

Myrtus
Myrtle MYRTACEAE

If I had to choose my all-time "Top 10" herbs, myrtle would feature in the list. The herb of "love" and dedicated to the goddess Venus, myrtle was grown around her temples – and Venus is often shown rising from the sea carrying a sprig of myrtle. Traditionally, brides carry a piece of myrtle in their bouquets as a symbol of love and constancy. Quite apart from its romantic history, myrtle looks wonderful grown in the garden or in containers. It smells fragrant, and is an excellent culinary herb. It goes particularly well with barbecued food to which it adds a distinctly Mediterranean flavour.

Berry is known as "mursins" in the Middle East where it is used as a spice.

How to grow

Herb	Soil	Propagation
Myrtus	**Sand**	**Softwood cuttings**

PROPAGATION In spring, separate the pulp of the ripe berry from the seed. Sow fresh, and place under protection at 15°C (60°F). Germination normally takes one to two months, but can take longer. Alternatively, take softwood cuttings in summer from non-flowering shoots. With both methods, pot up when well rooted, and grow on for two seasons before planting into a prepared site.

SITE Plant in well-drained soil in full sun. Myrtle is quite hardy but it is the wet that will kill it quicker than cold. *Myrtus communis* survives in temperatures of -10°C (14°F). Variegated forms are less hardy surviving at -5°C (23°F). In exposed sites, plant against a sheltered south- or west-facing wall. They grow well in containers, using a soil-based substrate. Do not pot-on too often; myrtle prefers being pot-bound.

MAINTENANCE Feed once in spring with well-rotted compost. Feed container-grown plants weekly during the growing season. Over-fed plants will not flower. In Mediterranean climates, trim myrtle in autumn. In colder climates, trim in spring.

HARVESTING Pick fresh leaves throughout the year. Harvest fresh flowers as required in summer. Pick berries in late autumn.

How to use

Add leaves and berries to stews and soups. Use flowers as a garnish. In rural areas of Italy and Sardinia, cooking is flavoured with the smoke of burning myrtle wood. Add myrtle leaves to the glowing coals of a barbecue to obtain a similar effect.

Medicinally, the oil from the berries is used externally to alleviate acne. A leaf infusion is used to treat urinary infections.

▲ *Myrtus communis* subsp. *tarentina* 'Microphylla Variegata'
VARIEGATED SMALL-LEAVED MYRTLE
A frost-hardy, evergreen shrub, with a height and spread of up to 1m (3ft). Very attractive, fragrant white flowers with golden stamens appear in summer, followed by blue-black berries. The small, oval, light green and white variegated leaves are aromatic when crushed. These leaves are the smallest of all the myrtles. This herb is hardy to -5°C (23°F); do not overwater in winter.

▶ *Myrtus communis*
MYRTLE

A hardy evergreen shrub, with a height and spread of up to 3m (10ft). Very attractive, fragrant white flowers with golden stamens appear in summer, followed by blue-black berries. The oval, dark green leaves are aromatic when crushed, and are a very good substitute for bay leaf in culinary dishes. This herb has the largest leaves and flowers of all the myrtles.

Leaf is oval and dark green and very aromatic when crushed

Flower is the largest of all the *Myrtus* species

Stem, as it matures, develops a bark which was used to tan leather

◀ *Myrtus communis* 'Variegata'
VARIEGATED MYRTLE

A frost-hardy, evergreen shrub, with a height and spread of up to 2m (6ft). Very attractive, fragrant white flowers with golden stamens appear in summer, followed by blue-black berries. The oval, variegated leaves are aromatic when crushed.

Nepeta

Catnip LAMIACEAE

This is a well-known feline aphrodisiac. Cats have been seen to destroy a plant as they roll about in ecstasy, or munch it to oblivion. On my farm, we named one of our cats after this herb because, as a kitten, he chewed his way through a vast number of these hallucinatory plants. Interestingly, it has a similar effect on humans and became a poor man's substitute for cannabis in the 1960s. Catnip tea was once commonly used in Europe as a relaxing hot beverage before real tea was introduced. Medicinally, it is mainly used as a calming and sleep-inducing herbal remedy, usually taken at bedtime.

How to grow

Herb	Soil	Propagation
Nepeta	Loam	Seed

PROPAGATION Sow seeds in early spring and place under protection at 18°C (65°F). Germination takes one to two weeks. In spring, propagate established plants by root division (see page 53). Avoid bruising the roots when you dig them up, or you will attract cats. In summer, take cuttings from non-flowering stems.

SITE Plant in well-drained soil in sun or partial shade. Catnip will adapt to most soil conditions, except clay or bog. *Nepeta cataria* is a very good companion plant. If planted between brassicas, it will repel flea beetles, and will deter ants and aphids.

MAINTENANCE Cut back hard after flowering to encourage a second flush of flowers and new growth. To protect a young plant from cats, turn a wire hanging basket upside down over it and peg it to the ground. Encourage the plant to grow through the wire. This system allows your cat to eat some leaves without rolling in it.

HARVESTING In spring, pick young leaves for culinary use. When the plant is in bud, pick leaves to dry for medicinal use.

How to use

Young leaves have a slightly bitter, minty flavour and go well with soups and sauces. Medicinally, they are used to treat childhood ailments, such as colic, colds, and coughs. Catmint leaves can also be made into an ointment for the relief of piles.

▲ *Nepeta* x *faassenii*
CATMINT
A hardy herbaceous perennial, with a height and spread of 45cm (18in). Clusters of small, lavender-blue tubular flowers appear in summer. The oval grey leaves are toothed and have a pungent aroma. This species of catmint has less effect on cats and no known medicinal properties.

▶ *Nepeta cataria*
CATNIP, CATMINT
A hardy herbaceous perennial, with a height of 1m (3ft) and a spread of 60cm (2ft). It produces clusters of pinkish-white flowers in summer that attract butterflies, especially the painted lady. The pungent, aromatic leaves are grey-green, toothed, and oval. The scent is said to repel rats.

Flowers are tubular and grow in clusters

Stem is square, ridged and slightly hairy

Leaf is grey-green and pungent when crushed. Recent research has shown that the dried leaf is a deterrent to cockroaches

Nigella
Black cumin RANUNCULACEAE

A delicate and pretty herb, Nigella's black seeds were found in the Tomb of Tutankhamun. Cumin is mentioned in the bible and has been used medicinally for thousands of years. It is also the "Muslim Miracle Herb" of which, according to an Arab proverb, it is said that "in the black seed is the medicine for every disease except death". Today, the seed of this herb is a popular spice in India, Egypt, and the Middle East. Do not confuse it with the garden plant love-in-a-mist (*Nigella damascena*); although they look similar, love-in-a-mist has no culinary or medicinal properties.

CAUTION Do not take *Nigella* medicinally during pregnancy.

How to grow

Herb	Soil	Propagation
Nigella	Sand	Seed

PROPAGATION In early spring, grow seeds under protection at 18°C (65°F); germination usually takes one to two weeks, but it can take three to four weeks and may be erratic. Alternatively, sow seeds in late spring into prepared open ground, when the air temperature does not fall below 7°C (45°F) at night; germination takes two to three weeks. In my opinion, sowing direct into open ground gives the best crop.

SITE Plant in well-drained soil in a sunny position. A better crop is achieved in open ground rather than when grown in a container.

MAINTENANCE A one-season crop. Prepare the site well prior to sowing. Do not feed with extra fertilizer once it has been planted out.

HARVESTING Collect the ripe seed pods and then crush and sieve the contents to separate out the black cumin seeds. The seeds are either dried and then their oil extracted, or used whole or ground for medicinal purposes or in the kitchen.

How to use

The seeds have a peppery aromatic flavour. Use in bread, cakes, sauces, curries, chutneys, and fish dishes. Medicinally, seeds are used in the treatment of respiratory conditions, allergies, fevers, flu, asthma, and emphysema. Research has shown that it inhibits certain forms of cancer. Sprinkling seeds in the folds of clothes acts as a moth and insect repellent. Commercially, the seeds are ground to make cooking oil.

▲ *Nigella sativa*
BLACK CUMIN, KALONJI
A half-hardy annual, with a height of 30cm (12in) and a spread of 23cm (9in). Small, pale blue to white flowers are produced in summer, followed by interesting horn-like seed pods, which contain black seeds. The grey-green leaves are finely serrated and divided.

Ocimum

Basil LAMIACEAE

A pasta or tomato dish without the aroma and taste of basil is now quite naked, since it has become an everyday herb. It is best if you can grow your own – supermarket basil is grown as a salad crop and only survives for three to five days; it never sees the light of day or experiences the elements. Organically grown herbs raised in the garden have a much more pungent flavour and when watered on a hot day, the aroma of the water drying on the leaf is fantastic. Basil has medicinal uses too – in Elizabethan times it was used as a snuff for colds, to clear the brain and to soothe headaches.

How to grow

Herb	Soil	Propagation
Ocimum	Sand	Seed

PROPAGATION Sow seeds in early spring. Cover with perlite or vermiculite (see page 44) and place under protection at 20°C (68°F). Keep watering to a minimum until germination takes place in five to ten days. Once germinated, water sparingly to prevent seedlings from rotting. As the seedlings emerge, move the pots to a warm, light position and grow on. Plant out in the garden when all threat of frost has passed, in a sheltered position. In warmer climates, with a minimum night temperature above 13°C (55°F), sow directly into a prepared site.

SITE Plant in a well-drained fertile soil in a sunny, warm site, which offers some shelter from the midday sun. It makes an ideal pot plant, especially in cool, temperate climates. Use a soil-based substrate. Basil is a good companion plant. It repels whitefly, aphids, and fruit fly from other plants, as well as house flies from the kitchen.

MAINTENANCE Mediterranean and Mexican basils are slightly hardier than the eastern basil, and are easier to grow outside in cooler climates. They are prone to attack from slugs, whitefly, and red spider mite. Always pick the growing tips to encourage bushy growth.

HARVESTING Pick leaves throughout the growing season from the top of the plant, to encourage new growth for use fresh or for drying. Pick flowers in the summer to use fresh or preserve in butter (see page 225).

How to use

Add fresh, torn leaves to salads, tomato, and pasta dishes. The flavour may be ruined if cooked for too long, The leaves used fresh with cold food aid digestion. The juice of basil leaves repels mosquitoes when rubbed on to the skin.

◄ ***Ocimum minimum* 'Greek'**
GREEK BASIL
A tender annual, with a height of 23cm (9in) and a spread of 15cm (6in). Clusters of small, white, tubular flowers are produced in summer. The leaves are small, green, oval and pointed. In Greece, terracotta pots of this species of basil are arranged on tables at mealtimes to keep away flies.

▲ ***Ocimum basilicum* 'Cinnamon'**
CINNAMON BASIL
A tender annual, with a height of 45cm (18in) and a spread of 30cm (12in). Clusters of small, pink-mauve tubular flowers appear in summer. It has dark purple-brown stems and olive to green-brown, oval, pointed, and slightly serrated leaves that have a very spicy flavour. Cinnamon basil tastes particularly good in stir-fry dishes.

▲ *Ocimum basilicum* **var.**
purpurascens **'Dark Opal'**
DARK OPAL BASIL, PURPLE BASIL
A tender annual, with a height of
45cm (18in) and a spread of 30cm
(12in). It has clusters of pink-mauve,
tubular flowers in summer, light purple
stems, and dark purple, oval, pointed
leaves with a spicy, warm flavour.
When added to rice and pastas, it
provides a stunning colour contrast.

Leaf is smooth
and highly aromatic
when crushed

Stem is square in
profile, becoming
woody with age

▲ *Ocimum basilicum*
SWEET BASIL, GENOVESE BASIL
A tender annual, with a height of 45cm (18in) and a spread
of 30cm (12in). Clusters of small, white, tubular flowers
appear in summer, and have a sweet, classic basil flavour.
The oval, pointed, leaves smell wonderful when crushed.
This is the variety most commonly found in the
supermarkets and used for pesto sauce (see page 227).

Ocimum

Eastern basil LAMIACEAE

Our knowledge of culinary herbs like basil has widened with our increased interest in the cultures of countries such as India, Thailand, and Vietnam. I am particularly fascinated by the uses of basil in different societies. Holy basil (*Ocimum tenuiflorum*), for example, is one of the sacred plants of India. This strongly flavoured herb plays a key role in ceremonies of worship in homes and temples; in Hindu weddings, the parents of the bride present the groom with a basil leaf. The leaves are rarely used in Indian cooking – more often they are mixed with Indian tea leaves to make a refreshing drink.

How to grow

Herb	Soil	Propagation
Ocimum	Sand	Seed

PROPAGATION Sow seeds in early spring. Cover with perlite or vermiculite (see page 44) and place under protection at 20°C (68°F), for germination in five to ten days. As these basils come from tropical climates it is important to water in the morning, never at night, which in turn will help prevent the seedlings from damping off. Once the seedlings are large enough to handle, pot up and grow on as a pot plant. Plant in the garden or place the container outside only when the night temperature remains above 13°C (55°F).

SITE Basils can only be grown in the garden in warm climates and even then need shelter from midday sun.

MAINTENANCE Only water in the morning. Keep picking the plant from the top to encourage it to bush out.

HARVESTING Pick leaves and flowering tops throughout the summer to use fresh or to dry, or conserve in oil.

How to use

In Thailand and other Asian countries, leaves are added to soups and fish dishes. The leaves are rarely used in Indian cooking. More often they are used to make herbal teas, combined with other herb seeds or simply with India tea leaves to make a refreshing drink. Medicinally, basil is used to treat bronchitis, colds, fevers, and stress. The juice of the basil leaves is used to alleviate skin complaints, and the essential oil is used to treat ear infections by means of drops and rubbed onto the skin as an insect repellent. Research has shown that it has the ability to reduce blood sugar levels, and it is now being used in the treatment of some types of diabetes.

▲ *Ocimum canum*
AFRICAN BASIL
A tender annual with a height and spread of 45cm (18in). Clusters of very pale pink-purple tubular flowers appear in summer. The mid-green leaves are oval and slightly serrated, with a hairy texture. The leaves have a strong scent, and a slightly minty aroma and flavour. African basil is used medicinally to treat persistent headache, migraine, fever, worms, and rheumatism.

▲ *Ocimum basilicum*
'Horapha Nanum'
THAI BASIL

A tender annual, with a height of 30cm (12in) and a spread of 20cm (8in). Clusters of mulberry-purple, tubular flowers appear in summer. The stem is dark purple to brown. The olive-green to purple leaves are oval and slightly serrated, with a hairy texture. The leaves have a strong scent and flavour and are used in Thai and Vietnamese cooking.

▲ *Ocimum* x *citriodorum*
LEMON BASIL

A tender annual, with a height of 30cm (12in) and a spread of 20cm (8in). Clusters of white, tubular flowers appear in summer. The light, bright green leaves are oval and slightly serrated, with a hairy texture. The leaves have a strong lemon scent and flavour, and are wonderful with fish, stir-fry dishes, and marinades.

▲ *Ocimum tenuiflorum* syn. *sanctum*
HOLY BASIL, TULSI

A tender annual, with a height of 30cm (12in) and a spread of 20cm (8in). Clusters of small, pink-mauve, tubular flowers appear in summer. The leaves are olive-green to brown-purple, oval, pointed, hairy, and slightly serrated, and have a very pungent scent and flavour. The leaves are an important component of Thai cuisine, and the plant is worshipped throughout India.

Oenothera

Evening primrose ONAGRACEAE

The potential of this herb is enormous because all parts of the plant are edible.
Evening primrose's value as a healing herb was recognized by the Native
Americans, who used it as a healing poultice for soothing itchy rashes and
bites. The seeds contain a rich source of essential fatty acids, which in modern
diets are often deficient. Oil extracted from the seeds of this plant is now used
to treat medical conditions including chronic fatigue syndrome, premenstrual
syndrome, hyperactivity in children, liver damage, and eczema.

CAUTION Do not take evening
primrose if you suffer from epilepsy.

How to grow

Herb	Soil	Propagation
Oenothera	Sand	Seed

PROPAGATION Sow seeds in either spring or autumn. Leave the
seed uncovered by substrate and place it in a cold frame. Germination
takes three to four weeks. If sowing in autumn, pot up and winter the
young plants in a cold frame before planting out. Alternatively, sow the
seeds directly into prepared open ground in autumn. Cover the soil with
twigs to prevent the birds from eating the seeds.

SITE Plant in well-drained soil in a dry, sunny position. *Oenothera
biennis* is not suited to growing in containers because it is too tall.
Shorter varieties are available, such as *O. speciosa*, but this species
does not have medicinal properties.

MAINTENANCE In autumn, cut back the flowerheads before the
seed pods open to prevent self-seeding. In winter, dig up the old roots
of second-year growth of the biennials.

HARVESTING Pick leaves to use fresh as required from spring
until midsummer. Pick the flowers in bud or as they open throughout
the summer. Dig up roots of the second year's growth in late summer,
before seeds have set – they are at their best for medicinal use at this
stage. Collect seeds in early autumn.

How to use

Add fresh young leaves to salads. Cook mature leaves like spinach. The
roots have an earthy, nutty flavour, and can be cooked like parsnips.
Use seeds in baking. Medicinally, the seed oil is used to treat dry skin.
The leaf and stem can be infused to make an astringent facial steam.

Flower has four petals
and is only scented in the
evening, when it opens

Leaf is textured
and lance-shaped

▶ *Oenothera biennis*
EVENING PRIMROSE
A hardy biennial, with a height, in the second season,
of up to 1.2m (4ft) and a spread of 90cm (3ft). The yellow,
trumpet-shaped flowers are night-scented. The flowers
appear in the second season and are followed by oval,
downy pods containing masses of small seeds. The green
leaves are lance-shaped.

Olea

Olive tree OLEACEAE

The olive tree, with its beautiful knarled bark and twisted trunk, is as old as the hills that it grows on. In the Old Testament, the dove returned to Noah's Ark with a sprig of olive in its beak, which showed that the flood waters were abating, and the olive branch has been the symbol of peace for centuries. The Greeks and Romans valued the oil produced by pressing the fruit, and the winners of the Olympic Games were crowned with olive leaves. Today, olive oil and the green and ripe black fruits remain a vital ingredient of the daily diet of Mediterranean people.

Fruit starts off green and ripens to black. It cannot be eaten straight from the tree.

How to grow

Herb	Soil	Propagation
Olea	Sand	Softwood cuttings

PROPAGATION First, scarify the seed (see page 45). In early autumn, sow fresh seeds and cover with coarse horticultural sand. Place under protection at 21°C (70°F) for three to four weeks. Then lower to 15°C (60°F). Germination takes from a month to a year. In summer, take cuttings from new growth but do not allow them to dry out. It takes four to eight weeks for them to root. In cool climates, grow all young plants on in pots under protection (cold frame, cloche or greenhouse) for four years before planting out.

SITE Plant in well-drained soil in full sun. It is a mix of wet and cold conditions, not just cold, that kills olive trees. In arid, temperate, and cold climates, grow as a container plant. Use a soil-based substrate.

MAINTENANCE In Greece, I have seen olive plants grown as a hedge, which proves that it can be clipped. Cut back in spring. To produce a good crop of fruit, do not allow the plant to dry out. Feed every autumn with well-rotted manure or compost. Feed container-grown plants from spring until autumn with liquid seaweed. Scale insect may attack container-grown plants.

HARVESTING Pick leaves to use fresh as required. Pick fruit either when green or black and soak before eating.

▶ *Olea europaea*
OLIVE TREE
An evergreen tree, with a height of up to 10m (30ft). Numerous clusters of small, creamy-white, fragrant flowers appear in early summer, followed by green olive fruits which ripen to black. The oval grey-green leaves are leathery in texture with silvery undersides.

How to use

To make the fruit palatable, it has to be soaked in brine, salt, or oil prior to eating. The leaves can be infused and used as an antiseptic wash for cuts and grazes, or made into a tea to lower blood pressure and reduce nervous tension. The oil is good for circulatory diseases and helps improve digestion. Olive oil is one of the safest laxatives.

Young, immature olive fruit follows flower

Leaf has a leathery texture, indicating that it does not need much water to survive

Origanum

Hardy oreganos LAMIACEAE

Oregano is a favourite in the kitchen. It combines particularly well with tomato dishes, pasta, meat (especially lamb) and fish. The heady aroma of this sun-loving herb fills the mountainous Mediterranean landscape, and it is credited with lifting people's spirits. The word oregano is derived from the Greek "oros" meaning mountain and "ganos" meaning joy and beauty, hence its full meaning "joy of the mountain". The ancient Greeks believed that wild oregano (*Origanum vulgare*) was a cure-all, including, as Aristotle suggested, an antidote for poison. Medicinally, it is probably one of the best antiseptics.

CAUTION Do not take medicinally during pregnancy. Do not take the essential oil internally.

How to grow

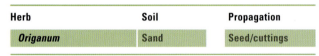

Herb	Soil	Propagation
Origanum	Sand	Seed/cuttings

PROPAGATION Mix the fine seed of *O. vulgare* with horticultural sand or flour to make it easier to handle. Sow in spring but do not cover the seed. Place under protection at 20°C (68°F). Germination takes ten to twenty days. The seedlings are prone to "damping off" so do not overwater. In summer, take cuttings from new growth. In warm climates, propagate established plants by division (see page 53) in spring or after flowering.

SITE Plant in a well-drained soil in a sunny position. The sun brings the aromatic oils up to the leaf surface and gives the plant its flavour and aroma. Oreganos attract bees and butterflies and so are good companion plants, encouraging fertilization of vegetable crops. All oreganos grow successfully in containers using a soil-based substrate, mixed with extra sharp grit or sand.

MAINTENANCE Cut back after flowering to encourage new growth which will give added protection in winter. Feed once in spring and once after cutting back, with comfrey liquid fertilizer (see page 39).

HARVESTING Pick leaves before flowering to use fresh or to dry. After the end of summer cut back, and use the fresh leaves immediately; fresh leaf flavour deteriorates quickly in cold climates.

How to use

Oregano and marjoram stimulate the digestive juices, helping to break down rich and heavy foods. The leaves are used fresh and dried throughout the Mediterranean, with meat and savoury dishes.

Medicinally, oregano is antiseptic due to its high thymol oil content. It is used to treat respiratory conditions like bronchitis and asthma.

▲ *Origanum vulgare* 'Acorn Bank'
OREGANO ACORN BANK
A hardy, herbaceous perennial with a height and spread of 45cm (18in). Clusters of tiny, tubular, pink flowers appear in summer. The golden-yellow leaves are oval and pointed in shape and have a hairy texture and are aromatic. In winter, the leaves die back to form a mat on the ground. Protect the plant from full sun, since these golden leaves are prone to sun scorch. This oregano variety can only be successfully grown from cuttings.

Flower has a classic herby flavour. Oregano flowers attract butterflies

▶ *Origanum vulgare*

OREGANO, WILD MARJORAM

A hardy, herbaceous perennial with a height and spread of 45cm (18in). Clusters of tiny, tubular, mauve flowers appear in summer. The dark green, hairy, aromatic leaves die back to form a mat in winter. The vigour and flavour of this plant is affected by the planting site, and hours of sunshine.

Leaf is very aromatic when crushed or eaten

Stem is square and covered in fine hairs

▲ *Origanum* x *onites*

FRENCH MARJORAM, FRENCH OREGANO

A hardy, herbaceous perennial with a height and spread of 45cm (18in). Clusters of tiny, tubular, pale pink flowers appear in summer. The aromatic, oval leaves are green with a hint of gold, and have a hairy texture. Like other oreganos, they die back in winter to form a mat on the ground. This oregano has a light spicy flavour and tastes good with vegetable dishes. Grow from cuttings only.

Origanum
Half-hardy oreganos LAMIACEAE

I am often asked to explain why some members of the *Origanum* family are called 'oregano' and others 'marjoram'. The only species to include marjoram in its Latin name is *Origanum majorana* (known commonly as sweet marjoram), so logic would suggest that this is the only true marjoram. In the rest of Europe, however, several edible oreganos are called 'marjoram', so perhaps the only way to be sure is to check the Latin name. In cooking, the flavour of *Origanum* species transforms an ordinary dish into a Mediterranean delight, and for personal well-being they act as a very good tonic.

CAUTION Do not take the essential oil of *O. majorana* internally. Do not take origanums as a medicine when pregnant.

How to grow

Herb	Soil	Propagation
Origanum	Sand	Seed/cuttings

PROPAGATION See page 166 for details.

SITE Half-hardy oreganos are ideal for rockery gardens, which simulate their native stony landscape. Plant in a well-drained soil in a sunny position. *O. majorana* is a good companion plant, as it deters aphids and is thought to improve the flavour of vegetables when planted between rows.

MAINTENANCE See page 166 for details.

HARVESTING See page 166 for details.

How to use

O. majorana is the species of marjoram most commonly found on pizzas and added to dried herb mixtures. It is an ingredient in bouquet garni (see page 228). Medicinally, sweet marjoram tea helps ease bad colds, headaches, and insomnia, and has a calming effect on the nerves. Chewing the leaf will give temporary relief from toothache. It is also said to reduce sexual libido.

▲ *Origanum dictamnus*
CRETAN OREGANO, DITTANY OF CRETE
A half-hardy perennial shrub, with a height of up to 15cm (6in) and a spread of 40cm (16in). The tiny, pink, tubular flowers are surrounded by grey-green bracts that turn pink-purple in summer as they mature. The rounded, grey-green leaves are highly aromatic, and are covered in a soft, woolly white down. The leaves have both culinary and medicinal uses.

Flower grows in clusters
in the shape of a knot

◀ *Origanum majorana*
SWEET MARJORAM

A half-hardy perennial shrub, often grown as an annual
in cool climates (because it dies in cold or wet climates
in winter), with a height and spread of 30cm (12in). Tiny,
white, tubular flowers grow around a green centre. The
oval, pale green leaves are soft and very aromatic. Other
half-hardy species worth growing include *Origanum
rotundifolium*, which has attractive, round bracts similar
to *O. dictamnus*. *O.* 'Dingle Fairy' is also very attractive,
with tiny flowers and interesting bracts.

Leaf is very soft and downy,
and has a strong oval shape

Pelargonium

Scented pelargoniums GERANIACEAE

John Tradescant (d.1638), the botanist and gardener to King Charles I, introduced the scented pelargonium to the UK from its native South Africa. Unlike the true geranium, pelargoniums have relatively small, unscented flowers but their fragrant leaves are present all year round, and will exude their scent when you brush past or rub a leaf between your fingers. Pelargonium leaves are still used to make geranium essential oil – an uplifting aromatherapy oil. Fascinatingly, the scent can vary depending on species and variety, from rose or apple to mint, which makes these plants eminently collectable.

How to grow

Herb	Soil	Propagation
Pelargonium	Loam	Softwood cuttings

PROPAGATION These species can be propagated from seed. Sow in spring at 18°C (65°F) and place under protection. Germination takes two to three weeks and can be erratic. A more reliable method of propagation is to take cuttings in early summer from new growth. Under protection, cuttings will take two to three weeks to root.

SITE In warm climates, when the night temperature does not fall below 9°C (48°F), plant in a well-drained soil in a sunny position, sheltered from cold winds. In cold climates, plant in a pot and sink the pot in the garden for the growing season. Dig up the pot and bring it inside before the first frost. Scented pelargoniums also grow well as container plants, using a loam-based substrate.

MAINTENANCE In cold climates, keep watering to a minimum in winter, and move potted plants to a frost-free environment. In spring, start watering slowly. For container-grown plants, water from the top and let the water drain through. Do not leave the plant to sit in a saucer of water. Feed weekly with comfrey liquid fertilizer (see page 39) from early spring until early autumn. To maintain plant shape, nip out the growing tips. Scented pelargoniums are prone to disease, including black leg virus, grey mould, leaf gall, and rust – destroy infected plants.

HARVESTING In spring and summer, pick scented pelargonium leaves to use fresh, or to dry for later use.

How to use

Rose-scented varieties can be used to flavour stewed apples and pears, as well as jellies. Fresh leaves of fruit-scented varieties can be infused in milk, cream, and syrups for puddings, custards, and ices.

▲ *Pelargonium* **'Lady Plymouth'**
PELARGONIUM LADY PLYMOUTH

A half-hardy, evergreen perennial with a height and spread of up to 60cm (24in). Clusters of small, pink flowers appear in summer. The grey-green and cream variegated leaves are deeply cut, and smell of a mixture of rose and peppermint when rubbed or crushed.

◀ *Pelargonium* 'Apple Scented'
APPLE-SCENTED PELARGONIUM,
APPLE GERANIUM

A half-hardy, evergreen, trailing perennial, ideal for containers, with a height of up to 60cm (24in) and a spread of 1m (36in). Clusters of small, white flowers appear in summer. The leaves are velvety, soft, and rounded with shallow lobes, and have an apple scent when rubbed or crushed.

◀ *Pelargonium* 'Chocolate Peppermint'
PELARGONIUM CHOCOLATE PEPPERMINT

A half-hardy, evergreen perennial with a height of up to 60cm (24in) and a spread of 1m (36in). The green and brown variegated, velvety leaves smell of peppermint with a hint of chocolate when rubbed or crushed.

Flower grows in small clusters

Stem has a velvety texture

Leaf is covered in fine hairs. It is highly scented when crushed

◀ *Pelargonium* 'Attar of Roses'
PELARGONIUM ATTAR OF ROSES

A half-hardy, evergreen perennial, with a height of up to 60cm (24in) and a spread of 30cm (12in). Clusters of small, unscented pink flowers appear in summer. The mid-green, three-lobed leaves are covered in fine hairs and smell of roses when rubbed or crushed.

Perilla

Shiso LAMIACEAE

The first time I displayed purple shiso (*Perilla frutescens* var. *purpurascens*) at the Chelsea Flower Show, its striking appearance caused a storm of interest. It looks very similar to *Solenostemon*. *Perilla* is one of the few aromatic plants used in Japanese cuisine and is also an ancient ingredient of Chinese medicine, traditionally used to treat the common cold. The common name "beefsteak plant" originated in the US, and refers to the size of the purple shiso's leaf, which looks like a large slice of raw beef. A useful culinary herb, the fresh leaf is excellent in stir-fry dishes and tempura.

CAUTION Can cause contact dermatitis.

How to grow

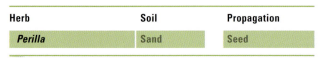

Herb	Soil	Propagation
Perilla	Sand	Seed

PROPAGATION Sow seeds in spring under protection at 20°C (68°F). Germination takes one to two weeks. Alternatively, sow in late spring into prepared open ground, when the night temperature does not fall below 8°C (45°F). In these conditions, it takes 14 to 20 days for germination to occur.

SITE Plant shiso out in fertile, well-drained soil that has been dug the autumn prior to planting with well-rotted compost or leafmould. Plant in the late spring in sun or partial shade. In arid climates, irrigation is necessary to keep soil moist. Use a soil-based substrate when growing shiso as a container plant.

MAINTENANCE Pinch out growing tips to maintain the plant shape and to encourage bushy growth. Feed container plants weekly with liquid comfrey (see page 39). Remove caterpillars.

HARVESTING Leaves can be picked at seedling stage to use as an intensely flavoured cress, or when they reach maturity for a spicier flavour. Pick the flower in late summer; harvest seeds in late autumn.

How to use

Purple shiso leaf is used as a natural dye for pickling vegetables and fruit like plums, and as flavouring in tea. The flowerheads are used as a seasoning for sushi. Green leaf shiso tastes of cumin with a hint of anise and cinnamon. In Japan, green leaf shiso is bought as a vegetable. The fresh leaves are used to wrap up rice, in salads, and tempura. The seed from this variety is used as a condiment. The flowering parts contain a substance even sweeter than sugar, and are used in Japanese confectionery.

◀ ***Perilla frutescens* var. *purpurascens***
PURPLE SHISO, BEEFSTEAK PLANT
A hardy annual, with a height of up to 1.2m (4ft) and a spread of 60cm (24in). It has dark purple leaves with crinkled edges, aromatic when crushed. In plants raised from seed, the flower spikes can be red rather than pink, and the leaf surface smoother.

▲ ***Perilla frutescens***
SHISO
A hardy annual, with a height of up to 1.2m (4ft) and a spread of 60cm (24in). It has strongly aromatic, pointed, mid-green leaves with a purple-brown underside, which have toothed margins and distinct veins. Tiny, white to violet-pink flowers appear in spikes in summer, followed by pale brown nutlets. Shiso is found from the Himalayas to Japan, and is naturalized in parts of North America.

Persicaria

Vietnamese coriander POLYGONACEAE

It is always interesting how new varieties of herb arrive at my farm – often by very circuitous routes. This plant was taken by some Vietnamese refugees to Australia, where it was given to a nurseryman, who in turn sent it to a friend in the UK who specialized in plants of the *Polygonaceae* family. He then gave it to me, knowing that I would be interested. It is a popular culinary herb in Thailand, Vietnam, and Malaysia, where it is also used medicinally. In Australia, the essential oil, called "kesom oil", is undergoing research for its use as a natural food flavouring.

CAUTION Do not confuse this herb with the inedible *Persicaria bistorta*.

How to grow

Herb	Soil	Propagation
Persicaria	Sand	Cuttings/layering

PROPAGATION Take cuttings in spring until late summer. Also, because plant stems that come into contact with the soil take root easily, you can propagate Vietnamese coriander by simply cutting one of these stems with roots and potting it up in a mix of bark and vermiculite. In spring until late summer, you can propagate established plants by division (see page 53).

SITE This tropical plant will need protection when temperatures fall below 7°C (45°F) at night. In warm climates, plant in a rich fertile soil in partial shade. It grows well as a pot plant in a soil-based substrate. It is a vigorous plant, so repot twice a year to keep healthy.

MAINTENANCE Because this plant is invasive, dig up and remove any surplus roots to keep it under control. In cool climates, Vietnamese coriander may disappear if you are reorganizing the garden, so take cuttings as insurance.

HARVESTING Pick the leaves of Vietnamese coriander to use fresh as required throughout the plant's growing season.

How to use

The baby leaves have a pungent coriander flavour, while the mature leaves have a hot, pungent, peppery flavour that can dominate. Use as a fresh leaf condiment, at the end of cooking. Important in Asian cuisine, this herb is used in noodle soups (pho) prepared from vegetables, seafood, or meat, and also in stir-fried meat and vegetable dishes.

Medicinally, it is drunk as an infusion to ease indigestion. To get rid of dandruff, the leaves are pounded to extract the kesom oil, which is then massaged into the scalp prior to washing.

▼ *Persicaria odorata*
VIETNAMESE CORIANDER, RAU RAM
A tender evergreen perennial, with a height of 45cm (18in) and an indefinite spread. Attractive, small, creamy-white flowers appear in summer, though rarely in cultivated plants or cold climates. The leaves are highly aromatic when crushed and have a very strong flavour.

Leaf has a V-shaped marking near its base

Stem is composed of many joints linked together by slightly bent "knots", which is typical of the Polygonaceae family

Petroselinum

Parsley APIACEAE

This culinary delight and natural breath freshener is without doubt the best-known and most popular herb I grow. It has been cultivated for thousands of years. The ancient Greeks associated parsley with death and so avoided eating it. Instead, they combined it with rue (*Ruta graveolens*, see page 183), as an edging plant. The Romans used it to disguise strong odours but believed that the seed had to go to the devil and back seven times before it would germinate. If you follow the simple techniques outlined here, you will find that parsley is not as difficult to grow as past civilizations imagined.

CAUTION Do not take medicinally if pregnant.

How to grow

Herb	Soil	Propagation
Petroselinum	Loam	Seed

PROPAGATION The secret to growing parsley successfully is to keep the temperature consistent during germination, and to keep the substrate or soil moist. Sow seeds in early spring and place under protection at 18°C (65°F). Germination takes two to four weeks. Alternatively, sow seeds in late spring, into prepared open ground when air temperature does not fall below 7°C (45°F) at night. Water the site well prior to sowing. Germination takes two to four weeks.

SITE Plant in sun or partial shade, in deep fertile soil that has been fed the previous autumn with well-rotted manure. Ideally, the site should be sheltered from the midday sun.

MAINTENANCE To deter carrot root fly, plant with either chives or garlic as their scent will discourage the fly. Or use horticultural fleece or a cloche to create a protective barrier over the crop, or improvise with a cut-off plastic bottle. Young parsley plants are also prone to slug attack. Sprinkle bran around the plants to protect your crop. Do not allow plants to dry out in summer. Feed weekly with liquid comfrey feed (see page 39).

HARVESTING Pick fresh parsley leaves for culinary or medicinal use as required during the growing season.

How to use

Parsley leaves are a key ingredient in bouquet garni (see page 228), and are widely used in cooking. Medicinally, parsley leaves are strongly diuretic, and a hair rinse made from the seeds is effective for killing head lice. Infuse one teaspoon of crushed seeds for ten minutes, strain and use as a final rinse.

◄ *Petroselinum crispum*
PARSLEY
A hardy biennial, with a height of up to 40cm (16in) and a spread of 30cm (12in). Flat umbels of small creamy-white flowers appear in the summer of the second season. The bright green leaf has a fresh, mild flavour. The leaves have a higher vitamin C content than an orange.

▼ *Petroselinum crispum* 'French'
FRENCH PARSLEY, FLAT-LEAFED PARSLEY
A hardy biennial, with a height of up to 60cm (24in) and a spread of 30cm (12in). Small, creamy-white flowers grow in flat umbels in the summer of the second season. The mature leaves are flat, dark green, and divided.

Leaf is strongly flavoured, and can be used in sauces or soups and added to salads

Phytolacca

Pokeroot PHYTOLACCACEAE

This herb is classed as a weed in the US, but in Europe it is valued as both a structural and ornamental garden plant. It was introduced to American settlers by the Native Americans, who knew it as "pocan" or "coccum", from which the name "pokeroot" originated. Herbalists use it with respect. It is currently being researched for its ability to stem the debilitating tropical disease bilharzia (carried by water snails) because the root is known to destroy snails. Traditionally, the young shoots were considered a wonderful culinary delicacy, but if prepared incorrectly this plant is poisonous.

Berry is toxic to humans but will attract birds to the garden.

How to grow

Herb	Soil	Propagation
Phytolacca	Loam	Seed

PROPAGATION In autumn, separate the seed from the flesh (see page 70) and either sow at once or the following spring (store seed in the refrigerator or in a cold, dry place). Sow into a pot and cover with coarse horticultural sand and place in a cold frame. Germination takes three to four weeks. In winter, protect autumn-sown seedlings in the cold frame. In either spring or autumn, propagate established plants by division (see page 53), replanting into a well-prepared site.

SITE Plant in fertile, moist soil, in sun or partial shade.

MAINTENANCE To prevent the plant from producing berries and self-seeding, cut off the flowers just after flowering.

HARVESTING Only pick fresh young leaves for cooking as mature leaves are toxic. In autumn, pick ripe berries to use medicinally or as a natural dye. For medicinal use, dig up the root of two-year-old plants in autumn.

How to use

The young leaves can be eaten like spinach but must be boiled for 30 minutes in at least two changes of water before they are safe to eat. Eat with care. Medicinally, this herb should only be taken under professional supervision. It is used to treat chronic infections and as a poultice or ointment for fungal infections and scabies. A crimson textile dye can be made from ripe berries.

CAUTION As the mature plant leaves and berries are toxic to humans, choose your site very carefully and, even though the cooked young leaves taste like spinach, never grow this plant in the vegetable garden.

▶ *Phytolacca americana*
POKEROOT, POKE BERRY

A hardy herbaceous perennial, with a height and spread of up to 1.5m (5ft). In summer, long clusters of small, cup-shaped flowers with a hint of pink, white, and green appear. They are followed by poisonous black berries on bright pink stems. The mid-green leaves are lance-shaped and, in autumn, the leaf edges turn pink and orange.

Flower is cup-shaped with a green centre

Leaf is oval and lance-shaped. When mature, the crushed leaf releases an unpleasant odour

Portulaca

Purslane PORTULACACEAE

This herb has been grown for thousands of years as a vegetable and as a medicinal herb. It was popular in England in the reign of Elizabeth I, but it is no longer fashionable as a culinary herb in Britain, even though it is a popular salad herb in Europe and Asia where it is also cooked as a vegetable. Research has shown that purslane contains a rich source of omega-3 fatty acids, which help to maintain a healthy heart and strengthen the immune system. Personally, I love the taste of this herb, and often eat fresh purslane leaves straight from the garden.

CAUTION Do not take medicinally when pregnant.

How to grow

Herb	Soil	Propagation
Portulaca	Sand	Seed

PROPAGATION Sow seeds in early spring and place under protection at 20°C (68°F). Germination takes one to two weeks. Alternatively, sow into a prepared site in late summer, when the night temperature does not fall below 10°C (50°F).

SITE Purslane will grow anywhere in light soil in temperate climates, but in cool and cold climates, sow each year in a well-drained, fertile soil in a sunny site. Plant into soil that has been fed with well-rotted manure in the autumn prior to planting – there is no need to feed again. It will grow in containers in a soil-based substrate mixed with a small amount of sharp grit, for extra drainage.

MAINTENANCE Cover seedlings with horticultural fleece to deter pests like flea beetles and check regularly for slugs, who adore young plants. It does not require feeding, but water regularly to prevent the soil from drying out during summer months. However, avoid over-watering as this plant does not like to sit in water.

HARVESTING Pick leaves, stems, and flower buds to use fresh throughout the growing season.

How to use

The leaves, stems, and flower buds of purslane can be eaten raw in salads or cooked as a vegetable. It is a good source of vitamins A, B, and C, and calcium. In the Middle East, it is an ingredient of a traditional salad called fattoush. It is often pickled in vinegar. The World Health Organization has included *Portulaca oleracea* in its list of most-used medicinal plants; it is a natural diuretic, and is used to clear toxins from the body and lower fevers. It also helps to build up the immune system.

▼ **Portulaca oleracea**
PURSLANE, PIG WEED

A hardy annual, with a height of up to 45cm (18in) and a spread of 60cm (24in). Its small yellow flowers open in the summer sun and close in the shade. It has thick, fleshy, spoon-shaped, mid-green leaves, which taste like a succulent version of mange-tout.

Leaves are fleshy and the juice is soothing when applied to insect bites and burns. It also soothes eczema

Stem is edible. Cut into bite-sized chunks to add crunch to salads

Primula

Primrose PRIMULACEAE

This pretty yellow flower with its delicate scent marks the arrival of spring. It is the flower of my childhood as I used to pick tiny bunches of primroses from the garden at Easter, tie them up with wool, and give them to my mother as a gift. Surprisingly, primroses are classified as a herb because the flowers possess useful medicinal properties. They were traditionally used to treat gout, respiratory tract infections, insomnia, and anxiety. Primrose flowers and young leaves are also edible and have a good flavour, and make an attractive addition to salads.

CAUTION Do not take medicinally when pregnant.

How to grow

Herb	Soil	Propagation
Primula	Loam	Division

PROPAGATION It is important to use fresh seed. Sow in late summer and place in a cold frame. Germination takes two to three weeks. Winter the young plants in the cold frame, planting out into a prepared site the following spring. It may not flower in the first season. In autumn, propagate established plants by division (see page 53).

SITE Plant in moist soil in semi-shade. In the wild, primroses thrive on west-facing banks, close to deciduous hedgerows and trees. Bear this natural habitat in mind when choosing a site in the garden. Primroses grow well in containers or as houseplants, using a soil-based substrate. Outside, shelter the container from the midday sun; indoors, keep it away from radiators.

MAINTENANCE All primulas need to be divided in the autumn to keep the plant healthy. Division also protects pot-grown plants from attack by vine weevil.

HARVESTING In autumn, dig up the roots of three- to four-year-old plants to dry for medicinal use. In spring, pick flowers and leaves to use fresh in salads or to dry for medicinal use.

How to use

Add flowers and young leaves to salads or puddings. Medicinally, the flowers, leaves and roots are used to treat respiratory tract infections, insomnia, and anxiety. The flowers are used in infusion ointments and tinctures to treat minor wounds. Do not take medicinally when pregnant or on anticoagulant drugs or if allergic to aspirin.

▲ *Primula vulgaris*
PRIMROSE, FIRST ROSE

A hardy herbaceous perennial, with a height and spread of 15cm (6in). Sweetly-scented, pale yellow flowers with a deep yellow centre appear in spring. The stems are covered in fine hairs. The mid-green, oval-shaped leaves are textured. The primrose has become increasingly rare in the countryside. It is now illegal to dig up plants growing in the wild anywhere in the UK.

Prostanthera

Australian mint bush LAMIACEAE

This native Australian herb is quite stunning when in flower, and I defy anyone not to want to try growing it in their garden. Historically, it was used by the Aborigines to treat chest complaints. The leaves are now used to make an essential oil, which is beneficial for treating stress and tension; the leaves also have both antibacterial and antifungal properties. The fresh leaves also work as a decongestant: simply place them in a bowl, pour boiling water over them, place a towel over your head, and inhale the steam. Remedies made from this herb should only be used externally.

How to grow

Herb	Soil	Propagation
Prostanthera	Sand	Softwood cuttings

PROPAGATION I have not known *Prostanthera* to set seed in the UK. After many trials, I have found it is best to propagate from cuttings taken from the current year's growth in late autumn or winter. Once rooted, restrict watering to the minimum possible and keep plants in a frost-free environment over the winter. Pot up plants in the spring and then grow on in pots, protecting young plants from winter frost for a further two years, before planting out.

SITE This alpine plant favours very free-draining soil and a sunny site. It prefers a neutral to slightly acid soil. It grows well in containers using a peat-based substrate, mixed with extra grit for drainage.

MAINTENANCE Do not overfeed this herb, otherwise it will not flower – only feed container-grown plants once a month. Feed plants outside in the autumn with leafmould. It dislikes wet and damp conditions, so from autumn onwards cut down on watering, but do not allow the substrate to dry out. In early spring slowly reintroduce watering weekly, depending on the weather. Container-grown plants are prone to sudden die-back. If a branch changes colour from green to brown, cut it back to the main stem, and burn the diseased branches.

HARVESTING Pick leaves in summer to make infusions and oils.

How to use

An essential oil from the leaves of the Australian mint bush is used externally to alleviate tension and to release emotional exhaustion. Rub the essential oil into the temples to ease headaches. It can also be applied to the skin as a mosquito repellent. Mix a few drops with almond oil for massage.

▲ ***Prostanthera lasianthos***
VICTORIAN CHRISTMAS BUSH
A frost-hardy, evergreen, large shrub with a height of 1–6m (3–18ft) and a spread of 1m (3ft). It has attractive, white, bell-shaped flowers with tiny purple spots in late summer. Its leaves are mid-green, long, spear-shaped, and mint-scented.

▲ *Prostanthera ovalifolia*
AUSTRALIAN OVAL-LEAVED
MINT BUSH

A frost-hardy, evergreen shrub with a
height and spread of 1.2m (5ft). Profuse
sprays of small, bell-shaped, purple
flowers on short, leafy racemes appear
in the spring and early summer. Leaves
are dark green, oval, and mint-scented.
The plant can only withstand a
minimum temperature of 5°C (41°F).

Leaf has a shiny,
leather-like texture

Flower has distinct
purple spots on the throat

▶ *Prostanthera cuneata*
AUSTRALIAN MINT BUSH, ALPINE MINT BUSH

A hardy evergreen shrub, with a height of 90cm (3ft) and
a spread of 60cm (2ft). It has attractive, white, bell-shaped
flowers with purple spots running down the flower's
throat. Each flower occurs singly close to the end of a
branch; they appear from late spring until early summer.
The small, dark green leaves are round with a wavy edge.
When crushed, the leaves release a strong mint scent.

Rosmarinus

Rosemary LAMIACEAE

If I had to choose one culinary herb to take with me on to a desert island, it would be rosemary. It is one of the most versatile and useful herbs in the kitchen, in the home, and medicinally. It is associated with remembrance and for hundreds of years it was used to improve the memory. Currently it is being tested in the treatment of senile dementia. There are many lovely stories associated with it; one of my favourites is about the Virgin Mary, who is said to have thrown her blue cloak over a rosemary bush during her flight into Egypt, which turned its white flowers blue.

CAUTION The essential oil should only be taken externally. Excessive doses of rosemary leaf may cause convulsions.

How to grow

Herb	Soil	Propagation
Rosmarinus	Sand	Softwood cuttings

PROPAGATION Sow seeds in early spring under protection at 21°C (70°F). Germination takes one to two weeks. After germination, do not overwater; the seedlings are prone to "damping off" (see page 54). Alternatively, you can take cuttings of new growth in summer after flowering. Pot up when well rooted, and grow on under cold protection for one season before planting out. In spring or autumn, rosemary can also be propagated by layering (see page 51). This is relatively simple, as plants often have branches that hang down to the ground.

SITE Plant in a warm, sunny site in well-drained, acid-free soil. This herb grows well in containers. Use a loam-based substrate and protect plants from wet or cold in winter.

MAINTENANCE Rosemary can, in temperate climates, be grown successfully as a hedge. Cut back after flowering in late spring. This plant is prone to a die-back virus. Immediately cut the infected branch right off to the main stem, and burn, do not compost the branch. Act quickly or the whole bush will die.

HARVESTING Pick fresh leaves from this evergreen herb throughout the year.

How to use

Rosemary leaf has many culinary uses (see page 218). Medicinally, it alleviates hangovers and restores the memory, and aids recovery from long-term stress and chronic illness. The essential oil is a good insect repellent, and can be rubbed onto the temples to alleviate headaches.

▲ *Rosmarinus officinalis* 'Roseus'
PINK ROSEMARY

A hardy perennial evergreen, with a height and spread of 80cm (32in). Small pale pink flowers appear in early spring and last until early summer, with, occasionally, a second flush in early autumn. It has short, needle-shaped, bright green leaves, with lighter undersides. These are highly aromatic when crushed.

▲ *Rosmarinus officinalis* 'Green Ginger'
GINGER ROSEMARY

A hardy perennial evergreen, with a height and spread of 60cm (24in).
Small pale blue flowers with a dark centre appear in early spring and last
until early summer with, occasionally, a second flush in early autumn. It has
short, fine, needle-shaped, mid-green leaves, which are highly aromatic with
a hint of ginger when crushed.

▲ *Rosmarinus officinalis* **Prostratus Group**
'Capri'
ROSEMARY CAPRI

A hardy perennial evergreen, with a height of 15cm (6in)
and a spread of 1m (3ft) Small, light blue flowers appear in
early spring and last until early summer, with, occasionally,
a second flush in early autumn. The leaves are needle-
shaped, dark green, and highly aromatic when crushed.

▲ *Rosmarinus officinalis*
ROSEMARY

A hardy perennial evergreen, with a height and spread
of 1m (3ft). Small, pale blue flowers appear in early spring
and last until early summer, with, occasionally, a second
flush in early autumn. The short, needle-shaped, dark
green leaves are highly aromatic. This is an important
culinary and medicinal herb.

Rumex

Buckler leaf sorrel POLYGONACEAE

This sour but refreshing herb takes its name from the old French word "surelle" (meaning sour). The ancient Egyptians and Romans ate sorrel to counteract rich foods, and in 15th-century England, it was considered one of the finest vegetables. I am also of the opinion that it is a wonderful herb to use in hot and cold sauces and soups, while the young leaves can add a lemony or fresh apple flavour to summer salads. Medicinally, it is a useful first-aid herb to relieve the unpleasantness of sunburn – try bathing the affected skin with a cooled infusion made from the leaves.

How to grow

Herb	Soil	Propagation
Rumex	Loam	Seed

PROPAGATION Sow seeds in early spring and place under protection at 15°C (60°F). Germination takes five to ten days. Alternatively, in late spring, sow seeds thinly into prepared open ground, when the air temperature does not fall below 7°C (45°F) at night. Germination takes two to three weeks. Thin seedlings to 30cm (12in) apart. Divide established plants in autumn.

SITE Plant in a rich, fertile acid soil that has been fed with well-rotted manure in the autumn prior to planting. It prefers sites shaded from the midday sun. Buckler leaf sorrel grows well in large containers. Use an ericaceous substrate and keep out of the midday sun.

MAINTENANCE The leaf flavour is best when the plant grows in cool soil. To prevent the leaves from becoming bitter in the summer months when the soil is warm, use a leaf or bark mulch (see page 36) to reduce soil temperature. Dry soil also impairs the leaf flavour, so keep the plants well watered. In autumn, feed around established plants with well-rotted manure. Feed container plants regularly throughout the growing season with liquid comfrey (see page 39). If plants become invasive, add lime to the soil to discourage growth.

HARVESTING Pick leaves of buckler leaf sorrel to use fresh throughout the growing season.

How to use

Eating buckler leaf sorrel in salads is thought to cleanse the blood and improve the haemoglobin content. Avoid overeating the leaves while breastfeeding, and do not take if you have a tendency to develop kidney stones. The fresh leaves of the plant can also be used as a poultice to treat boils and acne.

▲ *Rumex scutatus*
BUCKLER LEAF SORREL, FRENCH SORREL
A hardy herbaceous perennial, with a height of up to 45cm (18in) and a spread of 60cm (24in). It has small, inconspicuous green flowers that turn brown as seeds ripen. Its squat, shield-shaped leaves taste similar to crunchy green apples, and can be eaten fresh or cooked. Crushed leaves are good for removing ink stains or rust marks from clothes and furniture.

Ruta

Rue RUTACEAE

Rue has had some bad publicity, because when the skin brushes against the leaves in certain weather conditions it can cause phytol-photodermatitis (skin burn). However, it is highly beneficial medicinally and is used in a number of homeopathic remedies. It also makes an attractive addition to the garden when planted in a carefully chosen site. To the Greeks and the Romans it was considered the herb of grace, and all brides traditionally carried a sprig in their bouquet. It was also used as an antidote to snake venom and poisonous toadstools, and was thought to help preserve eyesight.

CAUTION If brushed against, rue can cause phytol-photodermatitis (skin burn) – take care in the garden.

How to grow

Herb	Soil	Propagation
Ruta	Sand	Seed

PROPAGATION Sow seeds in early spring and place under protection at 18°C (65°F). Germination takes one to two weeks. After germination, take care not to overwater because the seedlings are prone to "damping off" (see page 54). Take cuttings from new growth in late spring or early summer. Do not overwater; cuttings are prone to rot in damp conditions.

SITE Plant in well-drained, poor soil. Choose a sunny position in the middle or back of a border where it will not be disturbed by passers-by.

MAINTENANCE Cut back to maintain the plant's shape. Do this when the plant is dry, and wear gloves and cover your arms and legs to avoid being burned. Rue is prone to whitefly, followed by a black sooty mould. Use horticultural soap, following manufacturer's instructions, as soon as the pest appears on the plant. This soap will also control mould.

HARVESTING Pick leaves of the rue plant to use fresh or to dry for medicinal use as required.

How to use

This herb can be used in the kitchen, but is very bitter. A tastier culinary species is Egyptian rue (*Ruta chalapensis*). Medicinally, rue was traditionally used for reducing blood pressure. It is still used in Mediterranean regions to stimulate the onset of menstruation. In homeopathy, rue is used to treat back pain, sciatica, strained muscles, tennis elbow, and eyestrain – consult a fully trained herbalist or a general practitioner for advice and guidance on using rue as a herbal remedy. In the home, dried rue, strategically placed, will deter ants, and will also deter flies if added to floral displays.

▲ ***Ruta graveolens***
RUE

A hardy evergreen shrub, with a height and spread of 60cm (24in). Small, yellow, waxy flowers with four or five petals in summer. The green-blue leaves are divided into small, rounded, oval lobes and have an unusual musky scent, which is hard to describe. To avoid skin burn, take care not to brush against the leaves when they are wet after rain or watering, or when they are in sunlight.

Salvia

Sage LAMIACEAE

This Mediterranean herb has been in use for thousands of years. I never cease to be amazed by its healing and culinary properties. It was used to preserve meat, as an antiseptic, and as a cure for snake bites. Modern research has shown that it arrests the ageing process, and it is being tested as a treatment for Alzheimer's. In addition, sage makes an attractive garden plant. The foliage presents a soft backdrop of grey-green, which sets off its pretty blue flowers in summer. Sage flowers are also very good for attracting butterflies and bees to the garden throughout the summer.

CAUTION Overuse of sage can have potentially toxic effects.

How to grow

Herb	Soil	Propagation
Salvia	Sand	Seed/cuttings

PROPAGATION Sow seeds in early spring, under cover at 18°C (65°F). Germination takes one to two weeks. Or sow seeds in late spring into open ground, when the air temperature at night remains above 7°C (45°F). Germination takes two to three weeks. Thin seedlings to 30cm (12in) apart. Protect young plants for the first winter. Take cuttings (see page 50) from perennial salvias in late spring to early summer. Propagate established woody plants by layering in either spring or autumn (see page 51).

SITE Plant in a warm, sunny site in well-drained, acid-free soil. Hardy sages grow well in containers. Use a soil-based substrate and protect from wet or cold in winter.

MAINTENANCE Prune lightly in spring to encourage young shoots for strong leaf flavour, and again after flowering in late summer. Clear away dead leaves from under the plant in spring to prevent mildew in damp weather. To sustain leaf flavour, replace the plant entirely every four to seven years.

HARVESTING Pick fresh leaves throughout the year. In spring (before the plant flowers), the leaves have a mild, warm flavour. After flowering, they have a stronger, tannin flavour.

▶ *Salvia officinalis* **Purpurascens Group**
PURPLE SAGE, RED SAGE
A hardy perennial evergreen, with a height and spread of 70cm (28in). Grow from cuttings. Mauve-blue flowers appear in summer. The aromatic oval leaves are a mix of purple-red-grey colours, and have a soft texture. They have a mild flavour and combine well with vegetable dishes.

How to use

Before cooking, quickly immerse sage leaves in hot water to bring the leaf oils to the surface and enhance the flavour. Sage is known to be antiseptic, astringent, carminative, antispasmodic, and a systemic antibiotic. It is used to treat sore throats (as a gargle), poor digestion, hormonal problems, and to stimulate the brain.

▶ *Salvia lavandulifolia*
NARROW-LEAVED SAGE,
SPANISH SAGE

A hardy perennial evergreen, with
a height and spread of 45cm (18in).
Grow from cuttings. Attractive blue
flowers appear in summer. The leaves
are small, narrow, oval, textured, and
highly aromatic with an excellent
strong culinary flavour. The leaves
make a stimulating infusion. This sage
is ideal for growing in containers.

Flower petals form
a protruding lower lip,
which is characteristic of
the Lamiaceae family

Stem is square in profile
– a distinguishing feature of
this plant family

Leaf is highly aromatic
and velvet-textured

▶ *Salvia officinalis*
COMMON SAGE, GARDEN SAGE,
SAWGE

A hardy perennial evergreen, with
a height and spread of 60cm (2ft). It
has highly aromatic, oval, green-grey
textured leaves and mauve-blue
flowers in summer. This is the
standard culinary and medicinal sage.
Types of sage with variegated leaves
do not have such a strong flavour and
are less potent medicinally.

Salvia

Aromatic sages LAMIACEAE

The genus *Salvia* includes over 900 species of aromatic annuals, biennials, and perennials as well as evergreen shrubs. They are available in a choice of different colours and leaf fragrances, which gives them a special appeal. I am still amazed when crushing the leaf of pineapple sage (*Salvia* 'Scarlet Pineapple') at how it smells so distinctly of fresh ripe pineapple. Many of the aromatic sages are winter hardy; those that are not are so beautiful that it is well worth creating space in a conservatory or glasshouse to keep them in favourable conditions over the winter months.

How to grow

Herb	Soil	Propagation
Salvia	Sand	Seed

PROPAGATION Sow seeds in early spring under cover at 18°C (65°F). Germination takes one to two weeks. Alternatively, sow seeds in late spring into prepared open ground, when the air temperature remains above 7°C (45°F) at night. Germination takes two to three weeks. Thin seedlings to 20cm (8in) apart. *S. clevelandii* can only be grown from seed in warm climates. In late spring to early summer, you can take cuttings (see page 50) from the perennial species.

SITE Plant in a warm, sunny site in well-drained, acid-free soil. Half-hardy salvias will only tolerate outdoor night temperatures above 10°C (50°F). They grow well in containers using a soil-based substrate. In winter, keep watering to a minimum as wet conditions kill them quicker than cold.

MAINTENANCE Prune lightly in spring to encourage young shoots for a strong leaf flavour, and again after flowering in late summer. In autumn, collect the seeds from *S. viridis* and then remove this annual, digging over the patch. Before the first frost, lift half-hardy perennial salvia species, cut back flowering shoots, and pot up using a soil-based substrate. Protect in a glasshouse over the winter.

HARVESTING Pick fresh leaves from evergreen sages as required. For drying, harvest leaves before flowering. Pick flowers as they open, to use fresh or to dry.

How to use

The cooking process destroys the flavour of aromatic sage leaves, so only add leaves to dishes right at the end. As leaf flavours are strong, only use a small amount to start with.

▲ *Salvia viridis* **var.** *comata* **syn.** *S. horminum*
PAINTED SAGE, RED-TOPPED SAGE
A hardy annual, with a height of 45cm (18in) and a spread of 20cm (8in). Small purple and white or pure white flowers, which are dominated by a series of colourful leaf bracts in shades of purple, pink, blue, and white, which look like flower petals except that they are often marked with green veins. These bracts last all summer. The true green leaves are downy, rough-textured, and aromatic.

◀ **Salvia microphylla var. microphylla**
BLACKCURRANT-SCENTED SAGE
A half-hardy perennial evergreen, with a height and spread of up to 1.2m (4ft). Lovely raspberry-coloured flowers with a characteristic lower lip appear in late summer until early autumn. Oval mid-green leaves smell of blackcurrants when rubbed.

▲ **Salvia clevelandii**
JIM SAGE, CLEVELAND SAGE
A half-hardy shrub, with a height of up to 1.5m (5ft) and a spread of 90cm (3ft), and oval, wrinkled green, slightly sticky aromatic leaves. Beautiful blue flowering spikes appear in summer. The smell of this sage is the aroma of the California chaparral. Grow in very well drained gravelly soil. Cut back one-third of growth in autumn, a further third in winter, leaving a third for the following season.

Flower is narrow and trumpet-shaped with a protruding lower lip

▲ **Salvia elegans** 'Scarlet pineapple'
PINEAPPLE SAGE
A half-hardy perennial, with a height of 90cm (3ft) and a spread of 60cm (2ft). Stunning, trumpet-shaped red flowers appear from midsummer until early autumn. The oval pointed green leaves have a slight red-brown tinge to the edges and a wonderful pineapple scent when crushed or rubbed between the fingertips.

Sambucus

Elder CAPRIFOLIACEAE

This herb was once regarded as one of the most magically powerful of plants, offering protection against evil spirits. It is a truly useful herb – all parts of the plant have been used to make everything from wine to a musical instrument. It has many culinary and medicinal uses, and research shows that it can aid recovery from colds and flu. The berries are a good source of vitamins A and C, but require cooking before eating to avoid stomach upsets. The leaves smell unpleasant when crushed and are poisonous, but they can be used in the organic garden to make a potent caterpillar or fly repellent.

Berry must be cooked before eating. It is a good source of vitamins A and C.

How to grow

Herb	Soil	Propagation
Sambucus	Loam	Softwood cuttings

PROPAGATION In late summer, separate the seed from the pulp and sow fresh. Cover the seed with a coarse horticultural sand. In cold climates, place the potted seed outside to stratify it. Alternatively, mix the seed with sand in a glass jar and place in the refrigerator for four weeks before sowing. Germination takes four to six months. For the first winter, keep young plants in pots in a cold frame before planting out the following spring. Take cuttings from new growth in late summer.

SITE Plant in a fertile, moist soil in sun or dappled shade. Elder can grow up to 1.2m (4ft) in one season.

MAINTENANCE To maintain a good shape, and to keep rapid growth in check, prune back hard every three years during the autumn. Elder is not suitable for growing in containers as it becomes too large.

HARVESTING Pick the flowers in the spring just before they open fully. Gather berries in early autumn.

How to use

Fresh flowers are used to make elderflower cordial (see page 220). Medicinally, the flowers are used to treat coughs, colds, allergies, and arthritis. They are also used in skin lotions. The berries are mildly laxative and should only be eaten cooked in sauces, syrups, and pies. Elder spray is effective against aphids, caterpillars, carrot root fly and root maggots. Simmer 500g (1lb) leaves in 1 litre of water for 30 minutes, strain then dilute with 1 more litre of water. (Do not use the same pan for food.) Apply by spraying. All parts of the plant contain coloured pigment and can be used as natural plant dyes.

▼ *Sambucus nigra*
ELDER, COMMON ELDER, BLACK ELDER
A hardy deciduous shrub, with a height of up to 6m (20ft). Attractive, flat heads of lightly scented, creamy-white, star-shaped flowers appear in the summer and are followed by masses of small, round, black fruits. Its large leaves are made up of green, saw-edged leaflets.

Flower grows in large, flat clusters and has a sweet perfume

Leaves are large and serrated

Sanguisorba
Salad burnet ROSACEAE

Traditionally, this pretty herb was infused in a drinking cup of wine or beer as a cure for gout and rheumatism. The soft green leaves are deceptive, because salad burnet is an evergreen plant that survives winter conditions. Even in hard winters, salad burnet leaves will only die back for a short time, before reappearing in early spring. This hardy nature makes salad burnet a useful herb to grow in the kitchen garden. It can be harvested throughout the winter when most other green salad leaves have died back, and can be used as a substitute for parsley when it is out of season.

How to grow

Herb	Soil	Propagation
Sanguisorba	Sand	Seed/division

PROPAGATION Sow fresh seeds in autumn. Cover with perlite or vermiculite (see page 44), and place in a cold frame. Germination takes two to three weeks. Winter young plants in a cold frame. Alternatively, sow seeds in early spring, cover with perlite or vermiculite, and place under protection at 18°C (65°F). Germination takes two to four weeks. Divide established plants in autumn, replanting into a prepared site in the garden.

SITE Plant in a well-drained soil in sun or partial shade. In traditional herb gardens, salad burnet was often mixed with thyme and planted next to paths to perfume the air. This is a good system to follow, since paths give the gardener easy access to the plant, especially in winter. Alternatively, grow salad burnet in containers close to the house using a soil-based substrate.

MAINTENANCE In hot weather, the leaves become bitter as the sun brings tannin to the surface. Trim the bush to keep it compact, and to inhibit flowering. Cutting back will also promote new, tender growth. For plants in containers, water regularly in the growing season, and feed once a week with comfrey liquid fertilizer (see page 39).

HARVESTING Pick the fresh young leaves as required.

How to use

Salad burnet, as its name suggests, tastes good in salads. The leaf has a nutty, dry cucumber flavour, which also works well in sauces for grilled or poached fish. The young leaves can also be used in winter dishes as a substitute for parsley when it is out of season. Medicinally, chewing young salad burnet leaves aids digestion.

Leaves are toothed. Young leaves taste of cool cucumber

Flower head is shaped like a thimble. The flower is like a tiny powder puff

▶ *Sanguisorba minor*
syn. *Poterium sanguisorba*
SALAD BURNET, PIMPERNEL
A hardy evergreen perennial, with a height of up to 60cm (24in) and a spread of 30cm (12in). Tiny magenta flowers appear in summer, with compact heads. The flowering stalks stand out above grey-green leaves. In summer, the mature leaves become very bitter to taste; cut back to encourage new leaf growth.

Santolina

Cotton lavender ASTERACEAE

This silver-leafed herb is both useful and attractive in the herb garden. Medicinally, it was used by Arabian people as an eye wash, but today it is used in the home as an insect and moth repellent. Some sources suggest that the aroma of cotton lavender can also help to keep cats off the garden, but after testing this out, I can honestly say that it does not work. It is useful in herb garden design as an edging plant or as a dividing hedge within a larger bed, and is a suitable candidate for a dry or Mediterranean-type gravel garden.

How to grow

Herb	Soil	Propagation
Santolina	Sand	Softwood cuttings

PROPAGATION Sow seed in autumn in standard seed compost mixed with horticultural sand and place in a cold frame. Germination takes four to six months. Grow on in a cold frame for two years before planting out. Take stem cuttings from new, non-flowering growth in late summer. Winter young cotton lavender plants in a cold frame before planting out the following spring. In late summer, mature woody stems can be propagated by layering (see page 51). Cut off the flowers before you start the process.

SITE Plant in a well-drained soil in a sunny position. Avoid nutrient-rich soils for best results. Plant individual plants 45cm (24in) apart and hedge plants at 38cm (15in) intervals. Cotton lavenders grow well in containers. Use soil-based substrate. Feed once a week only during the growing season with a liquid seaweed fertilizer.

MAINTENANCE Cotton lavender plants can be clipped to shape in spring after flowering. In spring, cut out dead wood from established plants. In late summer, cut off the flowers to prevent the plant from becoming woody. In cold climates, do not cut back cotton lavenders in autumn because frost and damp will take hold and destroy the plant.

HARVESTING Pick cotton lavender leaves for drying from spring until just before flowering in summer. In late summer, harvest small bunches of flowering stems for drying.

How to use

Cotton lavender can be applied to surface wounds to encourage healing. It can also, when crushed, be rubbed on insect bites to ease the pain. The dried leaves are excellent for deterring moths.

▼ *Santolina chamaecyparissus*
COTTON LAVENDER, LAVENDER COTTON
A hardy evergreen shrub, with a height of 75cm (30in) and a spread of 1m (3ft). Yellow, button-shaped flowers appear from midsummer to early autumn. The aromatic silver leaves are divided and remind me of ocean coral.

Flower looks similar to the centre of a daisy that has lost its petals

Stem is covered in cotton-like hairs

Leaf is wispy and thin on the flowering stem, thicker and paler silver on the main body of the shrub

Saponaria

Soapwort CARYOPHYLLACEAE

As its name suggests, a natural lather can be made from the leaves, stem, and roots of this herb. When boiled in water, the plant releases saponins and produces a slippery substance that has the power to lift grease and dirt. Interestingly, soapwort was once used in the wool industry for cleaning new wool, and in the UK, colonies of soapwort plants can still be found growing close to old mills. It is still used by museum conservators to lift surface dirt gently from fragile antique textiles and paintings, and can be found growing wild on poor soils throughout Europe, Asia, and North America.

How to grow

Herb	Soil	Propagation
Saponaria	Loam	Softwood cuttings

PROPAGATION In my experience, it is far easier to grow soapwort from stem cuttings or by division than from seed, as it takes a long time for the seed to germinate and success is not always guaranteed. Take cuttings at the stem joint in late spring to early summer. Divide established plants in autumn after cutting back.

SITE This plant will tolerate any soil in a sunny position but if the soil is too rich in nutrients, soapwort growth will be too rapid and difficult to control. Avoid planting soapwort near fish ponds because it has creeping rhizomes which excrete a poison in wet soil that is harmful to fish. Dwarf species like *Saponaria ocymoides* are better suited to containers because of their size.

MAINTENANCE Cut back after flowering to tidy up the garden and prevent the plant from self-seeding. Cutting back will also encourage new growth and, in mild winters, a second flowering. In autumn, dig up any invasive roots.

HARVESTING Pick fresh leaves as required throughout the growing season.

How to use

Soapwort is used as a treatment for dry itchy skin conditions and as an anti-inflammatory. Mildly poisonous, it should only be used medicinally when prescribed by a qualified herbalist. In the home, it is used in both skin- and haircare products, particularly for those with sensitive skins. Simmer a handful of leaves for seven minutes, strain, and add to a bath to treat dry, itchy skin. Soapwort also makes a good cleaning product for delicate silk garments and upholstery.

Flower has five petals and grows in clusters

▶ ***Saponaria officinalis***
SOAPWORT, BOUNCING BET
A hardy herbaceous perennial, with a height of up to 1m (3ft) and a spread of 60cm (2ft) or more. Compact clusters of small, pretty pink or white, lightly-scented flowers are borne in summer until early autumn. The smooth leaves taper to a point.

Stem is notched

Leaf is soft and smooth to the touch

Satureja

Savory LAMIACEAE

The Ancient Egyptians used savory in love potions, whereas the Romans used it to flavour sauces and vinegars, and I also use it liberally in cooking to add a spicy taste to meat and fish dishes. The leaves, when crushed, are an excellent remedy for wasp and bee stings. Good specimens for the herb garden include: pink savory (*Satureja thymbra*) from the Middle East, which has pale purple flowers and a spicy flavour; lemon savory (*S. biflora*) from Africa, which has a spicy lemon taste; and winter savory (*S. montana*), which has a peppery taste and is a successful low edging plant.

CAUTION Do not take savory medicinally during pregnancy.

How to grow

Herb	Soil	Propagation
Satureja	Sand	Seed

PROPAGATION Sow seeds in early spring and place under protection at 20°C (68°F). Germination takes one to two weeks. Once germinated do not overwater because seedlings are prone to "damping off". Take cuttings of perennial savorys in summer from new stem growth. Once rooted, pot up and grow on in a cold frame. Plant out the following spring into a well-prepared site.

SITE Plant in a sunny position in well-drained, poor soil that has not been fed the previous autumn. Perennial savorys grow well in containers. Use a soil-based substrate, mixed with equal parts of coarse horticultural grit. Place the container in a sunny, dry, sheltered position.

MAINTENANCE Cut back perennial savorys after flowering. Keep picking summer savory from the top to maintain leaf supply for as long as possible. Do not feed garden plants with compost or liquid fertilizer. For container plants, feed once a week with a liquid seaweed fertilizer during the growing season.

HARVESTING Pick leaves either side of flowering to use fresh, and before flowering for drying. Pick the flowers in the summer for use fresh or for preserving in butter (see page 225).

How to use

Fresh savory leaves have a sweet aroma and pungent flavour, and can be used as a substitute for black pepper in cooking, though the flavour becomes less pungent when the herb is boiled for any length of time. Medicinally, species of savory have properties similar to thyme, rosemary, and oregano; they are antibacterial, antifungal, and antiseptic.

▲ ***Satureja hortensis***
SUMMER SAVORY, BEAN HERB
A half-hardy annual, with a height of 30cm (12in) and a spread of 20cm (8in). Small white flowers tinged with mauve appear in summer. The aromatic leaves are oval and pointed. A favourite in Europe and America.

▲ ***Satureja douglasii***
YERBA BUENA
A half-hardy evergreen perennial, with a height of 10cm (4in) and an indefinite spread, since it trails and creeps. This herb has very strong-flavoured leaves and can be used sparingly to make a herbal tea to reduce fevers.

Stem becomes woody with age

Leaf is narrow, oval and pointed

Flower is tubular, and can vary in colour from white to very pale pink or purple on the same plant

▶ ***Satureja montana***
WINTER SAVORY
A hardy semi-evergreen perennial, with a height of 30cm (12in) and a spread of 20cm (8in). Flowers are small and white, with a hint of pink-mauve; leaves are dark green, linear, and very aromatic. This herb is more pungent than summer savory, with a peppery undertone. It is ideal for culinary use.

Scutellaria

Skullcap virginia LAMIACEAE

Its common name "skullcap" is said to have originated from the shape of the flower, which was thought to resemble the helmets worn by Roman soldiers. It was used by Native Americans to treat women's menstrual problems, and in the 18th century, it was thought to be a cure for rabies, although this has been disproved. Personally, I grow this herb because it is very attractive in the garden. The botanical name comes from "scutella", meaning "small shield", which resembles the seed. The seeds are not only a good source of bird food, they also make a delightful sound in a light breeze.

> **CAUTION** This is not a culinary herb. It should only be dispensed by a trained herbalist.

How to grow

Herb	Soil	Propagation
Scutellaria	Sand	Seed

PROPAGATION Sow fresh seeds in autumn and place in a cold frame. Germination takes three to four weeks. Winter young plants in a cold frame. If there is no germination during this time, place the seed tray outside so the seeds can be stratified by the cold weather. In warm climates, place the seeds in the refrigerator for four weeks to stratify them. Germination can take a further five to seven months. It can flower in the first season from seed. Take root cuttings from the rhizomes in spring (see page 52), or stem cuttings in summer from non-flowering shoots. Divide established plants in autumn.

SITE Plant in poor, moisture-retentive soil in sun or semi-shade. Skullcap virginia will adapt to most soil types with the exception of acid and waterlogged soils. This plant is not suited for container growing because the rhizomes tend to rot if they are unable to spread out.

MAINTENANCE After collecting seeds, cut back to promote new growth. In autumn, dig up any plants that have started to spread. Divide established plants every third year to maintain health. Do not feed, as nutrient-rich soil will cause soft growth and excessive root spread.

HARVESTING Pick the leaves and flowers of skullcap virginia for drying in summer, for medicinal use only.

How to use

This is an important medicinal herb. It is often added to herbal nerve formulas in combination with valerian (see page 212) and other herbs. The whole plant is an effective soothing, antispasmodic tonic. It is also used to treat insomnia, stress, muscular tension, and for reducing high blood pressure.

Stem is square, and very rigid to the touch

Flowers grow on one side of the stem only

▶ *Scutellaria lateriflora*
SKULLCAP VIRGINIA
A hardy herbaceous perennial, with a height of 60cm (24in) and a spread of 30cm (12in) or more. The small, bi-coloured flowers are dark blue-purple on the upper lip and pale mauve on the lower. They blossom in summer and the flowers are followed by small, pale beige round seeds. The oval, mid-green leaves are crinkled.

Leaf has a mild scent when crushed. The texture on the leaf surface is raised and rough to the touch

Sempervivum

Houseleek CRASSULACEAE

This herb is an old family favourite. When my son was growing up, I encouraged him to keep houseleek leaves in his pockets to rub on nettle stings and cuts, as they have soothing and gently healing properties similar to *Aloe vera* (however, the two plants are not related). Historically, houseleeks were grown on the roofs of houses as it was believed that they would protect a thatched roof from fire and the occupants from witchcraft. The American settlers considered this such a useful herb that they took a supply with them to treat earache and ease toothache.

How to grow

Herb	Soil	Propagation
Sempervivum	Sand	Division

PROPAGATION Sow fresh seeds in spring or summer. Because these are very fine, mix with the finest sand or flour. Water from the bottom or with a fine spray, and cover the container with glass to keep the seed warm. Place in a frost-free environment like a cold frame. Germination takes one to six months. Once this occurs, remove the glass and cover the growing medium with fine sand. All houseleeks produce offsets that cluster around the base of the parent plant; in spring, each offset starts its own root system. Either pot up each individually, or plant each one directly into the garden.

SITE Houseleeks grow happily in very little soil as they have very short roots. Plant either in wall crevices, rock gardens, or in between paving stones. For growing in containers, use a soil-based substrate mixed equally with sharp horticultural grit to improve soil drainage.

MAINTENANCE In autumn, if the plant has become invasive, remove offsets and pot up to produce a new stock of young plants as insurance against a bad winter. Pests like vine weevils attack pot-grown houseleeks, so check the roots each autumn for infestation and repot if necessary.

HARVESTING Pick houseleek leaves to use fresh, for medicinal purposes, throughout the growing season.

How to use

Apply the sap-like gel directly to nettle stings and minor burns. Make an infusion from the leaves to treat bronchitis. To remove a corn, cut a leaf in half, bind the fleshy side to the corn for a few hours, then soak the foot in water. Try to gently scrape off the corn. Repeat as necessary.

Leaves are succulent, oval, and grey-green with darker tips

▲ *Sempervivum tectorum*
HOUSELEEK
A hardy evergreen succulent, with a height of 15cm (6in) when in flower, and a spread of 20cm (8in). Pink star-shaped flowers appear in summer, though it can take several years to flower. When broken in half, the succulent leaves release a sappy gel, which can be applied to minor burns, insect bites, or nettle stings. Plant in a container or into a niche in a garden wall. Each offshoot around the base of the mother plant has its own root system.

Solidago
Golden rod ASTERACEAE

This late-summer-flowering herb signals the change in season, hence its common names "cast the spear" and "farewell summer". It was much in demand in the 16th and 17th centuries as a remedy for loose teeth, for kidney stones, and as a wound-healer. Originally imported from the Middle East, it was later cultivated in the UK for its medicinal properties, and became naturalized in some regions; demand for the plant plummeted. A good companion plant, flowers are attractive to beneficial insects, especially lacewings, which control the whitefly and aphid populations in the garden.

How to grow

Herb	Soil	Propagation
Solidago	Sand	Seed

PROPAGATION The seeds need stratification to germinate (see page 45). Sow fresh in autumn and place the container outside to expose it to winter weather. In warm climates place seed in the refrigerator for four weeks, then sow, and place outside. Germination takes four to six months. Take root cuttings in spring. Divide established plants in autumn, replanting into a well-prepared site.

SITE Golden rod will grow in most soils, with the exception of rich soils. It favours a moisture-retentive soil in a sunny position. It can be grown in containers, but use a soil-based substrate mixed in equal parts with fine bark that is low in nutrients.

MAINTENANCE Lift the roots and replant every other year to prevent matting and invasive spreading. Repot container-grown plants every autumn to prevent the roots from rotting. As well as attracting beneficial insects, it also attracts the tortrix moth, whose caterpillars roll themselves up in the leaves. The only organic way to get rid of this pest is to use an elder leaf wash (see page 188) or hand-pick them off.

HARVESTING Pick leaves and flowering tops just before the flowers are fully opened to dry for medicinal use.

How to use

It is used medicinally to treat urinary infections, skin diseases, kidney stones, wounds, insect bites, and external skin ulcers. The leaves and flowers are also used to make a yellow plant dye for textiles.

▼ *Solidago virgaurea*
GOLDEN ROD, AARON'S ROD
A hardy herbaceous perennial, with a height of 80cm (32in) and a spread of 60cm (2ft). Spikes of golden-yellow flowers with clusters of golden stamens appear in midsummer until the first frosts. The leaves at the base of the plant are bright green, pointed, and lance-shaped, while the leaves on the flower stem are smaller and oval.

Flower is a small, golden daisy shape, typical of the Asteraceae family

Stem is smooth, with no hairs

Leaves smell similar to wild carrot when crushed

Stachys

Betony LAMIACEAE

This attractive flower is a worthwhile addition to any herb garden. Even though it is a wild plant, betony has adapted to the cultivated garden, giving a colourful display in the summer and attracting butterflies and bees. On the occasions when I have exhibited betony at flower shows, it has always drawn the crowds. Medicinally, it was claimed that it could cure over 47 different ailments, including "elf sickness" in the 10th century, and was used as a tobacco and snuff in the 18th century. It is taken for nervous disorders, and should only be used under medical supervision.

CAUTION The root of betony is toxic, and should only be used under medical supervision.

How to grow

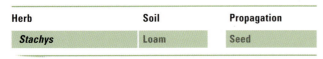

Herb	Soil	Propagation
Stachys	Loam	Seed

PROPAGATION Sow seeds when fresh in early autumn. Place in a cold frame. Germination takes two to four weeks but can be longer. Winter young plants in the cold frame before planting out the following spring, or sow directly into their planting position in autumn. Cover lightly with leafmould (see page 37). Mark the area where you have sown. Germination occurs the next spring. Divide established plants in spring or autumn. Replant 30cm (12in) apart.

SITE This herb tolerates most situations. For preference, plant betony in a fertile soil in sun or partial shade. Another favoured site for the plant is at the edge of deciduous woodland. I have also grown it to great effect in a container mixed with other wild flowers, using a loam-based substrate.

MAINTENANCE This plant needs little maintenance. In early autumn, save the seed before cutting back the flowers. In dry soils, mulch with a layer of leafmould (see page 37).

HARVESTING Collect the leaves for drying in late spring before the plant flowers. Pick flowers for drying just as they open. Gather leaves before and after flowering to use fresh.

How to use

Betony is used in Europe and the UK to treat diarrhoea, cystitis, and liver and gall bladder infections. A weak infusion of the leaves makes a refreshing cup of tea, which also treats headaches. A hair rinse made from an infusion of the leaves, to be used after washing the hair, will darken grey hair. All parts of the plant can be used as a yellow plant dye for textiles.

▲ *Stachys officinalis*
BETONY

A hardy herbaceous perennial, with a height of 60cm (24in) and a spread of 25cm (10in). Dense spikes of pink or purple flowers appear throughout summer. The dark green, oval leaves have scalloped edges. The leaf surface is perforated with glands that contain a bitter, aromatic oil.

Stevia

Stevia ASTERACEAE

Indigenous to South America, this truly amazing herb has been used for hundreds of years. Studies show that ¼ tsp of dried chopped leaf is equivalent in sweetness to 225g (8oz) of sugar! In the USA and Europe, stevia has been banned as a food or food ingredient, but is sold as a dietary supplement rather than as a sweetener in the USA. The Japanese have banned all artificial sweeteners with the exception of stevia, which they have used for years with no adverse effects. Personally, I will stop using this herb when it is proven to be unsafe but, to date, no such proof has been presented.

CAUTION Stevia is banned for sale as a food ingredient in the USA and EU due to inadequate evidence demonstrating its safety, but can be sold as a dietary supplement in the USA.

How to grow

Herb	Soil	Propagation
Stevia	Loam	Softwood cuttings

PROPAGATION Sow fresh seeds in spring under protection at 18°C (65°F); germination is erratic. Cuttings are by far the most reliable method of propagation for this herb. Take semi-ripe cuttings from non-flowering shoots in early summer.

SITE Outside the tropics, this herb can only be grown as an annual in the garden, where it should be planted in full sun in a light fertile soil that does not dry out in summer. In cool climates, this herb will grow happily in a container using a loam-based potting compost mixed in equal parts with composted fine bark. In autumn, bring the container in to a frost-free environment, cut the growth back to 10cm (4in), and reduce the watering to a minimum, but do not allow the plant to dry out. Reintroduce watering and pot up in the spring. Place the container outside once all threat of frost has passed.

MAINTENANCE In the tropics, this herb rarely needs maintenance. In cold and cool climates it is prone to mildew so water carefully, keeping watering to a minimum. Remove any infected leaves and burn – do not compost them.

HARVESTING Pick the leaves to use fresh as required from spring until late summer. The best flavour is from the young leaves. Pick the leaves for harvesting in early summer.

How to use

Stevia can be used as a sugar substitute in many dishes, but is very strong and sweet and should be used in moderation. It can withstand high temperatures but is not suitable for baking, because it lacks sugar's abilities to add texture, caramelize, or feed the fermentation of yeast.

▲ *Stevia rebaudiana*
STEVIA, SWEET LEAF, YERBA DULCE, HONEYLEAF, CAA'-EHE

A subtropical, evergreen perennial, grown as an annual in cold climates, with a height and spread of 45cm (18in). It bears clusters of small, white flowers in late summer and early autumn, and has mid-green, oval leaves with serrated edges.

Symphytum

Comfrey BORAGINACEAE

This invasive plant may be considered a weed by many, but the nutrients it contains are useful to the organic gardener. The leaves are naturally high in protein, potash, and potassium and make a wonderful mulch or liquid feed (see page 39) without having to resort to chemically manufactured products. Medicinally, its potential for healing external wounds and broken bones is unchallenged, hence its common names of "knitbone" and "boneset". Currently one of its key constituents, allantoin, which stimulates the growth of new cells, is undergoing research.

Root is fibrous with a blackish exterior. Internally it is fleshy, juicy, and white.

How to grow

Herb	Soil	Propagation
Symphytum	Loam	Root cuttings

CAUTION Do not take comfrey internally unless prescribed. Skin contact can also cause dermatitis.

PROPAGATION Sow seeds in autumn and place in a cold frame. Germination takes three to twenty weeks, but is very erratic. The easiest method is root cuttings taken in spring (see page 52). Established plants can be divided in autumn. Any piece of root that is left in the soil will root and create another plant.

SITE Comfrey prefers a moist soil in sun or partial shade. It is ideal for clay, though it will tolerate all but arid conditions. Choose the position in the garden with care; *Symphytum officinale* will self-seed erratically and, because of its very long tap root, it is nearly impossible to move once established. Comfrey can be grown in large containers. A dustbin with drainage holes is ideal. Use garden loam with ten per cent added coarse horticultural grit.

MAINTENANCE Comfrey sometimes suffers from rust (see page 148) and powdery mildew. With both diseases, cut the plant down to the ground and burn the contaminated leaves. When growing comfrey for leaf harvest, do not allow the plant to dry out in summer.

HARVESTING Cut the leaves before flowering from early summer until autumn to provide foliage for the liquid fertilizer (see page 39). Each plant is able to provide four leaf harvests per season. In autumn, dig up second-year growth roots for drying.

How to use

Medicinally, comfrey is used externally for cuts, as a compress, and to treat varicose veins, and was traditionally thought to heal broken bones. It can also be used for curing septic sores on animals, and as an animal feed. A golden yellow textile dye can be made from the leaves.

▲ ***Symphytum* x *uplandicum***
RUSSIAN COMFREY

A hardy herbaceous perennial, with a height and spread of 1m (3ft). It produces clusters of pink, purple, and blue flowers in summer and it has green, lance-shaped leaves covered with fine, slightly prickly hairs. A cross between *Symphytum officinale* and *S. asperum*, it does not self-seed but has the same nutrient-rich foliage properties as *S. officinale*.

Leaf is covered in bristly hairs. It decreases in size the higher it grows up the stem

Flower grows in one-sided clusters along a curving hairy stem

▲ *Symphytum officinale*

COMFREY, KNITBONE

A hardy herbaceous perennial, with a height and spread of 1m (3ft). Clusters of white, purple, or pink flowers appear in summer. The leaves are green, lance-shaped, and hairy. Young fresh leaves and shoots can be eaten like spinach, and are a rich source of vitamin B12.

Tagetes

Mexican marigolds ASTERACEAE

The following marigolds are from the *Tagetes* genus, rather than *Calendula* (see page 97), with which they are sometimes confused. *Tagetes* contains 56 species, including the plants known as Mexican, French, or African marigolds, which originated in Central and South America and were used as medicinal and ritual plants. I have chosen two Mexican marigolds that I find invaluable in an organic herb garden: the wild Mexican marigold (*T. patula*) for pest control, and *T. lucida*, whose fresh leaves have a flavour similar to French tarragon (see page 93), hence its common name, winter tarragon.

How to grow

Herb	Soil	Propagation
Tagetes	Sand	Seed/cuttings

PROPAGATION Sow in early spring under cover at 20°C (68°F). Germination takes fourteen to twenty-one days. Alternatively, sow in late spring into prepared open ground when the air temperature does not fall below 10°C (50°F) at night. Germination takes two to four weeks. Take cuttings of perennial varieties from non-flowering stems in summer. Winter young plants in a frost-free environment.

SITE Plant in a well-drained fertile soil in a sunny position. Mexican marigold is ideal for interplanting in the vegetable garden, repelling soil nematodes and also slugs and whitefly. *T. lucida* is a tender perennial that grows well in pots. Winter in a frost-free environment and use a soil-based substrate mixed with one-third coarse horticultural grit.

MAINTENANCE In early summer, pinch out or cut back the growing tips of young marigold plants to promote bushy growth. Deadhead flowers to prolong flowering.

HARVESTING Pick flowers for drying in summer. Harvest leaves in summer to use fresh or to dry. If protected from frost, the leaves of *T. lucida* can be picked up until midwinter.

How to use

Medicinally, *T. patula* is a diuretic and improves digestion. Externally, it relieves sore eyes and rheumatism. The yellow pigment in the fresh or dried flowers has been used to dye textiles. *T. lucida* grows in winter in cool climates under protection and so is a good substitute for *Artemisia dracunculus*. Leaves can also be burnt as an insect repellent. Medicinally, *T. lucida* treats diarrhoea, indigestion, and feverishness. It is used externally to remove ticks.

▲ *Tagetes lucida*
WINTER TARRAGON, SWEET MACE
A tender herbaceous perennial, with a height of 80cm (32in) in warm climates only, and a spread of 45cm (18in). Yellow flowers appear in late summer. The mid-green leaves are narrow and toothed, and have a strong aniseed scent and flavour similar to tarragon. In cool climates, this herb dies back in early spring, reappearing in early summer.

Flower is typical of the Asteraceae family. The daisy-like petals can vary in colour from golden yellow through to brown

Leaf shape is typical of *Tagetes* species

Leaf is highly aromatic with a pungent scent

◀ *Tagetes patula*
WILD MEXICAN MARIGOLD,
FRENCH MARIGOLD

A half hardy annual, with a height of 1.2m (4ft) and a spread of 45cm (18in). Clusters of single yellow flowers appear in midsummer, until the first autumn frosts. The mid-green leaves are deeply divided and lightly toothed. This species is a good companion plant – it deters nematodes in the soil and repels whitefly from ripening tomatoes.

Tanacetum

Tanacetum ASTERACEAE

Tanacetums are members of the daisy (Asteraceae) family, and thrive in the herb garden or herbaceous border. Silver leaves distinguish the silver tanacetums. Like many ancient herbs, they grow very successfully and become invasive, which is perhaps one reason why they have managed to survive for so long. Pyrethrum, a well-known insecticide, is made from the dried flowers of *Tanacetum cinerariifolium*. It is illegal in the European Union to use pyrethrum in spray form because insecticide sprays can also kill beneficial insects. However, it is non-toxic to mammals.

CAUTION Wear gloves when handling; the flower can cause a minor skin rash.

How to grow

Herb	Soil	Propagation
Tanacetum	Sand	Seed

PROPAGATION Sow seeds in spring and place in a cold frame. Do not cover. Germination takes two to four weeks. Plant out silver tanacetums when the seedlings are large enough to handle. Divide established plants in autumn or spring, replanting into a prepared site. Plant *Tanacetum cinerariifolium* seedlings 30cm (12in) apart and *T. balsamita* at 60cm (24in) intervals.

SITE Plant in well-drained, fertile soil in a sunny position. Both species are drought-tolerant and will adapt to most soils and conditions. However, they are unlikely to flower if planted in shade. Both grow well in containers. Use a soil-based substrate and feed once a month throughout the growing season with a liquid seaweed feed.

MAINTENANCE Deadhead regularly to promote new flower growth. Divide established plants every few years to keep them healthy and to prevent them from becoming too invasive. Do not feed with nutrients as this will encourage soft growth and disease.

HARVESTING Pick the leaves of *T. balsamita* before flowering to use fresh or to dry. Pick the flowerheads of *T. cinerariifolium* just as they open and dry on a muslin frame (see page 73). Store dried flowers in a dark glass jar out of direct sunlight.

How to use

Wearing gloves, sprinkle the powdered flowers of *T. cinerariifolium* by the back door to repel ants. *T. balsamita* was used for brewing ale.

◄ *Tanacetum balsamita*
ALECOST, COSTMARY

A hardy herbaceous perennial with a height of 1m (3ft) when in flower and a spread of 45cm (18in). Clusters of small, white, yellow-eyed daisy flowers are produced from mid to late summer. The soft, aromatic, silver-green leaves can relieve the pain of a bee sting or horse-fly bite.

▲ *Tanacetum parthenium*
FEVERFEW

A hardy herbaceous perennial, with a height of up to 1.2m (48in) and a spread of 45cm (18in). It has clusters of small, white, yellow-eyed daisy flowers, which appear from early summer until the first frosts. The leaf is mid-green, lobed, and divided with lightly serrated edges.

◄ *Tanacetum vulgare*
TANSY

A hardy herbaceous perennial, with a height of up to 1.2m (48in) and an indefinite spread. Clusters of yellow, button-like flowers appear from summer until late autumn. The dark green, feathery leaves have toothed edges. Dried bunches of aromatic tansy make effective fly repellents.

► *Tanacetum cinerariifolium*
PYRETHRUM, DALMATIAN DAISY

A hardy herbaceous perennial, with a height of 35cm (15in) when in flower, and a spread of 20cm (8in). White, yellow-eyed, single daisy flowers grow throughout the summer months. The grey-green leaves are finely divided. A powerful insecticide, also known as pyrethrum, is made from the powdered, dried flowers.

Flower is a classic white daisy with a yellow eye. It looks wonderful planted in big drifts

Stem is covered in a soft silvery white down

Leaf is grey-green on the upper surface. The underside is covered in a silvery white down

Teucrium

Germanders & wood sage LAMIACEAE

There has been a lot of confusion over species of *Teucrium*, and when purchasing plants for medicinal use, it is important to establish their correct identification. All the species mentioned here are native to northern Europe and have become naturalized in the UK. *T. chamaedrys* was traditionally used to treat digestive disorders, and *T. scorodonia* was used on the Channel Islands as an alternative to hops as the bitter element in beer-making. *T. scorodonia* was once called "hind heal", from the belief that the hind (female deer) will eat it when sick or wounded.

CAUTION Do not take internally unless under professional guidance.

How to grow

Herb	Soil	Propagation
Teucrium	Loam	Softwood cuttings

PROPAGATION Sow seeds in autumn, using a standard loam-based seed substrate mixed in equal parts with coarse horticultural sand. Place outside for the winter. The seeds need stratification to germinate (see page 45). In warm climates, place in a refrigerator for one month prior to sowing. Germination takes four to six months. When large enough to handle, plant out into a prepared site 20cm (8in) apart. A simpler method of propagation is to take cuttings in summer from new growth. Winter young plants in a cold frame, planting out in the following spring. Divide established plants in autumn, replanting into a prepared site.

SITE Plant in well-drained, slightly alkaline soil in a sunny position. This species tolerates temperatures as low as -29°C (-20°F) but it dislikes wet conditions. *T. x lucidrys* makes an ideal hedge. Plant 15cm (6in) apart. Germanders make good container plants, especially *T. x lucidrys*.

MAINTENANCE When grown as a hedge, clip germanders in spring and autumn to maintain their shape. If you do not cut back in the spring, it will produce pink flowers in late summer. After this, cut back fairly hard to encourage lower growth.

HARVESTING Cut leaves from *T. chamaedrys* and *T. x lucidrys* when the plant is in flower for drying, or for use in medicinal infusions. Pick leaves of *T. scorodonia* either side of flowering to use fresh or to dry. For culinary uses, pick in spring before the leaves become tough.

How to use

Rarely used in medicine, there is interest in it as an aid to weight loss. It is still used as a flavouring in spirits.

◄ *Teucrium chamaedrys*
WALL GERMANDER
A hardy herbaceous perennial with a height and spread of 25cm (10in). Pink flowers appear in midsummer until early autumn. The aromatic, matt green leaves are oval, pointed, toothed, and lobed.

▶ *Teucrium* x *lucidrys*
HEDGE GERMANDER
A hardy evergreen shrub, with a height of 45cm (18in) and a spread of 20cm (8in). Pink flowers bloom from midsummer to early autumn; the leaves are aromatic. This herb makes an ideal edging plant.

Leaf has a pleasantly spicy smell when rubbed

Stem is square in section

Flower is rose-coloured, with a large protruding lower petal and grows in groups of three or six

▲ *Teucrium scorodonia* 'Crispum'
CURLY WOOD SAGE

A hardy herbaceous perennial, with a height of 35cm (14in) and a spread of 30cm (12in). Pale, greenish-white flowers are borne in summer. It has soft, green heart-shaped leaves, with very ruffled crinkled edges, which can have a reddish tinge in autumn. This herb was much used by Gertrude Jekyll, the famous plantswoman, who recognized its aesthetic value in the garden.

▶ *Teucrium scorodonia*
WOOD SAGE

A hardy herbaceous perennial, with a height of 60cm (24in) and a spread of 24cm (10in). Pale, greenish-white flowers are borne in summer. The soft green, heart-shaped leaves have finely toothed edges. This natural woodland plant can be grown to great effect in a mixed herb garden. The leaves give texture and the flowers a subtle hue.

Flower, when fully open, has a lower petal which hangs down, making it look rather like a beard

Stem becomes thin and rigid as the plant grows

Leaf is soft with a textured upper surface. When crushed, it has a musty smell and it is bitter to taste

Thymus
Upright thymes LAMIACEAE

The classic culinary thyme has an upright habit, making it easier to pick than the spreading or mounding thymes. The leaves of this group can vary in scent and flavour from the classic thyme to the more exotic spicy orange. In their natural environment they grow at the edges of paths in rockeries and on escarpments – habitats which can be easily recreated in the garden. They also make a lovely edging for a path. Current research has shown that *Thymus vulgaris* helps to arrest the ageing process and is very beneficial in the treatment of stomach ulcers.

CAUTION Do not take thyme medicinally when pregnant.

How to grow

Herb	Soil	Propagation
Thymus	Soil	Softwood cuttings

PROPAGATION Sow the seed in spring. Because the seed is so small, mix it with fine horticultural sand or flour to make it easier to handle. Do not cover. Place under protection at 20°C (60°F). Germination takes five to ten days. Keep watering to a minimum; the seedlings are prone to "damping off". Always water from the bottom. Take cuttings from new growth before flowering in late spring. Winter late cuttings in a cold frame. Divide established plants in spring in cold, wet climates; in warm, hot, dry climates divide in autumn.

SITE Plant in well-drained soil in a sunny position. Thymes do not like wet winters or sitting in water. Make sure that the soil has adequate drainage. To improve drainage, dig in extra horticultural grit. To grow in containers, use a soil-based substrate.

MAINTENANCE In spring, lightly prune all upright and mounding thymes to encourage the growth of young shoots for strong leaf flavour, and prune the plants again after flowering in late summer to prevent them from becoming woody.

HARVESTING This evergreen herb can be picked all year round, for culinary or medicinal use. If the thyme leaves are to be used for drying, pick sprigs just before flowering.

How to use

Upright thymes are the classic thymes used in bouquet garni (see page 228). When added to cooking, the leaves aid digestion and help to break down fatty foods. They also have strong antiseptic properties. An infusion or tea of thyme leaves makes an excellent remedy for sore throats and hangovers.

◄ *Thymus* 'Fragrantissimus'
ORANGE-SCENTED THYME
A hardy evergreen perennial, with a height of 30cm (12in) and a spread of 45cm (18in). The narrow, grey-green leaves have a spicy orange scent. This thyme has a delightful warm flavour, which not only tastes good with meat and vegetables, but wonderful with sweet dishes like treacle tart.

▲ *Thymus* x *citriodorus* 'Silver Queen'
SILVER QUEEN THYME
A hardy evergreen perennial, with a height of 25cm (10in) and a spread of 45cm (18in). Terminal clusters of small pink flowers appear in summer. The leaves are small, oval, and grey variegated with silver. They have a strong lemon scent when rubbed or used in cooking, and this thyme combines particularly well with chicken and fish dishes.

Flower is small and tubular with a hanging lower petal

Stem is ridged to the touch. Young growth is green; mature growth brown

▶ *Thymus vulgaris* 'Compactus'

COMPACT THYME

A hardy evergreen perennial, with a height and spread of 30cm (12in). Terminal clusters of small, pale pink flowers appear in summer. The dark green leaves are aromatic with the strong classic thyme aroma. This thyme is identical to *T. vulgaris* in flavour and medicinal properties. The only difference is its neater growing habit.

Leaf is small, oval, pointed, and highly aromatic, with classic thyme scent

Thymus

Creeping thymes LAMIACEAE

There is nothing more romantic than coming across a bank covered in creeping thymes or walking across ground overrun with these aromatic plants, which release their delicious fragrance as they are crushed underfoot. Their creeping habit and robust leaves make them ideally suited to path or lawn surfaces. The right growing conditions are particularly important for creeping thymes; they originate from the Mediterranean, and so need a sunny, well-drained site. Their creeping habit can, however, make it difficult to pick enough for culinary use.

How to grow

Herb	Soil	Propagation
Thymus	Sand	Softwood cuttings

PROPAGATION See page 206 for details.

SITE To create a thyme path, prepare the site well before planting. Choose a sunny position. Thymes will not survive in shade, especially in wet climates. Dig the area over, removing all weeds. If the soil is heavy or cold add plenty of extra sharp horticultural grit. Lay a permeable membrane over the soil to inhibit weeds, while allowing rainwater to seep through to the soil. Cut slits into the membrane and plant the thyme plants through it, spacing them at 15cm (6in) intervals. Once planted, cover the membrane with a washed grit or fine gravel. right up to the "necks" of the plants, lying the green plant growth over the grit.

MAINTENANCE See page 206 for details.

HARVESTING See page 206 for details.

How to use

See page 206 for details.

◀ *Thymus* **Coccineus Group**
CREEPING RED THYME
A hardy evergreen perennial, with a height of 7cm (3in) and a spread of 1m (36in). Terminal clusters of small magenta flowers appear in summer, attracting bees and butterflies. The leaves are small, oval, dark green, and aromatic. This species can be grown successfully as part of a thyme walk.

▲ *Thymus serpyllum*
CREEPING THYME, WILD THYME
A hardy evergreen perennial, with a height of 7cm (3in) and a spread of 1m (36in). Terminal clusters of small pink, mauve or purple flowers appear in summer. It has small, oval, hairy, dark green, aromatic leaves. This thyme has strong medicinal properties and makes a potent natural antiseptic for use in the home.

▲ *Thymus serpyllum* 'Minor'
MINOR THYME

A hardy evergreen perennial, with a
height of 1cm (½in) and a spread of
15cm (6in). It has very short-stemmed
pink flowers in summer, but will only
flower in sunny, well-drained sites.
Its dark green leaves form a mat
on the ground. This tight-growing
thyme is able to withstand being
trampled underfoot.

Flower grows in
terminal clusters
flowering throughout
the summer

Stem is green when
showing new growth,
turning brown with maturity

Leaf is rounded
and highly aromatic

▶ *Thymus pulegioides*
BROAD-LEAVED THYME, MOTHER OF THYME

A hardy evergreen perennial, with a height of 25cm (10in)
and a spread of 45cm (18in). Small terminal clusters of
mauve flowers appear in summer. The dark green leaves
are small, rounded, and aromatic. It produces much leaf
with an excellent culinary flavour. Grow over a wall feature
or along the edge of a flower border.

Tropaeolum

Nasturtium TROPAEOLACEAE

Common nasturtium (*Tropaeolum majus*) is a valuable summer annual with its wonderfully bright flowers. It is a familiar sight in many gardens, but is rarely acknowledged as the useful culinary and medicinal herb it is. It was introduced into Europe from Peru in the 16th century and was first known as Indian cress (*Nasturtium indicum*), because of the peppery watercress-like flavour of the leaves. The practice of eating fresh petals and using them in tea originated in the Orient. There are now many more varieties, including those with variegated leaves and multi-coloured flowers.

How to grow

Herb	Soil	Propagation
Tropaeolum	Loam	Seed

PROPAGATION Sow annual varieties in pots in early spring and place under protection. Germination takes ten to twenty days. Alternatively, sow the seeds into prepared ground 20cm (8in) apart, when the air temperature does not fall below 9°C (48°F). Germination takes fourteen to twenty-one days. Unlike the annual, sow *T. speciosum* in autumn and place in a cold frame. Germination takes three to four weeks. If nothing happens, place outside for the winter. Germination can take as long as two years.

SITE Plant in well-drained soil in sun or partial shade. If soil is too rich, there will be too much foliage and little flower. Grows well in containers. Be mean with the nutrients in the substrate; dilute with ⅓ bark or coir.

MAINTENANCE Deadhead regularly to maintain flowering. Pick off seeds as they form to inhibit self-seeding. Water throughout the summer months. Nasturtium is renowned for attracting aphids and the caterpillars of the cabbage white butterfly. If the infestation is light, wash off, if severe, cut right back.

HARVESTING Use nasturtium fresh, picking the flowers, leaves, and seeds as required.

How to use

The seeds, leaves, and flowers all have a piquant taste and can be eaten in salads. Chopped leaves give a peppery flavour. Seeds can be pickled and used as an alternative to capers.

All parts of the plant are antibiotic. The leaves contain vitamin C and iron as well as an antiseptic substance, which is most potent before the plant flowers. Nasturtiums are thought good for the skin.

◀ *Tropaeolum majus*
'Empress of India'
NASTURTIUM EMPRESS OF INDIA
A half-hardy annual, with a height of 20cm (8in) and a spread of 30cm (12in). It has brightly coloured, helmet-shaped flowers with a long nectar spur that last throughout summer until the first frosts. A good companion plant, it deters woolly aphids from apple trees.

▲ *Tropaeolum speciosum*
FLAME NASTURTIUM, SCOTTISH FLAME FLOWER
A hardy perennial climber, with a height of up to 3m (10ft) and an indefinite spread. In summer, scarlet flowers appear, followed by bright blue fruits. The leaves are green and lobed. Plant the roots in shade, so they do not dry out in hot summers. This nasturtium flowers in three to five years if grown from seed.

Ugni

Chilean guava MYRTACEAE

I grow hundreds of different herbs, all are wonderful, but occasionally there is one that becomes a particular favourite. This is one of those. Chilean guava, a member of the myrtle family, is characterized by its charming shell-pink flowers, followed by lush, dark red fruit in autumn. The fruit tastes of wild strawberries and was apparently a great favourite of Queen Victoria, who requested that a jam be made for her from the sweet berries. It is now one of my dog's favourites – it is a race in autumn to see who will harvest the fruit first!

Fruit ripens to dark red. It should be just soft to the touch before eating.

How to grow

Herb	Soil	Propagation
Ugni	Sand	Softwood cuttings

PROPAGATION Either leave the berries on the bush until spring and sow fresh, or pick when ripe and store in a cold, dry place in a tray in a single layer until spring. Sow, and place under protection at 15°C (60°F). Germination takes one to two months but can take longer. Take softwood cuttings in summer from non-flowering shoots. For both propagation methods, pot up when the roots are established and grow on in a container for two seasons, before planting into a prepared site.

SITE Plant in a well-drained acid soil in full sun. Wet conditions will damage the plant quicker than cold. On an exposed, windy site, plant against a south- or west-facing wall. In warm climates grow it as a low hedge. It can also be grown in containers. Use an ericaceous substrate. Do not upgrade the pot size – it prefers being pot-bound.

MAINTENANCE Feed only once in spring with well-rotted compost. In containers, feed weekly during the growing season. Overfed plants will not flower. In warm climates, trim the plant in autumn to maintain its shape; in colder climates trim in spring.

HARVESTING Pick fresh leaves as required throughout the year. Harvest fresh flowers in summer. By late autumn the berries will be ripe and ready to eat.

How to use

The leaves of Chilean guava can be used to make a spicy-flavoured tea, or to add a warm spicy flavour to stews and casseroles. In Chile, the plant's seeds are roasted and used as a substitute for coffee. The dark red, ripe berries can be eaten raw or cooked. They become more tart in flavour when cooked.

▼ *Ugni molinae*
CHILEAN GUAVA

A hardy evergreen shrub, with a height of up to 2.5m (8ft) and a spread of 1.5m (5ft). Pretty pale pink flowers appear in summer, followed by round fruit, which ripen to a very dark red. The small, dark green leaves are leathery in texture and aromatic. In autumn, they may turn a slightly copper colour.

Flowers hang down and are pale pink and cup-shaped

Leaf is shiny on the upper surface, matt on the underside

Valeriana

Valerian VALERIANACEAE

The scent of the flowers is deliciously fragrant but the fresh root, when dug up, has a pungent odour. Cats, however, find the smell of the root even more seductive than catnip (*Nepeta cataria* – see page 158), as do rats, and so valerian root can be used as an enticing bait in rat traps as a chemical-free alternative to poison. Medicinally, valerian root is a well-known sedative and, combined with other herbs as a tea, tablet, or tincture, makes a good remedy for insomnia and restlessness. Do not take for an extended period or during pregnancy.

Root merges into short conical root stock. When broken, the root releases a strong, rather unpleasant aroma. This is the medicinal part of the plant.

How to grow

Herb	Soil	Propagation
Valeriana	Loam	Seed

PROPAGATION Sow seeds in spring and place in a cold frame. Germination takes three to four weeks. Plant out 60cm (24in) apart, when seedlings are large enough to handle. Alternatively, sow into prepared open ground in late spring. Leave uncovered, when the air temperature is above 9°C (48°F). Divide established plants in the autumn and replant into a well-prepared site.

SITE Choose the site carefully to avoid having to move the plant at a later date; the scent of broken roots will attract cats. Plant in sun or partial shade but keep the roots cool and damp in summer. It will grow well next to a pond. Valerian is a good companion plant for vegetables because the roots stimulate phosphorus and earthworm activity. Valerian also grows well in a large container placed in partial shade. Use a soil-based substrate and water regularly to keep the soil moist.

MAINTENANCE Cut back after flowering to prevent self-seeding. Place the leaves on the compost heap as they are rich in minerals.

HARVESTING Dig up the roots of a second- or third-year valerian plant to dry for later use.

How to use

Historically, this medicinal herb has been used as a sedative and relaxant. The roots, prepared into tablet, powder, capsule, or tincture form are a safe, non-addictive relaxant that reduces anxiety and promotes sleep. In the garden, spray an infusion of the root onto the topsoil to attract earthworms.

CAUTION Do not take for an extended period or during pregnancy.

▼ *Valeriana officinalis*
VALERIAN, ALL HEAL
A hardy herbaceous perennial, with a height of up to 1.2m (4ft) and a spread of 1m (3ft). Clusters of small, sweetly-scented flowers appear in summer. In spring, new leaf growth has an attractive bronze tinge.

Flower is very small, tubular, and grows in flat clusters

Stem is grooved and hollow

Leaf is made up of a series of lance-shaped segments. The underside is covered in fine hairs

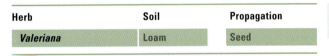

Verbena
Vervain VERBENACEAE

Although the flowers of this insignificant-looking herb have no fragrance and it is bitter to taste, vervain contains important medicinal properties. The ancient Greeks attributed magical properties to it, and wore amulets made from vervain flowers and leaves to protect themselves against demons and disease. In contemporary society, vervain is used by herbalists as an effective natural remedy to relieve nervous tension and anxiety. Take care not to confuse vervain (*Verbena officinalis*) with lemon verbena (*Aloysia triphylla* – see page 85).

CAUTION Do not take during pregnancy.

How to grow

Herb	Soil	Propagation
Verbena	Sand	Division

PROPAGATION The seeds of this herb need stratification before germination (see page 45). In cold climates, sow the seed into a pot and place outside for the winter. Germination takes four to six months. In warm climates, first place the seeds in the refrigerator for one month to stratify them, then sow into a pot or tray and place outside. Germination is erratic, so be patient. Once large enough to handle, leave the seedlings in pots outside and then plant out 30cm (12in) apart. Divide established plants in autumn or spring, replanting into a prepared site.

SITE Plant in any well-drained soil in sun or partial shade. Vervain plants will adapt to clay soils. To increase its visual impact, plant in groups against a dark backdrop like a hedge to help to show off the flowers. It will grow in containers, using a soil-based substrate.

MAINTENANCE Cut back after flowering to prevent self-seeding. To maintain healthy leaf growth, divide established plants in autumn or spring every third year.

HARVESTING Fresh vervain leaves can be harvested throughout the growing season. For drying, harvest the flowers in summer.

▶ ***Verbena officinalis***
VERVAIN, HERB OF GRACE
A hardy herbaceous perennial, with a height of up to 90cm (36in) and a spread of 30cm (12in). Tiny, terminal clusters of very pale lilac flowers appear in summer. Its green leaves are often deeply divided into lobes with curved teeth.

How to use

An important medicinal herb, it is used by Western and Chinese herbalists to treat nervous exhaustion, headaches, and liver and urinary tract infections. It can be administered as a medicinal tea, but this is very bitter.

Viola

Viola VIOLACEAE

These small pansies with their cheerful faces that always turn to face the sun are
a delight in any garden. Violas are a wild flower, and can be found throughout Europe,
North America, and Australia. They were made famous as a love potion by Shakespeare
in *A Midsummer Night's Dream*; many references are made to violas in romantic
literature, as they were often used to make love potions or to send messages. Each
colour represented a different sentiment, according to the language of flowers: purple
violas symbolized memories, white violas loving thoughts, and yellow violas, souvenirs.

CAUTION High doses can cause
nausea and vomiting.

How to grow

Herb	Soil	Propagation
Viola	Loam	Seed/division

PROPAGATION Sow seeds in autumn, leaving them uncovered
by substrate, and place in a cold frame for the winter. Germination will
occur by the following spring. Once large enough to handle, plant out
15cm (6in) apart. Divide established plants in autumn, replanting into
a prepared site.

SITE Violas are self-seeding and adapt to most soil types, but
dislike waterlogged sites. They favour sun or partial shade. They grow
well in containers, on their own or with other herbs. Use a soil-based
substrate in the container of your choice.

MAINTENANCE Deadhead flowers and pinch out growing tips
to maintain flowering throughout the season. Cut back in autumn to
encourage new growth and to help the plant survive the winter months.

HARVESTING Pick fresh flowers throughout the season. In
summer, pick the flowering parts for use in infusions or for drying.

How to use

Medicinally, violas are used as a detoxifying herb to treat arthritis,
whooping cough, bronchitis, and skin diseases. An infusion made from
the flowers, leaves, and stems will soothe itching skin. An infusion of
the flowers only has long been prescribed for mending a broken heart.
It is also beneficial when added to the bath, for easing aches and pains.
A cold infusion of the flowers, leaves and stems is diluted in drinking
water and given to racing pigeons to help them fly faster.

◄ *Viola odorata*
SWEET VIOLET
A hardy perennial, with a height
of 15cm (6in) and a spread of 30cm
(12in). White, dark purple, and
occasionally yellow, sweetly-scented
flowers appear from late winter until
mid-spring. The leaves are often a
broad heart shape.

Flower petals can vary in
colour from blue to yellow, white,
purple, and black.

◄ *Viola tricolor*
HEARTSEASE, WILD PANSY
A hardy perennial, often grown as an
annual, with a height and spread of
38cm (15in). Small, edible, tri-
coloured, pansy-like flowers with blue,
yellow, white, purple, and black petals
appear throughout the summer
until the first frosts. The leaves
are heart-shaped or oval.

Leaf becomes narrower
and smaller higher up the
flowering stem

Vitex
Chase tree VERBENACEAE

This aromatic shrub, indigenous to the Mediterranean and Central Asia, has been used medicinally for thousands of years. *Vitex agnus-castus* translates as "chaste lamb", which is the Christian symbol of purity. In the 4th century BC, Hippocrates used *Vitex* to treat female disorders, particularly diseases of the uterus. The common name, chaste tree, comes from the plant's ancient reputation for guarding chastity. Historically, the Christian monks chewed the leaves and ground the dried berries over their food to reduce their libido which gave rise to its local name, "monk's pepper".

How to grow

Herb	Soil	Propagation
Vitex	**Loam**	**Softwood cuttings**

PROPAGATION Sow fresh seeds in autumn into prepared plug module trays or small containers, using a seed compost mixed in equal parts with perlite. Place the container in a frost-free environment for the winter, and pot up rooted seedlings in the following spring. Cuttings are the most reliable method of propagation: take softwood cuttings in late spring to early summer from non-flowering shoots. Place the cuttings in a sheltered, warm environment; they do not need bottom heat. Once rooted, pot up and winter in a frost-free environment for the first two winters. Plants will flower in the second or third summer.

SITE Plant in a fertile soil. *Vitex* will tolerate dry and moist soils but not cold, heavy clay soils. In cold areas, plant against a south- or west-facing wall; the wall will help to cut the rainfall by 25 per cent, and will give added protection and warmth in winter. Alternatively, plant in full sun in a sheltered position; it will not tolerate shade. This is a good late nectar plant for butterflies.

MAINTENANCE In spring, prune back last year's growth to 5cm (2in); this will encourage new growth and maintain the shape of the plant.

HARVESTING The leaves are picked in early summer for use fresh, or for drying. The fruits are harvested in autumn for use fresh or for drying. However this plant rarely sets fruit in cool, cold climates.

How to use

In the kitchen, the dried berries can be used in Moroccan dishes and in a spice mixture called *ras el hanout*. Medicinally, the berries are taken in tablet or tincture form to treat menstrual and menopausal problems and infertility. It is also used to relieve spasms of pain, especially PMS.

▲ *Vitex agnus-castus*
CHASE TREE, MONK'S PEPPER, HEMPTREE, AGNUS CASTUS, CHASTE BERRY
A deciduous shrub, with a height and spread of 2.5m (8ft). Upright panicles of fragrant, tubular, violet-blue flowers appear in late summer until mid-autumn, and are followed by small, round, orange-red fruit. It has dark green, aromatic leaves, divided into five or seven lance-shaped leaflets.

THE KITCHEN

Using herbs in cooking

My enthusiasm for using herbs to flavour food follows a long family tradition: in the 1950s, my grandmother, Ruth Lowinsky, wrote several cookery books. My mother not only inherited her mother's love of cooking but was also a keen gardener, growing all her own vegetables and herbs; I was inspired by her, and have followed suit by setting up my herb farm. In the beginning, I only grew a limited selection of culinary herbs as at the time there was little public demand for anything other than parsley, sage, rosemary, thyme, chives, tarragon, and fennel.

Herbs in history

Today, tastes have moved on and I now grow a far more exotic, strongly flavoured selection of herbs, which are becoming as common in the kitchen as the standard Mediterranean ones. I believe the increase in the use of pungent herbs in modern cooking has a lot to do with people's desire to counter the bland flavour of the intensively farmed foods and mass-produced ready-made meals that have become so common. But, as the organic movement gathers momentum and locally grown and seasonal food becomes more popular, the future of good, flavoursome food is looking much brighter. Herbs, particularly home-grown herbs, are part of this desire to use fresh and simple ingredients.

Historically, herbs were used in the kitchen both as flavouring and as preservatives. Before refrigerators were invented, large households had underground cellars and cold rooms where they stored meat, which was covered in salt and wrapped in fresh sage leaves to preserve it. After shooting, fresh game was also left to hang to tenderize the meat with bunches of fresh thyme, which added flavour and imparted antiseptic properties to the meat to help prevent stomach upsets when it was eventually eaten.

Cooking with fresh herbs

Herbs have always been a part of the cooking process. Traditionally, they were used with all forms of cooked or preserved food to add flavour or other benefits. When you cook with fresh herbs they release a wonderful aroma, which not only smells fantastic but also makes your mouth water; this release of saliva actually helps to prepare your stomach for food, hence the old saying "whet the appetite". Classic herbs like thyme, sage, oregano, and rosemary are highly aromatic when cooked; they are also strongly antiseptic and help with the digestion of fatty foods, especially meats such as lamb. This goes some way towards explaining the tradition of preparing food with herbs – a tradition that continues to increase in popularity today.

Use your home-grown herbs and cook with fresh, organic ingredients for aromatic, delicious results.

◀◀ **Fresh sage leaves** (*Salvia officinalis*) are gathered from the herb garden for use in cooking.

◀ **Fresh mint leaves** (*Mentha*) are excellent with acid fruit, especially strawberries.

◀◀ **Sprigs of fresh thyme** (*Thymus vulgaris*) are laid over vegetables in preparation for roasting.

◀ **Basil leaves** (*Ocimum basilicum*) picked from a pot on the windowsill are delicious with savoury summer dishes.

◀◀ **A herb vinaigrette** made from mint (*Mentha spicata*) and hyssop leaves (*Hyssopus officinalis*) is poured over a herb leaf salad.

◀ **A gruyère tart** is flavoured with freshly chopped tarragon (*Artemisia dracunculus*), parsley (*Petroselinum crispum* 'French'), and fennel (*Foeniculum vulgare*).

Hot and cold drinks

There are many different hot and cold drinks that can be made from herbs. Herb teas, known as tisanes, can be drunk instead of ordinary tea, and can provide a simple and helpful supplement to the daily diet. One of my favourite herb teas is lemon verbena, which is refreshing when served hot or cold either on a summer's day or at the end of the day for a good night's sleep.

A herb drink is one of the best ways of extracting both the medicinal properties of the herb and its aroma and flavour. Tisanes (herb teas) usually have a light flavour; they can be made with fresh or dried herbs. Dried herbs are more pungent and intense; however, if the herbs are dried in poor conditions or stored incorrectly their flavour may be impaired. For a light, all-round flavour I recommend using fresh herbs, especially when in season. But remember, you need to use more fresh herbs than dried – fresh herbs are less concentrated because they still contain moisture in their plant parts. For advice on harvesting and drying herbs see pages 66–73.

Elderflower cordial

Makes about 2 x 500ml (17fl oz) bottles

1.2 litres (2pt) water

1.8kg (4lb) unrefined cane sugar

6 lemons, juice and peeled rind

30ml (2tbsp) of dry cider or
    white wine vinegar

20 heads of elderflower

METHOD Pour boiled water into a sterilized container. Add the sugar, stirring until dissolved. Cool. Add the lemon rind, lemon juice, white wine vinegar, and elderflowers. Cover with a muslin cloth and leave to infuse for 24 hours. Strain the cordial through muslin and pour into glass bottles with metal-levered caps. Once made, leave the cordial for two weeks. Then serve chilled, diluted with still or sparkling water to taste. Store in a cool, dark place. Use within three months.

HERB ALTERNATIVES

Lovage seeds add a celery flavour. Once the sugar has dissolved, add 25g (1oz) seeds. Use cider vinegar, not white wine.

Meadowsweet leaves add a warm herb flavour. Use four leaves.

Sweet cicely flowers have a light anise taste. Use 16 flowerheads.

Tisanes

5 fresh leaves, a 5cm (2in) sprig,
  2 tsp of dried herb,
  or 1 tsp of seed per cup of boiled water.

METHOD Place the herb on a piece of kitchen towel, lightly crush, and then add to the cup. Pour over the boiled water that has been cooled to just below boiling. Cover the infusion to prevent the herb leaf oils, which are medicinally beneficial, evaporating in the steam. Leave to infuse for five minutes. Strain if necessary. Tisanes may be sweetened with honey to taste. The teapot (right) contains lemon verbena leaves – a late-night tisane that aids sleep – and the tea cup, a sprig of rosemary for a refreshing morning pick-me-up.

HERB ALTERNATIVES

Chamomile flower tisane is lovely last thing at night to aid sleep.

Dill seed tisane is useful for calming griping pains in the abdomen.

Lemon balm leaf tisane is a mild antidepressant, and relieves headaches.

Peppermint leaf tisane drunk after a meal aids digestion.

Borage ice cubes

10 fresh borage flowers

METHOD Pick the fresh flowers when they are fully open. To keep the ice cube clear, use boiled water that has been left to cool. Fill the ice tray with the water, then add a single flower to each section. If you find the flowers difficult to handle, use a pair of tweezers to place the flowers in the ice-cube tray. Leave to set in the freezer for 12 hours. These flower cubes look lovely in drinks and added to fruit salads, or simply as decoration in an ice bucket.

HERB ALTERNATIVES

Chicory flowers, a lovely blue flower. Pick when fully open.

Heartsease flowers look lovely in fruit salads.

Pineapple sage flowers, a stunning red flower that looks magnificent in cocktails.

Primrose flowers, a charming yellow flower.

Salads and vinegars

Fresh herbs can be added to all types of mixed leaf salads and offer perhaps the best way to experience the unique flavour and fragrance of the herb along with the benefits of its medicinal properties. Chive, caraway, and basil leaves, for example, aid digestion, while chervil is high in vitamin C, and parsley is rich in iron.

To obtain the most intense flavour from fresh herbs in salad and their optimum medicinal qualities, it is best to use organically grown herbs. In growing herbs organically, the sun, rain and soil have all worked to boost their natural oil content. Personally, I find that pot-grown supermarket herbs, grown on artificial nutrients under glass to encourage fast growth, can lack taste and fragrance. In salads, limit yourself to no more than five herb leaves, or the flavours may become confused.

Herb flower salad

Heartsease flowers, green parts removed
Fennel flowers
Painted sage flowers and bracts
Wild rocket flowers

METHOD Make the herb leaf salad (opposite) and decorate with edible herb flowers. Before adding the flowers to the leaf salad, remove all the flower parts from their stems. Add the flowers to the salad, toss and serve. You can use a very light, mild vinaigrette made from olive oil and white wine vinegar, but do not add more herbs to the vinaigrette or it will overpower the flower flavours.

HERB ALTERNATIVES

Chive flowers add an onion flavour to salads.

Nasturtium flowers have a peppery taste.

Pot marigold flowers offer a mild, warm flavour.

Wild bergamot flowers add a strong herb flavour to salads.

Mint vinaigrette

45ml (3 tbsp) mild olive oil
15ml (1 tbsp) white wine or balsamic vinegar
Pinch of sea salt, to taste
Freshly ground black pepper, to taste
5ml (1 tsp) wholegrain mustard
5ml (1 tsp) honey or soft brown sugar
Handful spearmint leaves, chopped

METHOD Place the oil and vinegar in a bowl and whisk together. Add all the remaining ingredients and blend. Taste to check the seasoning, then pour over the salad. Toss the leaves, and serve. This simple mint vinaigrette is suitable for green leaf and apple salads.

HERB ALTERNATIVES

Chive and mint leaf vinaigrette for potato salad.

Dill leaf vinaigrette for courgettes.

Garlic and sweet marjoram leaf vinaigrette for tomato salad.

Tarragon and sweet basil leaf vinaigrette for cold fish.

Herb leaf salad

Use a generous handful of:

Buckler leaf sorrel

Chervil

Purslane

Salad burnet

Wild rocket

METHOD This herb leaf salad presents a lovely mix of flavours. The buckler leaf sorrel has a sharp, clean taste; salad burnet offers a hint of cucumber; chervil tastes of mild anise; wild rocket has a peppery edge, and purslane contributes a fresh, pea-like flavour. This selection of herbs works well served with fish, or as a starter to clean the palate. A wide range of leafy herbs can be used in a mixed salad and some other good alternatives are featured (right). Wash and dry the leaves before use if you do not know their place of origin. If home-grown, simply place the leaves in a salad bowl, since it is thought that water impairs their flavour.

HERB ALTERNATIVES

Chive leaves and flowers have an onion flavour that combines beautifully with salad burnet, purslane, and chervil.

French parsley leaves have a strong flavour that works well mixed with salad rocket, sorrel, and purslane.

Summer savory leaves have a peppery flavour that mixes well with salad burnet, chervil, and purslane.

Herb vinegar

575ml (1pt) white wine vinegar

2 handfuls of fresh tarragon leaves

METHOD This is a wonderful way to infuse vinegar with the fresh flavour of your home-grown herbs.

■ Fill a clean glass bottle full of fresh tarragon leaves. Make sure that they are packed in tight to the top of the container. Top up the bottle with white wine vinegar and seal. Do not use a metal top, because vinegar is corrosive.

■ Leave on a sunny windowsill for one month, shaking from time to time, so that the tarragon leaves can infuse the vinegar with their flavour. Strain off the liquid through unbleached coffee filter paper. Put a sprig of tarragon in the bottle for identification purposes.

■ For those who do not want to wait, here is a quicker method: put the herbs and vinegar into a covered ceramic bowl over a pan of cold water. Bring the water to the boil to heat up the vinegar, and infuse it with the tarragon leaf flavour. Then, remove the bowl from the pan. Leave it to cool for about two hours before using. You can infuse almost any herb with vinegar using either one of these simple methods. Tarragon vinegar is good for making salad dressing and sauces for white meat such as fish or chicken.

HERB ALTERNATIVES

Dill leaves and seeds make a vinegar that is wonderful for homemade gravlax. Use at least 1 teaspoon of crushed dill seeds.

Hyssop and spearmint leaves are good in sauces with vegetables or for making mustards.

Purple shiso leaves and caraway seeds are lovely in dressings for rice or pasta salads. The purple shiso makes the vinegar go a wonderful purple colour and the caraway seed adds a slight aniseed taste. Use 4 teaspoons of seed and two handfuls of leaves.

Wild bergamot leaves are very pungent. Use this vinegar for making pickles, sauces, and mustards.

Mayonnaises, mustards, & butters

In my opinion, there is nothing to beat the flavour of homemade preserves, and each of these recipes will contribute to a meal. One of my first cooking memories is helping my mother to chop herbs to make a herb butter to accompany grilled lamb cutlets. Equally, I remember my mother watching transfixed while I made a herb mayonnaise with a food processor – what took her hours, took me minutes.

My mouth waters at the thought of a homemade mayonnaise that has been blended with freshly harvested herbs to make a traditional, green mayonnaise. Depending on the herbs you grow, mayonnaises can be made to match many different dishes. I also find mustards indispensable as an accompaniment: they liven up sausages, and are great folded into a crème fraîche. Herb butters are not only a wonderful way to preserve the flavour of fresh herb leaves and flowers, but can also transform dishes – toss freshly cooked pasta in a sage butter for a quintessentially Italian alternative to a shop-bought sauce.

Herb mayonnaise

2 large egg yolks (at room temperature)
5ml (1 tsp) English mustard powder
Sea salt and freshly ground black pepper, to taste
275ml (10fl oz) light olive oil or sunflower oil
5–10ml (1–2 tsp) white wine vinegar, to taste
2.5ml (½ tsp) lemon juice
1 bunch parsley, finely chopped
2 sprigs fresh basil, finely chopped

METHOD Place the egg yolks, mustard, and salt into a bowl, and mix together. Add the oil, very slowly, one drop at a time, whisking until it starts to thicken. When half the oil has been added, add one teaspoon of white wine vinegar to thin the mixture. Now add the oil in a thin stream, whisking continuously. If the mixture is too thin, add a little more oil. When happy with the consistency, add the lemon juice, chopped herbs, salt and pepper to taste, and a little more white wine vinegar, if needed. Leave the mixture to infuse for one hour to bring out the herb flavours. Then use immediately as chopped basil leaves combined with vinegar may turn black on exposure to air.

HERB ALTERNATIVES

Chervil leaves create a delicate-flavoured mayonnaise that is good with rice dishes.

Garlic clove mayonnaise is wonderful with fish, and great with chips.

French tarragon leaf mayonnaise is good with fish, chicken, and rice.

Sorrel leaves make another classic green mayonnaise that goes well with fish and cold chicken.

Wild rocket leaves add a peppery, beefy flavour, which combines well with new potatoes or egg dishes.

Herb mustard

80g (3oz) black mustard seed
30g (1oz) white mustard seed
575ml (1pt) water
115g (4oz) English mustard powder
200ml (⅓pt) cider vinegar
5ml (1 tsp) salt
5ml (1 tsp) turmeric
50g (2oz) chopped dill

HERB ALTERNATIVES

Horseradish root is wonderful with red meats. Add 2 tablespoons of grated root to 50g (2oz) of coarse-grain and 50g (2oz) smooth mustard.

Oregano leaves taste good with goat's cheese and tomatoes. Add 25g (1oz) of chopped leaves to the mustard mix given above.

METHOD Place the mustard seed in a china or glass bowl, add the water, and soak for 24 hours. Then add the mustard powder, cider vinegar, salt, and turmeric. When thoroughly mixed, sit the bowl over a saucepan of water, but do not allow the bottom of the bowl to touch the water. On a low heat, gently cook the mustard seed for four hours, stirring occasionally. Check that the water in the saucepan does not evaporate, and do not allow the mixture to boil or the mustard will lose its flavour and become bitter. Once cooked, allow to cool and add the chopped dill. Cover and keep in the refrigerator. Alternatively, you can cheat and simply buy some good coarse mustard and a smooth Dijon mustard and mix together 50g (2oz) of coarse-grain mustard and 50g (2oz) of smooth mustard with 50g (2oz) chopped dill. If the mustard is too thick, add a small amount of white wine vinegar to thin it.

Herb butter

2 tbsp thyme leaves, chopped
125g (4oz) unsalted butter

METHOD Remove the leaves of the thyme by rubbing your fingers up and down the stems. Once removed, chop up to release the leaf oils, then mix with the soft unsalted butter. It is important to use salt-free butter so that the herb flavour will come through. Use a fork to blend the herbs and butter. When thoroughly mixed, pack the butter into a roll of greaseproof paper and place in the refrigerator for up to 24 hours to set. The longer you leave it, the better the flavour.

HERB ALTERNATIVES

Coriander leaf and garlic clove butter can be rubbed over trout before grilling. Use 1 tbsp chopped coriander leaf and two cloves of garlic.

Dill leaf butter is ideal for salmon. Use one handful of dill leaf, chopped.

Parsley and lemon thyme leaf butter can be pushed under the skin of a chicken before roasting. Use 2 tbsp of chopped herb leaves.

Rose-scented geranium leaf butter is excellent for making cakes. Use three leaves, chopped.

Sage leaf butter is great for using on grilled pork chops. Use three leaves, chopped.

Spearmint leaf and elderflower butter is very good for making a sweet sauce for ice-cream. Use 1 tbsp of chopped spearmint leaf and two heads of elderflower.

Sauces and marinades

Fresh herbs are ideal in sauces, giving colour, texture, and flavour. Simply by warming the sauce, the natural oils contained in the leaves of the herbs are released, and will infuse the sauce with their flavours. A good sauce can transform a simple pasta or rice dish, and liven up grilled fish or meat. Herbs can equally be used to flavour and perfume sweet sauces, like the aromatic herb custard below.

In Europe, sweet cicely was considered a natural sugar and was used as a sweetener for custards and milk puddings and to counteract sharp fruit flavours, such as gooseberry, rhubarb, and strawberry. In India, cardamom is still used to flavour rice pudding, and is combined with fennel seeds to make a sweet pancake syrup.

A marinade will tenderize and give flavour to meat, fish, or vegetables before cooking or serving chilled. This marinading time will also endow the food with the herbs' beneficial properties: for example, oregano, sage, or thyme will work as an antiseptic. Most marinades also contain an acid ingredient, which acts as the tenderizer.

Herb custard

560ml (1 pt) milk
5 bay leaves
6 egg yolks
85g (3oz) white sugar

METHOD Place the bay leaves and milk in a pan and bring to the boil to infuse the milk with the herb flavour. Whisk the egg yolk and sugar together until they change colour from a deep gold to pale yellow. Pour in the hot milk and bay leaves. Stir over the heat in a double boiler for ten minutes until the custard thickens. Take the pan off the heat, remove the leaves, and pour it into a cold jug. Serve with summer fruits.

HERB ALTERNATIVES

Cardamom seed custard is delicious served with a steamed dried fruit pudding. Use two teaspoons of ground cardamom seeds.

Scented pelargonium leaf custard is lemon-flavoured. Use four pelargonium leaves, whole. Serve with fresh apricots.

Pesto

1 tbsp pine nuts

4 tbsp chopped rocket leaves
  (alternatively, try using basil, chervil, or coriander)

2 cloves of garlic, chopped

75g (3oz) Parmesan cheese

6 tbsp sunflower or olive oil

Salt and freshly ground black pepper

METHOD Blend the pine nuts, herb leaves, and chopped garlic cloves in a food processor or blender until smooth. Add the oil slowly, a little at a time, continuing to blend until you have a smooth, thick paste. Mix in the Parmesan cheese, and season to taste. The pesto can be served with cooked pasta or rice, or spread on bruschetta. It will keep in a sealed container for a week if covered with a thin layer of oil, or can be frozen (before adding the Parmesan) and used within a month.

Herb marinade for fish

500g (1lb) cod fillet or other meaty white fish

For the marinade

200ml (8fl oz) white wine vinegar

Juice of 1 lemon and juice of 1 lime

1 tbsp sea salt

2 garlic cloves, sliced

2 handfuls of finely chopped parsley, dill,
  lemon thyme, mint, and basil

METHOD Mix all the marinade ingredients together. Slice the fish into 2.5cm (1in) pieces and place in a shallow glass or ceramic dish. Pour the marinade over the fish, cover the dish with a lid, and refrigerate for four hours, turning the fish every half an hour so that it is completely saturated in marinade liquid. Drain the fish and pour over a herb vinaigrette (see page 222). Toss the fish with the herbs, return, covered, to the refrigerator, and leave for one hour. Serve the fish chilled, with salad and crusty bread.

> **HERB ALTERNATIVES**
>
> **Chives, chervil, salad burnet, and fennel leaves**
> can be chopped finely and added to this marinade in any combination.

Cooked dishes

There is nothing more comforting than to enter a house and be greeted by the aroma of a casserole being cooked with fresh herbs, or vegetables being roasted with herbs and olive oil. This is how food should be cooked and enjoyed, for the pleasure of family and friends. Herbs are well-suited to this slow style of cooking, as it allows time for the herbs to add fragrance and flavour to the dish.

A bouquet garni is the classic herb flavouring for casseroles and stews, but many other herbs also work well in cooked dishes, and some also have marvellous medicinal benefits. Fennel and tarragon impart a delicious aniseed taste, and also work medicinally to help break down cholesterol in the bloodstream. Chives thin the blood and help to improve the metabolism. The addition of herbs to recipes like the herb and gruyère tart recipe outlined below will also aid digestion of cheese and eggs, which some people find difficult. By using herbs in cooking you not only create a wonderful meal, but a healthy one as well.

Herb tart

350g (12oz) shortcrust pastry made with lard,
  or ready-made pastry

2 x 180g (6oz) packets of gruyère cheese

500ml (15fl oz) crème fraîche

3 large eggs

salt and pepper, to taste

1 tsp brown sugar

1 clove garlic, crushed

2 handfuls each of finely chopped tarragon,
  parsley, and fennel

METHOD Preheat the oven to 200°C (400°F). Finely grate one packet of gruyère cheese and finely dice the second packet. Roll out the pastry and line a metal, loose-bottomed tin 28cm (11in) in diameter. Refrigerate for an hour so that the pastry does not shrink during cooking. Place the diced gruyère on to the pastry base. For the filling, beat all the other ingredients together, and pour into the pastry case. Bake for 40 minutes, turning occasionally so that the top of the tart does not burn. Serve immediately or at room temperature, with a sharp salad and herb vinaigrette (see page 222) to counteract the rich taste.

HERB ALTERNATIVES

French parsley, chives, and sweet marjoram – use two handfuls of each herb.

Mint, rosemary, and French parsley – use two handfuls of each herb.

Summer savory, hyssop, and dill – use two handfuls of hyssop and dill but less summer savory as it has quite a strong flavour.

Bouquet garni

1 bunch of parsley

3 sprigs of thyme

1 clove of garlic, peeled

2–3 bay leaves

METHOD Tie the herbs together with a long piece of string, so that they can easily be removed from the casserole or stew at the end of cooking. Alternatively, tie the herbs in a muslin bag attached to a long piece of string. Add the bouquet garni at the start of cooking, and leave in the dish for two hours.

HERB ALTERNATIVES

For fish Fennel, lemon balm, French parsley, and sweet marjoram.

For meat Oregano, thyme, bay, and lovage; rosemary, sage, thyme, and parsley; thyme, sage, parsley, and bay.

For poultry Parsley, tarragon, chervil, and myrtle; bay, lemon thyme, lemon balm, and lemon grass (the grass tips); rosemary, summer savory, hyssop, and bay.

For wild game Myrtle, bay, orange-scented thyme, and parsley; luma, juniper berries, garlic, and parsley; winter savory, thyme, sage, and oregano.

Roasted vegetables with herbs

Serves 4

1¼kg (2½lb) mixed root vegetables

2–8 garlic cloves

4 sprigs rosemary

4 sprigs classic thyme

salt and freshly ground pepper, to taste

3 tbsp olive oil

METHOD Use the tough leaves from evergreen herbs like rosemary, because soft green leaves will disintegrate at high roasting temperatures. Chop up your chosen vegetables, such as onions, potatoes, carrots, and parsnips. Place them on a baking tray and scatter the herbs over them. Sprinkle with salt and pepper to taste, and drizzle with olive oil. Roast the vegetables in a preheated oven at 180°C (350°F) for 30–40 minutes. Turn the vegetables every 15 minutes.

HERB ALTERNATIVES

Bay leaves add a warm flavour. Use three to four leaves.

Luma sprigs add a rich spicy flavour. Use two sprigs.

Myrtle sprigs add a warm spicy flavour. Use four sprigs.

Winter savory leaves add a peppery flavour. Use eight sprigs.

THE HOME

Using herbs in the home

Today, in our busy and industrial world, using herbs in the home as natural alternatives to chemical cleaning products, for first aid, or simply to pamper yourself is, I am pleased to say, experiencing a revival – not only is it beneficial for you and your family, it is also very beneficial for the environment in which you live. If you grow herbs in the garden, herbal products are not only healthy but inexpensive and fun to make. Marigold cream (see page 240) and rosemary oil (see page 241) are classic examples, and also make great presents for your friends and family.

Herbal uses

Historically, herbs were central to the household, where they were used not only to flavour and preserve food but to sweeten and purify the air. Herbs were woven into roof thatch, scattered over floors, used to clean and polish furniture and ornaments, and to disinfect kitchen utensils and work surfaces. Although in the developed world the use and knowledge of herbs has decreased, in the third world, from the Amazon rainforests to the remote mountains of north Thailand, herbs are an important part of daily life.

Animals can benefit from herbal remedies as much as we can (see pp.246–247) for recipes and ideas.

Herbs as medicine

Traditionally, herbs have long been used as medicine for people and livestock. A basic herbal first-aid kit is useful to have in the home for treating minor ailments: herbs like aloe can be rubbed on to minor burns to relieve the pain, and a cup of herbal tea at the end of the day aids relaxation and helps sleep. Using herbs medicinally for more serious complaints is a complex issue, and self-treatment is not recommended. When I am ill, I consult a fully trained herbalist or a general practitioner. When taking herbs internally, it is important to remember that they are the foundation of all our manufactured medicine, and many contain potent medicinal properties and should be treated with the greatest respect. My animals also benefit from being treated for minor ailments with herbs, which make their coats glossy and their temperaments relaxed.

Herbs for relaxation

One of my favourite uses for herbs in the home is in the bath (see pages 244–245 for some of my favourite herbal bath recipes). Not only do herbs smell wonderful when they are infused in warm bath water, but they also help to relieve the aches and pains that accumulate after a day of physical work on the farm. I am also a great believer in herbal foot baths, infused with lavender and bay, lovage, or sweet marjoram, to soothe tired feet, and herbal pillows filled with hops or lavender (see page 245) to aid sleep and relaxation at night.

◄◄ **Water infused** with fresh or dried lavender (*Lavandula angustifolia*) makes a fragrant, natural room spray for the home.

◄ **Fresh tansy leaves** (*Tanacetum vulgare*) rubbed into a dog's coat will deter fleas.

◄◄ **Lemon verbena leaves** (*Aloysia triphylla*) mixed with vinegar, water, and liquid soap make an effective natural window cleaner.

◄ **Dried sprigs of southernwood** (*Artemisia abrotanum*) are a good moth repellent. Place them between bedlinen and clothes in drawers and cupboards.

◄◄ **Lemon balm leaves** (*Melissa officinalis*) and beeswax make a wonderful natural furniture polish with a fresh lemon scent.

◄ **Aloe gel** (*Aloe vera*) is a good natural remedy for soothing sunburn, minor burns, and insect bites.

Herbs for furniture and fabrics

There is nothing better for cleaning and restoring wooden furniture than a good old-fashioned beeswax polish, scented with fresh herbs. Soapwort shampoo is also wonderful for cleaning curtains or delicate upholstery fabrics. The gentle cleansing power of the plant's saponins (see page 191) makes this natural shampoo ideal and, because of its cleansing properties, soapwort is still used as the main ingredient in manufactured cleaning products.

Beeswax polish and soapwort shampoo are easy to make at home and offer a "green" alternative to commercial cleaning products, which contain a mixture of synthetics and chemicals. Natural products are not only better for your furniture but also for the health of you and your family, especially if you have babies or toddlers at home. They are also gentle on your hands, and do not pollute the air or the waste water. In the following recipes, all the herbs smell wonderful, and also work as a mild antiseptic.

Natural furniture polish

275ml (½ pt) water
1 large handful of fresh lemon balm
275ml (½ pt) pure turpentine
60g (2oz) beeswax
60g (2oz) soapflakes
2 x 500g (1lb) screw-top tins

HERB ALTERNATIVES

Lavender stems or sweet marjoram leaves
– use a large handful of dried herb, or six drops of essential oil.

METHOD Make a herb infusion by placing the lemon balm leaves and stalks in a bowl. Boil the water and pour over the leaves. Cover and leave to stand for 15 minutes. Melt the beeswax and turpentine in a basin over a saucepan of simmering water. Take care when heating beeswax and turpentine since it has a low flash (ignition) point. Place the strained infusion and soapflakes into another saucepan and heat gently. Cool both mixtures a little and then stir the two together to make a thick cream. Pour into the tins and seal. Use a soft cloth to apply the polish to wood, metal, or painted surfaces. Buff to a shine with a clean soft cloth.

Upholstery shampoo

15g (½oz) dried or fresh root of soapwort
  or 2 handfuls of fresh stems
750ml (1½ pt) water

METHOD Wash the fresh soapwort root thoroughly in water. There is no need to peel it. If using dried soapwort root, prepare it by soaking in water overnight. Put the soapwort into a saucepan with the water. Bring to the boil, cover, and simmer for 20 minutes. Allow to stand until cool. Strain the liquid into a bottle and store in the refrigerator. To use, dampen a sponge with the solution and rub the fabric lightly. Allow it to dry before applying again, if necessary. If you wish to perfume the shampoo add six drops of essential oil to the strained liquid. Lavender, thyme, rosemary, or rose-scented geranium oil are all suitable.

Herbs for surface cleaning

Using products made with herbs to clean surfaces will leave your home smelling delightfully fresh and fragrant, and they are just as effective as proprietary cleaners. You can make these natural cleaners with just a few basic store-cupboard ingredients, including fresh lemon, vinegar, baking soda, liquid soap, table salt, and fresh herbs, so there is no need to rely on chemical sprays to keep surfaces and windows clean.

There are several advantages: the ingredients are easy to obtain; they are inexpensive and have no damaging effects on the environment; they contain no additives, so are unlikely to cause allergic reactions; and they are not tested on animals. Instead, an all-purpose surface cleaner (see below) can be made with 100 per cent natural ingredients, and a handful of fresh sage leaves will add a natural disinfectant. Fresh lemon verbena leaves mixed with white wine vinegar, liquid soap, and water will help make your windows sparkle and smell fresh.

All-purpose surface cleaner

1 handful fresh sage
300ml (½ pt) water
2 tbsp baking soda
8 drops lemon juice

METHOD Put the sage leaves and stems into a saucepan, add the water, cover and bring to the boil. Once boiling, reduce the heat and simmer for 20 minutes. Remove from the heat. When the liquid is cool, strain through a fine mesh to remove any impurities. Pour the cooled liquid into a bottle, add two tablespoons of baking soda and eight drops of lemon juice. Put a top on the bottle, and shake well. The liquid can be used to clean sinks, and bathroom and kitchen surfaces. Store this all-purpose cleaner in the fridge for up to a week.

HERB ALTERNATIVES

Thyme sprigs – use two handfuls of the herb.

Rosemary sprigs – cut to fit into the pan. Use a handful.

Window cleaner

1 handful lemon verbena leaves, either fresh or dried
230ml (8fl oz) water
30ml (2 tbsp) white vinegar
3–4 drops liquid soap

METHOD Add a handful of fresh or dried lemon verbena leaves to a saucepan, pour over the water, bring to the boil, and reduce the heat to a simmer. After ten minutes, turn off the heat and allow to cool. Strain through a fine mesh into a bottle. Add two tablespoons of white wine vinegar and a few drops of liquid soap. Seal and shake well. Store the liquid in a labelled spray bottle, and use within three weeks. If you apply this solution to your window panes and then rub with an old newspaper, it will increase the shine.

HERB ALTERNATIVES

Lemon balm leaves – use one handful, fresh or dried.

Wild bergamot leaves – use one handful, fresh or dried.

Herbs for home fragrance

Keeping your home fresh and sweet-smelling not only makes it a pleasant environment to live in, but can also help to deter insects. For centuries, fresh and dried herbs have been used in the home to improve the air quality and add a wonderfully refreshing fragrance, and are far more beneficial than synthetic room sprays, which are particularly harmful to those who suffer from asthma and allergies.

In the Middle Ages, rosemary and marjoram were strewn in doorways and, as they were crushed underfoot, they released their perfume and helped to prevent the spread of disease. In Elizabethan times, ladies carried a "tussie-mussie", made up of sweet-smelling herbs, to hide the odours of the street and to give protection from the plague. Bunches of tansy leaves were hung in windows to repel flies, and mint sprigs were added to flower arrangements to repel mosquitoes. Like my grandmother, I still tuck sprigs of southernwood between wool jumpers to deter moths, and every time I smell this herb, I am reminded of her.

Herbal room spray

2 large handfuls of fresh lavender flowers
or 1 large handful of dried lavender flowers
or 10 drops of lavender essential oil

300ml (½ pt) water

METHOD Place the lavender flowers into a saucepan, add the water, cover, and bring to the boil. Lower the heat to a simmer. Simmer for 15 minutes, then turn off the heat. Leave the lavender to cool in the water. Strain using a fine mesh to remove all impurities. Pour the clear liquid into a spray bottle, adding a fresh sprig of lavender to the strained liquid if desired. Alternatively, use the essential oil for a quicker recipe. Add it to the cold water (hot water will cause the oils to evaporate). Shake the container well to mix the oil and water together. The scent from the essential oil is slightly sharper than fresh lavender sprigs.

HERB ALTERNATIVES

Rose-scented geranium leaves – use either two large handfuls of leaves or ten drops of rose geranium essential oil.

Sage leaves – use two large handfuls of leaves.

Sweet basil leaf fly repellent

Place a sweet basil plant (*Ocimum basilicum*) by a window or just outside the kitchen door. If flies are persistent, crush a leaf to release a more pungent aroma.

Herbal sachets for clothes drawers

1 handful of dried lavender flowers

METHOD Dry the lavender flowers on stretched muslin (see "Herb garden pot-pourri", below). Loosely fill sachets with the flowers or leaves, taking care not to overfill. You can intensify the fragrance by adding a few drops of lavender essential oil. The scent of lavender perfumes clothes and repels moths.

> ### HERB ALTERNATIVES
>
> **Alecost leaves** – these have a warm, minty but camphorous scent when dried. Alecost is also a good moth repellent.
>
> **Lemon verbena leaves** – the dried, lemon-scented leaves make clothes smell wonderful.
>
> **South African wild rosemary leaves** – these have an aroma similar to a mixture of southernwood and rosemary.

Southernwood moth deterrent

Simply dry sprigs of southernwood (*Artemisia abrotanum*) on a stretched piece of muslin (see below). When dry, lay whole branches between woollen clothes to deter moths.

Herb garden pot-pourri

6 tbsp peppermint or spearmint leaves

4 tbsp rosemary leaves

4 tbsp lemon balm leaves

2 tbsp oregano flowers and leaves

1 tbsp sage leaves

1 tbsp bay leaves

1 tbsp thyme flowers and leaves

2 tsp coarse salt

2 tsp orris root powder

5ml (1 tsp) rosemary essential oil

5ml (1 tsp) oregano essential oil

METHOD Start by drying the leaves in single layers on a piece of muslin stretched over a frame, as shown below. Dry the herbs in small batches; do not mix herb types, as their drying times vary. Keep the frame in a warm, dry place out of direct sunlight. When each batch is dry and crisp, put the herbs into individual jars with tight-fitting lids. Before sealing the lids, sprinkle over two teaspoons of coarse salt and two teaspoons of orris root powder. Put the sealed jars into a dark cupboard for three weeks. Mix all the dry ingredients in a bowl, sprinkle over the essential oils, and place in a room away from direct sunlight. Stir occasionally to allow the fragrance of the pot-pourri to perfume the room.

> ### HERB ALTERNATIVES
>
> **Incense plant flowers and bracts** – use these on their own or mixed with bay leaves.
>
> **Myrtle and juniper berries and cardamom pods** – this mix gives a spicy aroma.

Herbs for first aid

Herbal remedies can provide quick, effective relief for a whole range of household accidents, from wasp stings to minor burns or sprains; many of these can be treated by using the leaf picked straight from the plant. Aloe vera and pennyroyal, for example, are rubbed directly on to the affected area. Other remedies take longer to prepare, but there is something reassuring about homemade products. Before using any plant medicinally, do check that it has been correctly identified. If you are in any doubt about using a herbal remedy, seek professional medical advice and always seek help for more serious accidents.

Natural healing with herbs

I have aloe vera (see page 84) and the burn jelly plant (*Bulbine frutescens* – see page 95) growing in pots on my kitchen windowsill, because I am renowned as something of a clumsy cook. When I burn myself, I simply cut off a bit of leaf of either of these herbs and rub the glutinous gel straight on to the burn (see below), reapplying if the burn becomes uncomfortable. The burn then heals without blistering. Aloe vera and burn jelly plant gels are not only good for healing burns; they can also be used to control acne and eczema, and to relieve itching caused by insect bites and allergies. In cool climates, the succulent leaves of houseleek (see page 194) can be used in the same way, as can St John's Wort oil (see page 128). The mashed-up leaves of pennyroyal (see page 148) offer immediate relief from ant, mosquito, and horse-fly bites. Lemon balm (see page 146) is also indispensable, as an infusion of the leaves is a wonderful soother for cold sores.

Herbal first-aid kit

A good first-aid kit needs to cater for all basic minor ailments including stings, grazes, allergies, and sprains. Choose which natural herbal remedies from the following pages will suit you and your family's needs best, make them up, and keep them in your bathroom cabinet or refrigerator. Ensure that you do not store any of the remedies for longer than the recommended time, or they may lose their potency.

▲ **Aloe vera** plants will grow happily in containers on a windowsill, which makes them ideal for use in the kitchen.

◀ **The beneficial gel** of the aloe vera plant is in the centre of the leaf stem. It will stain, so take care to keep it away from clothing and other fabrics.

Aloe (*Aloe vera*) gel for cuts, burns, sunburn, or poison ivy. Use fresh from the plant or as a homemade gel (see page 241).

Arnica (*Arnica montana*) ointment for painful bruises and muscle pain. Only use when the skin is unbroken.

Chamomile (*Chamaemelum nobile*) dried flowers and leaves for an infusion to help sleep and relaxation. Chamomile cream treats eczema and skin rashes (see pages 240).

Comfrey (*Symphytum officinale*) ointment for bruises and cuts. It encourages the growth of scar tissue (see page 240).

Lavender (*Lavandula angustifolia*) oil for insect bites, stings, burns, and headaches. It has excellent antiseptic and antibacterial properties.

Marigold (*Calendula officinalis*) as a cream for inflamed or minor wounds, skin rashes, and sunburn (see page 240).

St John's Wort (*Hypericum perforatum*) oil for burns, grazes, and rashes; a good substitute for aloe vera when travelling (see page 241 for hot infused oil recipe). It can also be used to make a cream to treat cramp and neuralgia (see page 240).

Lemon balm (*Melissa officinalis*) dried herb infusion for stomach upsets, and as a relaxant. It is a good herbal treatment to give to children (see page 241 for an infusion recipe).

Herbal remedies

The recipes on this page show just a few of the ways in which your homegrown herbs can be used to create simple, natural, and effective herbal remedies. Marigold cream can be applied to minor wounds, skin rashes, or sunburn, for example. A herbal infusion is the simplest way to prepare the leaves or flowers of herbs as a remedy for specific ailments, or as a relaxing or revitalizing tea.

Marigold cream

150g (5oz) emulsifying ointment
70g (3oz) glycerol
80ml (3fl oz) water
30g (1oz) dried marigold flowers (*Calendula officinalis*)
  or 75g (3oz) fresh whole flowers

METHOD Melt the ointment in a glass bowl over a pan of boiling water. Add the water and glycerol and keep stirring until melted. Add the herb, stir well, and simmer for three hours. Check the water does not boil dry. Strain through a wine press or jelly bag fitted into a jug. Once strained, stir constantly to prevent separation. When set, fill a dark glass jar, cover, label, and store in a refrigerator for up to two months.

HERB ALTERNATIVES

The following creams are made from the flowering parts of the herb in exactly the same way as marigold cream:

Chamomile (*Chamaemelum nobile*) cream for eczema and other allergic skin conditions.

St John's Wort (*Hypericum perforatum*) cream for cramp and neuralgia (the cream will be pink in colour).

Comfrey ointment

500g (1lb) petroleum jelly or soft paraffin wax
60g (2oz) dried or 150g (5oz) fresh comfrey leaves
  (*Symphytum officinale*), finely chopped

METHOD This ointment promotes the healing of bruises and cuts, helping the scar tissue to form. Melt the petroleum jelly in a glass bowl over a pan of boiling water. Add the leaves and simmer, stirring continuously for about an hour. Pour the mixture into a jelly bag or a muslin bag. Wearing rubber gloves, squeeze the mixture through the bag into the jug. Pour the ointment into a jar before it sets. Place the lid on the jar, without securing it. When cool, tighten the lid. Store in a refrigerator for up to three months.

HERB ALTERNATIVES

Arnica (*Arnica montana*) for bruises, sprains, and chilblains. Only use on unbroken skin. Use the whole plant – flowers, leaves, and stalks – to make the ointment.

Heartsease (*Viola tricolor*) for skin rashes. Use the flowers, leaves, and stalks to make the ointment.

Aloe gel

1 aloe vera leaf (*Aloe vera*), taken from top of the plant
   (do not use the leaves at the base as these are very bitter)

4 drops of lavender essential oil

METHOD Use this gel to treat sunburn, minor burns, and insect bites. Peel the tough outer skin off the leaf using a potato peeler or paring knife. Extract the clear gelatinous gel and place it in a blender. For every 50ml (2fl oz) of gel, add four drops of lavender essential oil. Mix thoroughly. Pour the mixture into a glass jar or plastic-lined tin, seal, and label. Store in the refrigerator for three to four weeks.

Rosemary oil

250g (8oz) dried rosemary sprigs (*Rosmarinus officinalis*),
   or 500g (1lb) fresh herbs, finely chopped

750ml (25fl oz) olive, sunflower, or other good quality
   vegetable oil

METHOD This hot oil is good for aches and pains. Stir herbs and oil together in a glass bowl over a saucepan of boiling water. Cover the bowl and simmer the water gently for two hours – do not let the pan boil dry. Cool the oil, strain, then pour into glass bottles, seal, and label. Place in a cool cupboard out of direct light. The oil will keep for up to a year.

Medicinal infusions

1 tsp of dried herb or 2 tsp of fresh herb per teacup
Freshly boiled water

METHOD Place the herb leaves or flowers in a cup and pour over freshly boiled water. The water should be just off the boil, to avoid the valuable plant oils evaporating in the steam. Cover and infuse for five to ten minutes, then strain. Sweeten with honey if required. Some herbs are too strong to be taken daily; always check the recommended dosage and quantity. Do not drink more than two cups of any one medicinal herb in 24 hours, unless under guidance from a qualified practitioner.

WARNING None of the plants marked * should be taken during pregnancy. See individual herbs (pages 74–215) for further cautionary notes and information.

HERB ALTERNATIVES

Bergamot (*Monarda fistulosa*) for nausea and flatulence. Use four fresh leaves or 1 tsp of dried herb per cup.

Cardamom (*Elettaria cardamomum*) for indigestion. Use four crushed seeds per cup.

*Catnip (*Nepeta cataria*) for a chill, catarrh, or insomnia. Use five fresh leaves or 1 tsp of dried herb per cup.

Chamomile (*Chamaemelum nobile*) for insomnia. Use four fresh flowers per cup.

Dill (*Anethum graveolens*) for stomach pains and indigestion. Use 1 tsp of crushed seeds per cup.

Fennel (*Foeniculum vulgare*) for indigestion and as a diuretic. Use 1 tsp crushed seeds per cup.

*Gotu kola (*Centella asiatica*) is a diuretic that cleanses toxins (see page 103). Use 1 tsp dried leaves per cup; infuse for 15 minutes and strain.

*Hyssop (*Hyssopus officinalis*) for coughs and catarrh. Use 1 tsp of dried or 2 tsp of fresh leaves per cup.

Lemon balm (*Melissa officinalis*) for tension, headaches, and upset stomachs. Use five fresh leaves per cup.

Lemon verbena (*Aloysia triphylla*) for insomnia and congestion. Use five fresh leaves or 1 tsp dried per cup.

Peppermint (*Mentha x piperita*) for indigestion. Use five fresh leaves or 1 tsp dried per cup.

Rosemary (*Rosmarinus officinalis*) for halitosis, and to improve concentration. Use 5cm (2in) of a rosemary sprig or 1 tsp of dried leaf per cup. Drink no more than one cup a day.

Herbs for beauty

Herbs have been used cosmetically for thousands of years. The ancient Egyptians perfumed their hair with marjoram oil, and used many other herbs in beauty preparations, for ceremonial occasions and religious rituals. Roman soldiers also used fragrant herb oils, such as lavender, to rub into their skin after bathing. This acted as an insect repellent, and helped to heal skin wounds after battle.

Today, a whole commercial industry is based around beauty products, and it is big business. Many such products contain chemical preservatives, synthetic perfumes, and artificial colourings, but by making your own cosmetics, you can ensure control over the purity of the ingredients. You can also experiment with the various herbal ingredients to find the combinations that work best on your skin and hair, as well as the fragrances that you like best. There are also therapeutic reasons for using herbs in your daily beauty routine, plus their wonderful herbal aroma will promote a sense of well-being when you use them.

Toning face pack

2 tbsp dried lady's mantle leaves and flowers,
    dried spearmint leaves, and dried mallow leaves

1 tsp crushed fennel seed

1 tsp crushed juniper berries

575ml (1 pt) water

2 tbsp ground oatmeal, almonds, or Fuller's earth

METHOD Combine the herbs in a pan with the water. Cover, bring to the boil, and simmer for 15 minutes. Remove from the heat, strain, and cool. Put the two tablespoons of ground oatmeal into a bowl. Add two to three tablespoons of the herbal infusion and mix well to form a paste. Spread thickly over your face, avoiding the area around the eyes and mouth. Leave for 10 minutes. Rinse with warm water. Use once or twice a week to tone the skin.

HERB ALTERNATIVES

For oily skin: Chamomile, yarrow, parsley, and peppermint to equal either two handfuls of fresh leaves or 2 tbsp of dried herbs.

For dry skin: Two handfuls of fresh houseleek, mallow, and borage leaves, or 2 tbsp of dried herbs and 1 tsp of crushed flax seed.

Facial steam

3 tbsp dried herbs, comprising equal
    parts chamomile, chervil, lavender,
    lemon balm, spearmint, curly mint,
    and thyme

1½l (3pt) freshly boiled water

> **WARNING** Avoid facial steams if your skin is very dry or has visible red veins, or if you suffer from a heart condition or asthma.

METHOD Place the herbs in a bowl, pour over the slightly cooled, boiled water. Hold your face over the steam at a distance of 30cm (12in), or 45cm (18in) for those with sensitive skin. Cover your head, shoulders, and the bowl with a bath towel, and inhale for five to ten minutes. Rinse your face with tepid water, then splash with cold water. To close up pores, dab on an infusion (see page 241) of elderflower or peppermint with cotton wool.

HERB ALTERNATIVES

For oily skin: Pot marigold flowers, dried horsetail, sage leaves, and yarrow leaves.

For mature skin: Dried elderflowers and tansy flowers, plus dried tansy and lemon verbena leaves.

Hair shampoo

1 tsp dried soapwort root or 10 fresh soapwort stems
    with leaves each 15–20cm (6–8in long)

850ml (1½ pt) water

METHOD Soapwort makes a slight lather when added to water, but it does not sting the eyes like some synthetic shampoos. You can use soapwort on its own or combine it with other herbs that benefit your hair type (see Herb Alternatives). Crush the soapwort root or roughly chop up the fresh stems. If using dried soapwort, soak the root overnight in water. Put the soapwort and other herbs in a saucepan with the water, cover, bring to the boil, and then simmer for 20 minutes, stirring occasionally. Remove from the heat, cool, and then strain the liquid through a fine sieve or piece of muslin. Store the shampoo solution out of direct light for up to a week.

HERB ALTERNATIVES

For oily hair: Add 1 tbsp dried or 10 leaves fresh mint; 1 tbsp dried or one sprig fresh rosemary; 1 tsp dried sage or three leaves fresh sage.

For dry hair: Add 1 tbsp dried or 10 leaves fresh mallow, chamomile, or sweet marjoram, or 1 tbsp dried or one sprig of fresh rosemary.

Herbs for relaxation

As the Greek physician Theophrastus noted, fragrant herbs have an instant healing effect as the smell travels directly from the nerves in the nose to the part of the brain concerned with intuition, emotion, and creativity. He noted that when an aromatic herb poultice was applied to a leg it could produce fragrant breath as its essences would permeate the skin and enter the circulatory system.

A warm bath infused with herb oils or dried herb ingredients helps relaxation and has a soothing effect on the nervous system. By adding herbs to warm water we are encouraging them to release their natural oils, which in turn help us relax our body and mind. As you stretch out in the bath, breathe in deeply and inhale the herbs, and then slowly exhale several times to get the maximum benefit. When you have been sitting in front of a computer all day an eye compress is wonderfully relaxing, and a herb or hop pillow is a great remedy if you have a racing mind and cannot sleep; simply smelling the herbs and imagining a warm summer's day does the trick.

Bath tonic

1 large handful of common thyme stems and leaves
575ml (1pt) water

METHOD I do not think that I could cope with the strenuous work on my farm without being able to soak in a relaxing herbal bath at the end of a hard day. It not only washes away the physical aches and pains but also restores my equilibrium. This is one recipe I use frequently to alleviate backache. Place the thyme sprigs into the saucepan of water. Cover, bring to the boil, reduce the heat and simmer for ten minutes. Remove the infusion from the heat and carefully strain the herbs through a sieve – it is not romantic to have leaves floating in the water because when you get out they stick to the skin. Add the thyme infusion to a hot bath and soak.

HERB ALTERNATIVES

Lemon balm leaves relieve insomnia and soothe the nerves. Use two large handfuls of fresh leaves. Simmer for five minutes.

Basil and sweet marjoram leaves Use two large handfuls (one of each herb) of fresh leaves, and simmer for five minutes. This bath relieves muscular cramp.

Bath bag

2 tbsp dried or 6 fresh chamomile flowers
2 tbsp dried or 6 sprigs of fresh lavender
2 tbsp dried female flowers or 6 fresh female hop flowers

METHOD One of the easiest ways of adding herbs to a bath is to hang a bag made from muslin under the hot water tap. Fill the bag with either a single dried herb or a mixture of herbs and allow the hot water to run through it, so infusing the water and the air in the bathroom with herbs.

HERB ALTERNATIVES

Eau-de-cologne mint – one generous bunch of the fresh or dried herb makes a refreshing bath.

Chamomile, valerian, rosemary, horsetail, and peppermint – one large handful of each of the fresh or dried herbs mixed together makes a very soothing bath.

Hop pillow

2 handfuls dried female hop flowers
1 handful dried chamomile flowers
1 handful dried lemon verbena leaves

METHOD Hop pillows are well-known for their ability to aid sleep. If you do not like the beer-like aroma, mix them with other more aromatic herbs, like chamomile flowers and lemon verbena leaves. This will not detract from the hops' sleep-inducing properties. To make the herb pillow, sew a small muslin or cotton cover and simply fill it with the dried herbs and stitch it up. It will last for up to six months.

HERB ALTERNATIVES

Sweet marjoram leaves and lavender sprigs – mix one handful of each dried herb to induce sleep and to lift the spirits.

Chamomile flowers and rosemary sprigs – mix one handful of each dried herb to prevent nightmares and to refresh the mind and body.

Relaxing eye compress

5 leaves or 1 tsp dried mint leaves
200ml (7fl oz) water

WARNING Eyes are very delicate. Before use, test the solution on a tender patch of skin, such as underarm, for an allergic reaction.

METHOD Place the herbs in a ceramic bowl, pour over freshly boiled water, cover and allow to infuse for ten minutes. Strain through an unbleached coffee filter paper, and leave to cool. To reduce dark circles under the eyes, dip two cotton wool pads in the liquid and place on the eyelids for 10–15 minutes.

HERB ALTERNATIVES

Cornflowers to soothe the eyes and reduce puffiness in the eye area. Use one handful of fresh or dried flowers.

Fennel leaves reduce inflammation and brighten eyes. Use one teaspoon of crushed dried herb.

Herbs for petcare

Wild animals naturally turn to herbs if they are feeling unwell. Our domesticated animals have not lost this instinct and will treat themselves if, for example, they get a burr stuck in their throat, by eating grass. We can use herbs to alleviate our pets' simple ailments. For instance, you can add parsley to a dog's diet to cure bad breath, or rub his coat with tansy (*Tanacetum vulgare*) to deter fleas.

Cats and dogs and other small creatures have much shorter digestive systems than humans, and do not digest fresh herbs in the same way as we do. For this reason it is easier and safer to administer herbs to pets either as a herbal infusion or as drops of herb tincture; either can be added to drinking water or food. Make the doses compatible with your pet's size – small amounts for small animals, larger amounts for large animals. I use a drop of valerian tincture on a dog biscuit to calm my dog, Hampton, before long car journeys. But if your pet is unwell, consult a qualified vet for advice and treatment rather than attempting to treat it with herbs.

Flea powder

1 tsp dried rosemary

1 tsp fennel seeds, crushed

1 tsp dried wormwood

1 tsp dried rue

METHOD Mix together the dried herb ingredients, and comb sparingly into your pet's hair. Alternatively, you can pick a handful of tansy (*Tanacetum vulgare*) and rub your pet's coat with the crushed leaves. This will soothe your pet and deters fleas. Alternatively, you can bathe your dog in a strong rosemary (*Rosmarinus officinalis*) infusion (see page 241). This infusion can also be used to wash your dog's bedding and to soak its collar – both are effective ways to deter fleas.

Lice deterrent

METHOD Free-range hens will control their own lice infestations by taking dust baths. You can help control lice in the coop by hanging large bunches of dried wormwood (*Artemisia absinthium*) inside the coop and placing dried leaves in the hens' bedding straw. Dried bunches of pyrethrum (*Tanacetum cinerariifolium*) will deter flies and tansy (*Tanacetum vulgare*) will deter mice.

Calming tonic

METHOD Pets, like humans, can be frightened by thunder storms, car travel, or loud noises. Here, a hamster is being given a few drops of chamomile tea (*Chamaemelum nobile*). It calms the nerves and is an excellent cleanser and toner of the digestive tract, helping to expel worms and parasites and so improve the appetite. It also helps to control dry, flaking skin. For cats, add 1 tbsp of chamomile tea to their feed; for dogs up to 3 tbsp, depending on the dog's size. Another calmative is valerian (*Valeriana officinalis*), which works well for anxious cats. Cats are notoriously fussy about their food but are partial to valerian, which reduces anxiety and soothes the nervous system. Add three to four drops of valerian tisane to food using a pipette.

Worming mixture

½–1 raw garlic clove, grated or minced (depending on pet's size)

1 tsp–2 tbsp of brewer's yeast powder (depending on pet's size)

WARNING This mixture is not suitable for dogs under six months old.

METHOD Garlic is very beneficial for dogs, acting as a wormer, a flea deterrent, and as an all-round tonic for the immune and cardiovascular systems. Some dogs are happy to eat garlic grated on to their food, but others will refuse it. To disguise the aroma of garlic, add brewer's yeast to it to make a more palatable worming mixture, which is also good for conditioning your dog's coat.

Cat toy

METHOD My two cats both adore the two species of catnip (*Nepeta cataria* and *Nepeta* x *faassenii*). They can be found lying outdoors in ecstasy amongst the fresh plants in summer. To give them year-round pleasure, dry catnip leaves, and use them to fill a small cat toy, or make a small cotton sachet and sew it up.

Index

Page numbers that appear in italic in this index indicate an illustration and/or its caption; page numbers that appear in bold indicate a main entry (with illustrations) for a particular herb.

Resources

B&Q
They have an independently verified organic gardening range; for information telephone 0845 609 6688.
More information and details of local branches are available at www.diy.com.

Chelsea Physic Garden, Royal Hospital Road, London SW3 4HS
Tel: 020 7352 5646
www.chelseaphysicgarden.co.uk
Founded in 1673 by the Society of Apothecaries; one of Europe's oldest botanic gardens containing important herb and medicinal collections.

Garden Organic, Ryton Organic Gardens, Coventry, CV8 3LG
Tel: 02476 303517
Email: enquiry@gardenorganic.org.uk
www.gardenorganic.org.uk
The UK's leading organic growing charity has been at the forefront of the organic horticulture movement for 50 years, and is dedicated to researching and promoting organic gardening, farming, and food.

The Herb Society (UK), Sulgrave Manor, Sulgrave, Banbury OX17 2SD
Tel: 0845 4918699 (or +44 (0)1295 768899 from outside the UK)
www.herbsociety.org.uk
Aims to increase the understanding and use of herbs and their benefits to health.

Jekka's Herb Farm, Rose Cottage, Shellards Lane, Alveston, Bristol, BS35 3SY
Tel: 01454 418878
Email: sales@jekkasherbfarm.com
www.jekkasherbfarm.com
Please visit our website for details of our farm's open weekends and our plant and seed mail-order catalogue.

The National Herb Centre, Banbury Road, Warmington, Warks OX17 1DF
Tel: 01295 690999
Email: info@herbcentre.co.uk
www.herbcentre.co.uk
The National Herb Centre was started in 1997, to provide the public with an opportunity to see, enjoy, and learn about herbs, as well as to further research for the food industry.

The Organic Gardening Catalogue, Riverdene Business Park, Molesey Road, Hersham, Surrey, KT12 4RG
Tel: 01932 253666
www.organiccatalogue.com
The official catalogue of Garden Organic: organic seeds, fertilizers, other sundries, and publications.

Royal Botanic Gardens Kew, Richmond, Surrey, TW9 3AE
Tel: 020 8940 1171
www.kew.org
One of the world's most important botanic gardens where many mature herb species can be seen grown to full size.

The Royal Horticultural Society, 80 Vincent Square, London SW1P 2PE
Tel: 0845 260 5000
Email: info@rhs.org.uk
www.rhs.org.uk
The UK's leading garden charity, dedicated to advancing horticulture and promoting good gardening.

The Soil Association, South Plaza, Marlborough Street, Bristol BS1 3NX
Tel: 0117 314 5000
Email: memb@soilassociation.org
www.soilassociation.org
Membership charity promoting planet-friendly food and farming through education, campaigns, and community programmes.

Further reading

Deni Bown
RHS Encyclopedia of Herbs
Dorling Kindersley

Andrew Chevallier
Encyclopedia of Medicinal Plants
Dorling Kindersley

John Gerard
Herbal
Bracken Books

A.M. Grieve
Modern Herbal
Peregrine Books

Lawrence D. Hills
Guide to Organic Gardening, Month by Month
Thorsons Books

Home Herbal
Dorling Kindersley

Jekka McVicar
Jekka's Complete Herb Book
Kyle Cathie Ltd

Jekka McVicar
Seeds: the ultimate guide to growing successfully from seed
Kyle Cathie Ltd (with the RHS)

Penelope Ody
Home Herbal
Dorling Kindersley

Pauline Pears
HDRA Encyclopedia of Organic Gardening
Dorling Kindersley

Directories

RHS Plant Finder
Editor: Tony Lord
Dorling Kindersley
Also available at www.rhs.org.uk

The Seed Search
Karen Platt
Karen Platt 2002
Over 40,000 seeds and where to buy them worldwide

Acknowledgments

This book would not have been possible without Mac's continuous love and care, William's constant companionship whilst writing the first edition, Hampton's boundless energy and moral support during this edition, and not forgetting Hannah and Alistair's encouragement and love.

I would like to thank all of the team at the Herb Farm for keeping the farming going while I was writing, and all the DK team for producing a beautiful book, especially Sarah Ruddick, Vicky Read, Esther Ripley, and Alison Donovan.

Thanks to Chelsea Physic Garden, the Royal Botanic Gardens Kew, and Emma and Anton Buckoke for allowing the team to photograph in their beautiful gardens.

Thanks to all the marvellous chefs I have met over the years, including Jamie Oliver, Nigel Slater, Raymond Blanc, and Jonray and Peter Sanchez-Iglesias, who are all inspirational in their use of herbs, and to Camilla Goslett at Curtis Brown for stepping in at the last minute.

Publisher's acknowledgments:
Dorling Kindersley would like to thank Becky Shackleton for editorial assistance, and Louise Waller for design assistance.

Photography credits

Sarah Cuttle Page 6, 9 except cr and bl, 14–15, 19, 34, 41tr, 57, 67, 74, 77

GAP Page 73c, 102t, 127, 174

Garden Picture Library Page 87br, 104t, 146t

Getty Page 227tl

Craig Knowles Pages 1–5, 8, 10, 11, 16, 18, 21, 22–23, 28–29, 36–39, 42–43 except 43bl, 44–55, 58–65, 68–73 except 73c, 76, 78, 80–85, 87l, 88t, 90–91, 93r, 96, 100t, 101, 102b, 104–105 except 104t, 106b, 108–109, 111, 113–121 except 117t, 123–125, 128–133 except 129b, 134–135 except 134bl, 136–141 except 137tl, 143, 144–145 except 144t, 146b, 147r, 148–149 except 149tl, 150 b, 151br, 152, 154, 155t, 156t, 157r, 158br, 161br, 163tr, 164–165, 167r, 169–171, 173, 175, 176, 179r, 180, 185bl, 188–195, 198–199, 201, 202t, 203r, 204–209 except 205tl, 210–212 except 210t, 212, 214, 218, 232, 239, 247

Jekka McVicar Page 9cr and bl, 12, 15 t, 25, 26–27, 31, 32–33, 35, 40–41 except 41tr, 79, 86, 88–89 except 88t, 92–93 except 93r, 94–95, 97, 99, 100b, 103, 106–107 except 106b, 110, 112, 117 top, 122, 126, 129b, 134bl, 137tl, 142, 144t, 147bl, 149tl, 150t, 151tl, 153, 155b, 156b, 157bl, 158–159 except 158br, 160–161 except 161br, 162–163 except 163tr, 166–167 except 167r, 168, 172, 177, 178–179 except 179r, 181–187 except 185bl, 196–197, 200, 202b, 203tl, 205tl, 210t, 213, 215

Harry Smith Collection Page 98

Tim Winter Page 216, 219–230 except 227t, 233–238, 240–246

All other images © Dorling Kindersley